WHEN DATING HURTS

A MEMOIR

Bill Mitchell

WHEN DATING HURTS

Published by Bill Mitchell

Copyright © 2020 by Bill Mitchell

All rights reserved. No part of this book may be reproduced or transmitted in any form or by any means, electronic or mechanical, including photocopying, recording, or any information storage and retrieval system without the written permission of the publisher.

You can stop dating violence in your community.
Join our community. Work to end dating violence.

Learn more about Kristin's story
WhenDatingHurts.com

The When Dating Hurts podcast series
is on most popular podcast players

Twitter
@WhenDatingHurts
#WhenDatingHurts

Facebook
Facebook.com/WhenDatingHurts

Questions or Comments
Email: BillMitchell@WhenDatingHurts.com

Printed in the United States of America.

Library of Congress Control Number: 2019920087

ISBN: 978-1-7342537-0-2
ISBN: 978-1-7342537-1-9 (eBook)

WHEN DATING HURTS

First Edition

When Dating Hurts is a memoir. Memoirs, by definition, are written depictions of events in people's lives. They are memories. All events in this story are as accurate and truthful as possible. Many names and places have been changed to protect the privacy of others and to keep a promise I made to people who assisted with this work. Mistakes, if any, are caused solely by the passage of time.

"Bill writes with a deep personal understanding of the ultimate price of domestic violence. Readers will be touched by the impact Kristin's death had, not only on her family but on the expanding circles of people who did not have the privilege of knowing her. The Mitchells' sharing what they have learned is a gift to all who may someday need this information. *When Dating Hurts* is a 'must-read' for parents and other adults who are in a position to provide guidance to teens and young adults."
— **Beth Sturman, Executive Director, Laurel House Domestic Violence Agency**

"*When Dating Hurts* is heartfelt and horrific. Bill's writing quickly captivates you and tugs at your heart while taking you into the depths of his tragedy. This is every parent's worst nightmare and every educator's promise to proactively protect. As educators, parents, partners, and protectors, we must read this even when it hurts our hearts."
— **Dr. Beverly R. Bryde, Dean, School of Education, Cabrini University**

"This is a must-read for every parent, educator, aunt, uncle, grandparent, friend, co-worker (the list goes on), to understand dating violence and the toll a murder by an abuser can take on an entire family. Bill, Michele, and David Mitchell's 'superpowers' are to stop dating violence in the name of their beloved daughter and sister, Kristin. In *When Dating Hurts*, the raw, true emotion of their lives is real, honest and heartbreaking. Bill's words carry the reader through their journey as he tries to make sense of a senseless death. Thank you, Mitchell family, including friends of Kristin, for being her voice and the voice of so many victims of domestic and dating violence. Kristin will forever be alive in your hearts (and ours)."
— **Colleen Lelli, EdD, Associate Professor of Education & Director of the Jordan Center for Children of Trauma and Domestic Violence Education, Cabrini University**

"Kristin Mitchell was a beautiful St. Joseph's University graduate with a bright future ahead... but her 'boyfriend' destroyed her life in a horrific murder. Her family faces an ugly criminal trial outside of Philadelphia and begins a painful journey to understand 'why.' Bill carefully weaves together the tragic story of his daughter's murder and the 'red flags' almost everyone missed until it was too late. This is a guide for us to avoid a similar fate. *When Dating Hurts* is a precious gift to you or someone you love."
— **Ben & Connie Clery | Clery Center for Security on Campus, Inc.**

"Every family's worst nightmare is having a child murdered. This story of a family's heartbreak is one of courage, resiliency, and strength. Rather than falling apart, the Mitchells focused on healing and drawing attention to the tragedy of dating violence that is far too prevalent in our culture. In a raw, authentic way, Bill brings Kristin to life. Her story has already saved the lives of so many young women. This is a must-read for every parent—and all of us who work to end dating violence. It is a call to action to ensure that no other family is forced to endure what the Mitchells have."
— **Raquel Kennedy Bergen, Ph.D., Professor, Director of Gender Studies St. Joseph's University**

"This book is about awareness, about enlightening our sons and our daughters; our brothers and our sisters; our friends, both male and female. It's about all of us knowing what to look for and what to listen for, about erring on the side of safety, about saying something and doing something!"
— **Cpl. David R. Thomas (ret.), Montgomery County Police, Montgomery County, Maryland National Domestic Violence Expert**

DEDICATION

To Kristin, and all women
taken from us before their time by
the epidemic of dating violence.

RECOLLECTION

You Feel Sorry for Me?

On a warm June afternoon in Washington, D.C., a film crew from ABC's *Good Morning America* interviewed my wife and me for a segment on dating violence. Two other pairs of parents were interviewed following us. Their daughters had also been victims of violent acts caused by their boyfriends.

I had been told that parents who lost daughters in violent crimes were in "the club nobody wants to join." If included, you immediately felt close to the other members like a support group.

In the early evening, the interviewed parents collected at a posh D.C. restaurant. John and Mary, from a northeastern state, lost their daughter four months after our daughter was killed. Mary was in town to advocate for a national law to mandate teaching about dating violence in every high school in the nation.

My wife, Michele, was chatting with Mary and a single mother named Sheila, who was from Buffalo, New York.

John, on my left, leaned over to me.

"Bill, I gotta say, man, I feel sorry for you..."

Taken off guard, I responded, "*You* feel sorry for *me*?"

John continued, "I do. You see, we lost our daughter too, but our situation's different." I wondered where this was going. It felt personal, considering we had only met minutes before.

"See Sheila there, talking with your wife? The guy who killed her daughter had the decency to kill himself after he shot her. She doesn't need to deal with him anymore. He's gone and that's that ...

"Then there's our guy. He killed my daughter and got nailed with first-degree murder. He's in prison for the rest of his miserable life. He's not coming out. But, believe me, if I had the chance, I'd still kill him."

John was scary. His anger was so close to the surface—as if he could explode at any moment.

But he felt sorry for me? Then, he pointed right at me.

"Bill, let's talk about your guy. What'd he get? Thirty years?"

Taking it gently, I replied. "Thirty years, but mandated to do only fifteen. Then he'll face annual parole boards until his thirtieth year."

John, with eyebrows raised, said, "What did I tell you? See? That's why I feel sorry for you ... You have all of that ahead of you. Mary and I don't. Neither does Sheila."

Suddenly, I felt sorry for me, too.

June 3, 2005

It's a Friday evening. Ugly and drizzling. But the weekend's here, and I'm good with it.

Tonight's venue is Snyder's Willow Grove, a family-style restaurant near Baltimore's BWI Airport. Snyder's has seen better days, but decades ago. Muzak performs a duet with periodic roars from outbound air traffic. It's part of the ambiance.

What A Wonderful World.

For my just-past-eighty-year-old parents, Snyder's is their go-to supper spot. No one can make out who is older: the patrons or the waitstaff.

Chances are excellent I will be referred to frequently tonight as *Hon*, as in, "*Hon*, can I getcha s'more wooder?" Kind of cute in what we call a Baltimoron way.

When plates are cleared, I delight my parents with a photo of their granddaughter, Kristin. Wearing her mortarboard, gown, and sweet smile, she is the personification of accomplishment and triumph. Her college graduation was twenty days ago.

Mom and Dad love it. They love Kristin.

After studying Kristin's photo, Mom says, "Oh, we brought you a little gift, too." From under the table, she hands me a strange ten-inch robotic bird with a button on its wing. "We got one for Aunt Marie years ago. We saw this in Frederick and got you one."

I squeeze the button, the beak begins to move, and then it belts out "What a Wonderful World" by Louie Armstrong in full Satchmo. The restaurant is almost empty, so there is negligible disturbance. "I see trees of green, red roses too ... "

"After we gave one to Marie, darned if your Uncle Joe didn't pass soon afterward," Mom tells me.

Trying not to appear discourteous or superstitious, and keeping it light, I have to ask, "Why'd you want me to have one?"

"We liked the song and thought it was cute."

The Call

On the rainy ride home from seeing Mom and Dad at Snyder's, my Ford Explorer's wipers slap away on high. It's challenging to discern road from not-road. The singing bird is facedown on the passenger seat, nice and quiet.

Nearing 8:30 p.m., my cell phone rings. I shouldn't be fumbling to find it under these tense conditions, but who's calling me at this hour on a Friday?

"Hello, I'm Police Lieutenant Detective Vicki Stewart with the Howard County Police Department. Is this Mr. William Mitchell?"

What on earth is this about? Who is this, I mean, really?

"Uh, *who* are you?"

"Police Lieutenant Detective Vicki Stewart with the Howard County Police. Are you William Mitchell?"

"Yes, this is William Mitchell."

"Mr. Mitchell, I need to meet with you and tell you something. Are you available to speak with me this evening?"

"You need to meet with me? And why is that?"

I'm ready to hang up so this person can move on and bother someone else.

"Mr. Mitchell, we can't do this over the phone, sir. It has to be in person. Can I meet you at your home?"

My home? This person knows where I live?

For some reason, she is absolutely determined not to tell me what's happening. Between driving in a downpour and dealing with Detective Whoever-This-Is, tonight is becoming weird and dangerous.

"Meet at my home...?"

"Can I meet with you at your home, Mr. Mitchell? Will you be there any time soon? We were there, and no one was home."

I can't imagine where this is going; I give it one final try.

"Help me. What is it you need to tell me?"

"This cannot be done by phone. I'm very sorry. We've been to your home a couple of times. No one was there. But I need to meet with you, Mr. Mitchell. In person."

She will not let this go.

"So, how can I be sure you are who you say you are?"

"Mr. Mitchell, you can call our Northern District Headquarters and give them my name. Tell them I'm trying to speak with you. You'll find this is all legitimate police business."

I pull off the road, and she gives me a number.

Then I snap back with, "Look, I'll call you back, okay? Does that work for you?"

I want to get off the phone and take a moment.

Before I contact headquarters, I call my wife, Michele. She's with our sixteen-year-old son, David, celebrating a friend's high school graduation an hour away. When she hears I've just been contacted by a police detective, she cuts in, "Is this about Kristin?"

"*Kristin?* Why on earth would *local police* be contacting me about Kristin? She lives two-plus hours away in Philadelphia."

Such an absurd thought.

Kristin is totally out of this area; she is 120 miles north of us. How could this be about Kristin?

Obviously, I've never fully grasped the truth: all mothers possess special powers acquired while carrying their babies from inception to first breath. I should never have discounted those nine months of mother-child interdependence. I tell Michele I'm going to meet this detective, or whoever she is, someplace safe.

"We're coming home right now," concludes Michele with her mother-sense on high.

I resist her. "Hold on. We don't even know what this is about. Let me meet with her and call you back."

That doesn't do it for Michele; she is set on coming home.

I acquiesce. "Okay, look, how about letting David drive?"

David is a rookie driver, but his eyes and reflexes will be sharper and quicker than his mother's, especially in rain at night.

David wouldn't think it is about Kristin any more than I do.

Silly men.

This is a Bad Dream

It would be wise to have a few people around in case things get crazy with this detective. Is this a setup? Is this real? As a semi-safe location, I pick a grocery store. A Giant near home. There is a chance this Vicki Stewart person is not who she says she is.

Why does she have to meet with me? What happened? Does she think I did something? Will it be handcuffs and a jail cell for me tonight? Maybe she thinks I know about a crime on my cul-de-sac today? If so, I missed it. I was cooped up at work, and later, I was at Snyder's with my parents.

I call Detective Stewart back and suggest the Giant.

There's no good place to hear bad news.

By half past nine, Detective Vicki Stewart has not appeared. Only a few customers enter or leave through the automatic doors. I lean back on one of the store's large glass windows. On my left, a bright orange ten-gallon Gatorade container sits, reminding me of jubilant football teams dumping these over head coaches after playoff victories. A complete contrast to how I feel. I feel like doom is coming my way.

No detective comes out on a rain-soaked evening to tell someone good news. The only thing left to wonder is how bad is it? And here she is, driving a silver Honda Civic with a dark-blue compact right behind it. Two get out of each car. I'm already outnumbered.

Police Lieutenant Detective Stewart, a demure blonde with a slight build, is all-business, just like she was on the phone. After studying her face for a second, I notice she is holding a badge in front of me.

Detective Stewart wastes no time. "Mr. Mitchell, I'm Vicki Stewart with the Howard County Police Department. This is my partner, Detective Cody."

I have to tilt back to see Cody's face. This man towers over me and does nothing to diminish my feelings about being here. He shows me a badge. Detective Stewart introduces two grim-looking women standing beside a blue car; both are wearing dark business suits. I miss the names and job titles; it is too much to take in.

My mind pinballs around why I'm here.

"Would you prefer to talk in my car?" the detective offers.

Her car? Why would I? Why trust anything? I want to know the *Something* that could not be told over the phone. The *Something* that can only be told in person. I want to hear it—*but not in her car.*

I gesture with my right thumb.

"How about in that Subway there?"

Detective Stewart frowns. "No, I don't think we should go there."

Really? Why not?

Again, Detective Stewart recommends her car. I picture getting in and never being seen again. I'm not getting into that car.

I feel better about staying here by the automatic doors and the Gatorade.

The Something

"Mr. Mitchell, I regret to inform you your daughter, Kristin, was murdered by her boyfriend earlier today," Detective Stewart says with as much consideration as she can bring.

Okay. Stop right there. I get it.

That is plain enough. Kristin is dead. Dead? Murdered? Her boyfriend? Just like that? She is in Philadelphia. We are here. These are local police. I never thought of this possibility. My wife was way ahead of me.

I can't feel a thing. I'm still processing.

At this moment, it is now only about hearing the details, I guess. Whatever they are, the outcome will be the same.

Kristin is dead. There can be no, "But then … "

Dead is dead.

With a second to think, I see myself placed in such a pitiable role. I am the emissary of the most tragic information I have ever heard. I see myself telling it thousands of times like a nightmare on infinite repeat. Tonight, I will begin by telling Kristin's mother, brother, and grandparents.

As I contemplate what this means, Detective Stewart inquires, "Mr. Mitchell, are you okay, sir? You seem to be taking this very well."

I am? Why? Because I'm not doing anything? Because I'm not falling on the sidewalk screaming like people do in movies? Pounding my fists. Crying. Flipping out.

"I'm acting."

Why did I say that? *Stupid.* What does that even mean? It was all that came to mind. I'm acting the way I feel. There is nothing I can do. I'm helpless. I cannot do a damned thing about this.

Are we finished here? Is there more?

Detective Stewart tells me a detective in Philadelphia is prepared to share details with me any time this evening.

I walk over to her silver Civic and sit in the passenger seat with the door open, feet out, prepared to run at any second. I feel weak. Detective Stewart hands me a legal pad and a Bic, then calls the Philadelphia detective.

"Jim? Yes, hi, it's Vicki Stewart in Maryland. I have Mr. Mitchell here. Is this a good time to speak? Thank you."

She hands me her cell phone and says, "This is Detective Jim McGowan."

Detective Jim McGowan says just above a whisper, "Mr. Mitchell? Sir, I'm so sorry about what happened with your daughter ... "

"Thank you. What can you tell me?"

Jim McGowan tells me all he knows. There was an argument. It ended violently. It appears Kristin's boyfriend killed her in her apartment very early this morning. With a knife. He's been in custody all day. They expect to learn more after interviewing a few people.

I notice how calm McGowan is. It must take practice. Must be a hard job.

There is nothing more to be obtained. It is still early even though it happened over fifteen hours ago. I want to know more, but that is all he has. I know whatever I hear, it will never be good.

"I'm so sorry about what happened..."

"Thank you for all you're doing, Detective. I appreciate you speaking with me."

"I'm very sorry, sir."

The way he sounds, I picture this man with a tear in his eye.

Since there's nothing more to talk about with Detectives Stewart and Cody, I thank them, and they drive off. The two bereavement counselors, the ones whose names and titles I didn't catch at first, follow me while I drive the short distance home.

Important events carousel around my mind. Each one appears and disintegrates. No birthdays. Poof. No Christmases. Poof. No wedding day. No grandchildren ...

I force myself to stop doing this. Do I really need to review everything we once had to look forward to? All of that is obliterated. Gone. The end. Taken away by the *Something*.

My cell phone rings. Michele is rightfully demanding an answer. "What did that detective tell you? Was Kristin in an accident? Is she okay?"

Her mother-intuition thing is so powerful.

"Look. Let's meet at home, okay? We can talk about it when you get there. Take your time. Okay?"

For some reason, that's enough for her. She lets it go at that.

I'm about to tell my family something that will alter each of their lives. While I think about that, the passing streetlights allow me glimpses of the weird singing bird on the seat next to me. Uncle Joe and now Kristin? I don't see me keeping this thing. I toss him onto the backseat.

I want this moment to end.

Kristin is dead? No, she isn't. This is confounding. And soon, Michele, David, and my parents will have to suffer knowing this too. It's news that has no reversal. It's as bad as it gets, and it's permanent.

I call my parents and ask Dad to drive Mom to our home.

"Please take your time. No need to rush. Racing here isn't going to make any difference."

He does not ask why we need to meet.

How does anyone get mad enough to kill someone?

On our cul-de-sac, the bereavement counselors' car is parked across from our home.

"I guess it's part of your job to be around in case someone faints on the pavement. Or loses it ... ?" I ask.

"Mr. Mitchell, can we help you in any way?"

I ask more pointedly, "Do you need to be here when I tell my family? I mean, is that mandated?"

"Only if you want us to ..."

"There's no need to stay. Thanks, I've got this."

Kristin Mitchell
BABY

Parents will tell you their baby is perfect. But Kristin really was. Born at 4:17 p.m. on a bright Saturday, August 24, 1983, she entered the world exactly the way she left it. Beautiful. I could never take enough photos.

By the time Kristin reached her second birthday, Michele and I realized we had met our match in a battle of wits.

"This is one iron-willed child. We're in for the time of our lives," I repeated to Michele when the terrible twos arrived in full force before she reached eighteen months.

No matter, I believed the day would come when her pluck would pay off. It might take twenty years, or maybe by the time she reached her late twenties, but she would never put up with an overly assertive boss or an irritating coworker. Or some demanding boyfriend. She would need no urging to stand up for herself. Her resolve was locked in. She was one determined little lady.

As a babe in arms, she was continuously mistaken for a blonde-headed boy. No matter how pink Michele dressed her, we would hear, "Isn't he the cutest little fellow?" Or, "What's his name?"

Kristin's hair took its time to grow. But when it did, it was glorious. More like platinum than blonde. Well worth the long wait.

Kristin could be funny. When she noticed her grandmother and grandfather were laughing at something she did, she would serve it up again with a slight variation to keep it fresh. She captivated everyone she met. Kristin was our little bright spot and a people magnet. One happy little girl.

Our first cat, Rockwell, was a handsome Siamese and more like a doll than a cat to Kristin. She could play with his ears and tail or dress him in doll clothes. He loved the attention. Kristin adored cats and goldfish, hermit crabs, and later, hamsters and horses. Rockwell vaulted up into any open window to recline in the sun and watch birds and squirrels. His warm naps were cat nirvana.

One Saturday, when Kristin was just over a year old, Rockwell did another window leap. Michele and I distinctly heard little Kristin cry out, "Rocka jum window!"

Had we just heard her first complete sentence?

For a guy who worked sixty miles away, I was fortunate to be there and hear her first noun-verb-object statement. To be exact, I was twice blessed because I also saw her first triumphant walk of any remarkable distance.

In those fledgling days, Kristin's attempts to pronounce "Grandma" came out as "Gaga." It was unique, and it stuck. From that point on, both of her grandmothers were her "Gagas."

Each grandfather was "Poppy." Very cute. Very Kristin.

Kristin and Michele were inseparable in those nascent days, but sometimes they wrestled over who was controlling whom. An illustration was when potty training came to a standstill.

Kristin wanted to graduate from diapers to big girl pants, but it meant surrendering to what her mom wanted. Progress hit an impasse. To change the dynamics, we decided Kristin should spend a day at Gaga Mitchell's. There were no control issues there. Gaga could encourage Kristin to use the potty as a personal favor.

The road trip to Gaga's house worked. Pleasing her grandmother benefited us all. Upon her triumphant return home, Kristin was one victorious little heroine when she told Mommy and Daddy what she had done that day for her grandmother.

Kristin and Gaga Mitchell

The Worst News

A psychologist friend offered me a bit of wisdom.

"Bad news should be held on to for as long as possible."

He was originally from Ireland and probably in his mid-seventies. With that old-world accent, his words held special gravitas.

He told me, "Before telephones were widely used in the Irish Republic, it could take months to get a letter to relatives here in the States. Let's say we lost a family member. Well, the circumstances wouldn't change, but depending on how slow the mail moved, it allowed the family a bit more time before getting hit with the devastating news nobody could change. In a way, it was more merciful then."

He was correct, but tonight I cannot hold on any longer.

Gaga and Poppy join Michele and David in our family room. They can tell by the way I look so dejected that their lives are about to be sent to an unrecognizable place.

"Michele, you were right. The call from the detective was about Kristin."

I detail what I know while the four begin to weep. From my first call to Michele, she has known something was wrong. David and Michele have called and sent unanswered texts to Kristin. They were suspicious. Kristin had always gotten back to them right away.

But not tonight.

For my parents, at their age, this of course will not be the first close family member they had lost, although later they told me it was more stunning than losing their first son when he was only six months old. He was a baby, but Kristin was a fully-grown woman of twenty-one. She was a multi-dimensional, young adult with a life and a blossoming future unfolding for us to watch and share.

After explaining the inexplicable with everything Detective McGowan told me, there is nothing more to say. It's late. Tomorrow will bring a torrent of imperatives.

We have no cemetery plot or, to be honest, anything we need. There's a lot to do, and none of it is welcome.

Looking from the outside in, people will be watching, studying, to see how our family handles this catastrophe. No different from drivers rubbernecking on an expressway after a mishap; they cannot help but look over and be thankful it's not them in that wreck.

I know my family will get through this somehow. Will we stay in the house and pull the shades down and avoid people? That's not us.

I know we will face this head-on as we always have. But this one is an Everest to climb. I know something this bad has to be answered in time by something good. I have no idea what form this will take.

Funeral Homes

I awaken. I feel horrible. Is our nightmare over?

No, it's gaining momentum.

In our present reality, we start every morning with an immediate cry. Then we stop cold. Just like that. On and off. Odd.

This morning, calls and emails go out. Michele, David, and I will interview funeral home salespeople and walk cemeteries in search of the perfect spot to lay to rest our twenty-one-year-old daughter, a young woman with so much promise who was prepared to launch a job she had won and a future she earned on her own merits.

But it's all gone.

As early June days go, this Saturday morning is insufferably hot starting at sunup. Twenty-one days ago, I hugged and praised Kristin at her graduation. That Saturday seems so long ago.

When we are not figuring out arrangements, we are fielding calls from detectives working the case and people at the apartment complex where the murder took place thirty hours ago. That feels like such a short time, but so much has taken place since then.

Michele and I will be working the clock forward and backward trying to get a wake and funeral scheduled. I take the lead searching out details of a killing we still cannot believe happened. I want to know what took place. Maybe it's to prove to myself this actually happened.

We visit three funeral homes. Two are so dreary we cannot wait to leave. In the third, Andy, the funeral director, intuits what we are going through. With a light touch, he asks insightful questions and puts us more at ease. He knows what he's doing and we feel better here.

After a brief look at three viewing rooms, Andy asks which one we'd like to reserve. There is a small room, a medium one, and an overly large one. We rule out the overly large room since Kristin has been at college in Philadelphia for four years. We doubt many people will travel over two hours to Maryland. She has been away from home so long; we do not expect many from this area will attend either.

Andy says with conviction, "I've seen this before. This place will be packed. A tragedy like this happens, and anyone who ever knew your daughter will be here. This place will be filled. Neighborhood friends and families. High school friends she hasn't seen since her graduation. You'll be surprised how many students and faculty from Philadelphia will come here for this. I'm telling you, I've seen it. You will need the large room."

Michele and I take Andy's advice and set aside the large room which can open to a large entry area in case we need it. A young person's death brings out those never expected.

While Andy is asking whether we would like a wooden or metal casket for Kristin, David asks to walk outside alone. I wonder how his sister's horrific death is hitting him and hope he is not going to do something drastic when we are not watching. We have not had much time to ask how he's doing. It is hard to think of everything at this time.

I wait a moment while Andy and Michele are discussing costs, then ease out of the room to a window in the reception area and watch David sitting on a battered concrete bench. He leans forward with his head down.

Let it out, Dave. We know how much you love her.

The next part on this dreadful day requires Michele, David, and me to visit the caskets on display downstairs. Surrounded by dark wood paneling that I associate with a 1960s basement club room, there are full-size caskets lined up with lids open for inspection. After a brief survey, Michele says, "I think Kristin would like white. She wouldn't want a dark wooden one."

I never imagined a conversation about how Kristin would like her casket. But it's happening.

I say to Michele and David, "Can't speak for you two, but I really don't want to be here ... " The irony isn't lost on them, even under these circumstances. It's a bizarre time for that remark, but our lives will be strange from here on out.

We are perusing the oddest place. Like a new-car showroom for caskets. For colors and finishes they have gold, silver, bronze, white, and various shades of brown. There are metal and wood. You can go with a custom color, but it adds waiting time and cost.

The lids are padded if we want. Interiors can be white, blue, pink, beige, or silver. Fabrics come in taffeta, crepe, plush, twill, or velvet. There are various grades and styles for flower holders, picture holders, and flag holders. Pillows are standard, but there is a casket head panel selection catalog to help. You can get praying hands, the flag, or flowers. All kinds of options for someone who is not present to appreciate any of them. As far as we know.

So many bells and whistles for the dead. Had Kristin been a long-suffering elderly woman, what I'm feeling would be different. Maybe it would be more tolerable. There is no relief in this, just a total emotionally crushing feeling.

The day before yesterday, Kristin was sunning herself beside a pool with a college friend. Both would soon be trying on shiny-new careers and all that life has to offer. She had training scheduled in Minneapolis in three short weeks and a small company car coming her way. She was on course for a sales associate position that could set her up for long-term success. A well-earned start was inked on her calendar—only days away.

The day before yesterday, Kristin was also writing thank-you notes for her graduation presents, including the digital camera that captured her last few smiles.

Only yesterday morning, Kristin was having an argument with her boyfriend. And then complete hell broke loose.

Okay, I need to concentrate. Now is what's important.

My daughter was murdered yesterday, and our mission is to choose a casket. Then go and find a decent cemetery plot.

The casket was a relatively easy decision to make. Kristin would like the glossy white one. Fine. Add it to the bill with a few options. Done.

The Cemetery

We search the immense, sun-scorched 350-acre Leighton Park Cemetery, established in 1835. A good number of Mitchells are interred here. To help us, Gaga and Poppy Mitchell set up an appointment with Roberta, a sales representative who will meet us in the main building.

Roberta says she is new at her job, and several times she shows how new. She constantly misinterprets maps that indicate available plots. We need one for Kristin but are looking for four in a row. Who knows what the future might hold for our family?

She points in the distance.

"How about over there? By that tree?"

No, too close to a rough-looking neighborhood where we hear kids yelling at each other. It's rest in *peace*, remember?

"How about in that area? Where there are no headstones," I suggest.

Roberta checks and frowns. "No, all of those are taken."

She is struggling, but to be fair, this cemetery is over 150 years old, and her map has tiny handwritten notes that make deciphering them complex. Added to that, every plot map has been copied countless times.

We reenter the Explorer and continue our crawl around the cemetery. This heat makes me wonder if we will survive the search.

I wondered about finding plots in proximity to my buried relatives. You never know. The last one, my paternal grandmother, Mildred, was interred here in 1972.

Roberta becomes excited. She thinks she's found four plots in a row. Maybe this is coming together.

She waves to a groundskeeper standing by a dusty green dump truck. We will be here for a few scalding hours, but this is Fred's day job. It's my guess he's in his late thirties. Under his soiled light-green jumpsuit, both arms are tattooed from his wrists to halfway up his neck. Fred's hair is mostly brown but the summit looks home-bleached; his face showcases deep creases burned in by the relentless sun. I take it back; Fred could be in his late twenties—or early forties.

When Fred starts talking about this cemetery, we feel relieved. He knows this place as if he was here when it opened. He quickly figures out what we already know: Roberta is not in sync with the plot map.

"You're tryin' to find four in a row *right here?*" Fred asks while pointing at the map Roberta is holding. "Well, *this here* is *three*. Three numbers open. See? That'n there don't count."

Roberta hands the map over to Fred. He looks, does an about-face, and walks off without saying a word. Is he leaving us? Please don't. Twenty paces away, he turns back.

"Over this way ... " He points with his thumb. "Right there, yeah, that there's four in a row."

Four plots. A short fifty paces from the final resting places of my two Mitchell great-grandparents, my two Mitchell grandparents, my two Mitchell uncles, and my brother, Robert Mitchell. Robert is a brother I never knew. He was only six months old when he died, three years before I was born.

Four in a row. We'll take them. Good location. Goodbye. We have so much more to do today.

Mitchell relatives are buried less than fifty paces from Kristin's final resting place.

We find a measure of comfort knowing Kristin will be laid to rest close to family. We hope our daughter and these other deceased relatives have met on *the Other Side* by this time.

That's what we believe. Good thing. Because we need to believe in something.

Home

It's Sunday, two days after we got the news.

Our home is taken over by friends, family, and Michele's coworkers pouring out their hearts by helping. We're relieved they're here. We dub them *The Angels*. They must be imagining what we are going through and probably praying it never happens to their families.

The doorbell rings. Each time, it's someone dropping food off at our front door. In the living room, someone's running the vacuum. When we try to do anything, we're redirected nicely with, "Let me take care of that for you." Michele, David, and I often retreat upstairs to collect our thoughts, make calls, and try to make sense out of things.

I'm so proud of my wife and son. We, as a threesome, have become a synchronized force. Each of us is emotionally numb but supporting each other.

What next? Oh, there is plenty.

We need to select burial clothes for Kristin. Call detectives working the case. Call a friend or family member and break their hearts by breaking the news. We have to call the apartment complex people again to see what is happening there. We explain the tragedy again and again.

I see us existing in two states of mind: observers but simultaneously participating in everything. Without coaching, we know what to do, and we keep it together, but we do not understand why.

Kristin is dead.

Can I bargain for one more hour with her? A minute? One more conversation? I already know the answer. The answer is: I am in denial, and it's going to take a long time before I accept this.

Monday and Tuesday

It's Monday.

My suit pants need the waist let out a merciful inch. I tell the people at the cleaners I need this altered today, and then I tell them why. They do it while I wait. They tell me how sorry they are about our circumstances. No charge.

I am interviewed by two newspapers. They query with "how and why" she died. "How she lived" is apparently not interesting to them. I hurriedly email them photos of Kristin and send her résumé along with other information they request.

Kristin's clothing is another critical concern. The catch is she was living in Philadelphia, and we will not be able to access what's there in time. Kristin's favorite colors were pink and black. Michele asks her close friend, Donna, if she can shop for a pink sweater. It is no easy task considering this is the beginning of June.

Then it's Tuesday, and an article in Baltimore's largest newspaper was written to be sensational. It fits neatly under crimes of passion. They use the killer's police interview as the thread of the story. I didn't know his interview was available. The article states Kristin precipitated an argument that escalated, and then she was killed in the ensuing violence. Their story is based on the words of her killer? There is nothing from the interview I gave.

What a horrible insult to a devastating injury. Later that week, I school the reporter on how thoughtless her decision-making was. "Imagine this happened to your child," I fire at her.

She says she doesn't have a child; her editor made the decision.

Time flies attending to the must-do's that are continuing to mount up. But the easiest decision of the week is to cancel our subscription to that newspaper.

Scheduling the funeral is impossible since our daughter's body is still in Philadelphia. Her body is technically held as evidence. A call finally comes, and we learn we can bury her Thursday, nearly a week after she was killed.

Donna comes through with burial clothing. It took an entire day in malls and specialty shops for her to find a pink sweater and it looks handpicked by Kristin. Perfect. Our daughter will also wear a black skirt with black dress gloves to hide her damaged hands. A beautiful pink and white chiffon scarf hides Kristin's injured neck.

Wednesday, the Day of the Viewing

The early afternoon heat is oppressive. We gain relief when we enter the air-conditioned funeral home. It has been a long while since one of our family members was the one being waked.

Bouquets lines the walls on both sides of the white casket. Michele, David, and I walk gently over to Kristin. This is the first time we see her since graduation. Nobody is ready for this.

She appears peaceful. Nothing like what she experienced days ago in her apartment. She will be twenty-one forever.

Forever young. Forever beautiful. Forever lost.

Through a veil of tears, Michele sees her lifeless daughter. Immediately catching her attention is a pair of black gloves. They function to conceal horrendous defensive wounds to Kristin's beautiful hands. Michele imagines the horror and pain Kristin endured throughout the fatal attack. Now, in the uncomfortable silence of this moment, Michele realizes she will never hear Kristin's voice again. It's part of a future to be lived without her.

My heart learns what it's like to break completely. I feel it mostly for my wife and son. David shared a supportive and encouraging relationship with his sister. They would have enjoyed their entire lives together in such a beautiful affiliation. This scene was nowhere in the script. Although four years apart, they fit perfectly from the day he was born. It was unconditional love. It was magical to watch.

I don't want my son or wife here anymore than I want my daughter here. This is all wrong. This is loathsome.

We say goodbye to Kristin until this evening's wake. The three of us are almost outside when David stops. He walks back over to Kristin and stands by her casket. Brother and sister.

What is he thinking? When he rejoins us, he whispers softly, "That's not Kristin." He says she is more than the body she lived in. She has moved on. It gives him comfort believing her body is no longer "her," considering what she has been through.

The Viewing

It is good the funeral director urged us to take the large visitation room. A train of mourners is surging in without a break in the line.

This evening's viewing moves through hour numbers two and three, and the head count is lost at 500 participants—with more arriving. Mourners trail out onto a sidewalk that remains excessively hot. Someone tells me street traffic is at a standstill.

We tick past the fourth hour with no letup. Michele and I never once leave a floor position three feet in diameter. We fail to remember some names, but nobody corrects us.

This is a lot to process.

Our son, with Gaga and Poppy at his side, creates a second receiving line so people are able to enter and gain relief from the heat. It seems everyone we have ever known is arriving tonight.

Several feet to my left, I see the side of my daughter's face. At her May 14 graduation, she was buoyant and enthusiastic. She was magnificent. Now she is silent. Tomorrow, she will be buried.

A tall man steps in front of me. Wait, didn't he live across the street from me? We met when we were seven. Richard? I haven't seen him in four decades.

I will be the first to admit that Richard was considered Mr. Dreamy in high school, back when all of the girls threw themselves at him. Tall, handsome, thick hair, Crest smile, and an athletic build. Richard made the most of high school and after. He was one lucky guy in the looks department. It is said that "nature bats last," and I see how time has leveled the playing field. Baldish, thick face, and a thick body have rendered him mortal. Just another mid-fifties man like me.

It appears Richard hasn't had a good cry in years because it is all pouring out tonight. He weeps for me, and I try to console him. His assessment of my family's regrettable circumstances underscores how bad things must be for us.

The wake rolls into hour five. Michele and I have no idea what time it is. It is only *now*. I'm okay with the distraction of having hundreds of people paying their last respects to my daughter. We hug, kiss, and shake hands with many we haven't seen in over half of our lives. Friends. Family. Neighbors. Co-workers. Acquaintances. It is likely we will never see most of these people again after tonight. It took this degree of devastation to bring so many out.

Most mourners take a moment and approach Kristin's casket. That's when they see her hands are concealed within those black wrist-length gloves. These were mandatory to cover what her attacker did to her a week ago. She looks peaceful now, and she will never suffer again.

While the viewing continues, at the rear door of the funeral home, a woman slips in without anyone noticing. Patricia is a teacher at the high school where Kristin graduated four years ago.

Earlier in the day, Patricia abandoned any notion of attending this viewing. She was a home room teacher for Kristin at Mount de Sales Academy during her junior year. She assumed that tonight's viewing would be crowded and thought a few concentrated prayers at home would suffice.

Her mind abruptly changed. She is on a mission tonight.

At all times, Patricia wears two distinctly different lockets. One is silver; one is gold. Both contain locks of hair from her deceased daughters, Colleen and Erin. In September 2001, they were killed on the campus of the University of Maryland by a tornado, an unusual event for Maryland. The car they were traveling in was picked up and propelled over an eight-story dormitory.

Patricia asks if someone could point out the closest friend of Kristin's mother, Michele. A woman who knows the Mitchells motions toward Donna Watkins, Michele's dearest friend since they taught together thirty years earlier.

Patricia's emotions make explaining herself challenging, but she finds a way to tell Donna the story of her daughters and her lockets. She connects her compelling story with this night.

While Patricia speaks, Donna is transfixed by the way she clutches these lockets close to her heart. Patricia grips them almost as if she is protecting them. There is nothing symbolic about it. This mother had to say goodbye to both of her daughters, and this is real. She carries Erin and Colleen with her wherever she goes. Kristin's passing has brought the past to today.

Patricia realizes if she couldn't find a trusted individual at the viewing tonight, Michele would never possess a locket for herself. Locks of Kristin's hair have to be obtained soon. The funeral is early tomorrow.

After depicting her intent, Patricia leaves discreetly by the door she entered. At the end of the viewing, Donna sees to it that an ample amount of Kristin's hair is snipped for safekeeping.

Patricia's actions on this night are a crucial component in a story some will later come to call a true miracle. This will take time to play out.

As we are all nearing the point of exhaustion, the viewing for Kristin Marie Mitchell ends. Outside, on the parking lot, the heat is suffocating. Gaining a full breath is virtually impossible. The sun might have taken the night off, but the next day is anticipated to be hotter.

We will lay our daughter to rest—a young woman whose future is shattered. The dreams almost fulfilled will be carried by pallbearers into a church, prayed over by hundreds, and finally lowered into her grave.

There is nothing anyone can say or do to make this one scintilla better.

And I need to attend to a eulogy.

The Eulogy

I write and rewrite. Is there a perfect sendoff for saying goodbye to our child? If so, I cannot imagine it.

It is three a.m.

At precisely this moment one week ago, Kristin was being attacked. I close both eyes and say a prayer. This is so bad.

I know I will not be capable of speaking this tribute in seven hours. When I read these words aloud, I halt and choke up. This needs to be spoken by someone else.

Our printer malfunctions. Another instance of electricity playing a role in the story of this week. All writing is done by hand. I need to rewrite this so someone is able to read it without my edits and scratch-outs.

I'm jolted when an errant tear smacks the paper. In a house this silent, any noise is abrupt.

I'm attempting to sum up a girl I loved months before she was born. A girl I held in my arms with so much pride in the delivery room. I remember taking 35mm photos of her at birth and rushing to a one-hour photo shop so I could share them with Michele that same day. A big breakthrough back then.

The hospital scrubs top I wore in the delivery room hangs in an upstairs closet. It reminds me of the day we became a family.

I am distracted by thinking back to those days of wonder. Tonight, I wonder why this happened to her. I ask Kristin "why" aloud since everyone else is sleeping, but there is no answer.

So much adrenaline, but finally, blessed sleep.

Kristin Mitchell
CATS, HORSES & KIDS

Cats were Kristin's first love, but on her third birthday a new animal was added. She received a rocking horse with special springs added that brought greater bounciness to her galloping. Once she settled into that plastic saddle, she had the horse leaping and jumping as far as it could go. Everyone feared she would topple over or shoot off, but she stayed on, laughing hilariously. It lit a fire in her to become an exceptional equestrian one day.

The moment Kristin's love for riding horses kicked in.

When Kristin was two and a half, our first Siamese cat, Rockwell, named after the famous illustrator, became sick from both feline leukemia and infectious peritonitis. He was my wedding present to Michele but had to be euthanized on our tenth anniversary.

Rockwell was succeeded by Gatsby.

Gatsby and Kristin became soulmates from the moment they met. We could feel their love. He was her cat; she was his best friend. They played together, napped together. The perfect twosome.

Her love of cats and horses carried throughout her life. She was always holding a cat or preparing for a horse-riding practice or event.

Kristin and Gatsby. Love at first hug.

When children played in the neighborhood, Kristin kept everyone happy with appealing ideas about what to do next. As a preschool and later as elementary school student, she brought friends home when she was not already invited to play at their homes. She loved to improvise backyard shows with her friends to be enjoyed by their parents. These spontaneous performances were remarkable.

Funeral Mass and Burial

Someone decided to hold the reception at our home. From a bedroom window, I see men and women busily raising tents, assembling tables, and bringing chairs to our backyard.

Michele recognizes colleagues from her school where she teaches. They're giving up time to help with this. In the driveway, a coal-black limousine backs in. This dreadful day officially begins.

The church fills with faces we saw at the wake. No tears this morning; everyone looks drained and expressionless. I give them the "I cannot believe we are here" headshake.

A woman from the Howard County Domestic Violence agency comes to our pew and presents a business card. "You can call if you feel you might want some counseling. We are here to help you."

I thank her and I offer my help. How exactly I'd help makes no sense, but I'm trying to be nice.

She says, "Mr. Mitchell, today is about your family. We can talk later."

She makes more sense than what I said.

Five priests are conducting this funeral Mass. Having five priests is extraordinary. Father Gerald McGlone is from Saint Joseph's University, Kristin's alma mater for a mere twenty days. Father Jack Dennis is from our son's high school, Loyola Blakefield. Father Mike Jendrek and Father James McGovern are both from our parish. Monsignor Francis Seymour from Kearny, New Jersey, is my mother's cousin. He married Michele and me over thirty years ago. Plus, a deacon also assisted with this funeral service.

So many in attendance at Kristin's somber funeral Mass.

Our daughter's casket is wheeled up the main aisle. Soon, Michele, David, and I stand with our right hands resting on it. This is our child in there. If only she could climb out, and we could go home arm in arm.

Let's call off this nightmare which is too much to fathom.

St. Paul Catholic Church was founded in 1838. The two-story ashlar granite church itself was the place of worship where Baltimore's Babe Ruth was married on October 14, 1914. Our daughter had her First Holy Communion here.

This funeral, today, is the history we will attach to this church from this day forward. There are eulogies by Felicity followed by Samantha, Kristin's best friends in high school and college, respectively. Their faces and words describe how much they love Kristin. This loss will hurt them forever, too.

Collin, who dated Kristin for a short while in high school, was her date for senior prom. He steps to the podium with a boom box. I am not sure about this. Collin pushes a button, and we hear "Shine Your Light," a beautiful anthem sung by Robbie Robertson. It fits the moment perfectly.

With David and Michele. Our right hands rest upon Kristin's coffin.

Next, David touches every heart with beautiful words for his sister. He is the next best thing to having Kristin speak to us today. Everyone is so touched when he says, "Kristin will forever be twenty-one. She will be forever young." David speaks to Kristin more than to this assembly of mourners. He connects profoundly with every person here. What an excellent way to picture our daughter: forever twenty-one. But, honestly, forever spoken of in the past tense.

Kristin's grandfather, Poppy Mitchell, adds loving words to his grandchild's eulogy. Besides this tribute today, in his home workshop, he is creating an adorable white cross to mark her grave. It will suffice until a headstone can be prepared. Poppy will fashion commemorations for each and every birthday, Christmas, and Easter, which are placed lovingly on Kristin's grave.

Michele and I approach the podium. My friend, who could almost be called my brother, Dick Parker, stands by us to deliver my eulogy.

Somehow a sense, a calmness, rushes over me. A feeling of peace. I describe our daughter as the sweet and generous person she was. I refer to the generous ways she brought joy into people's lives. This is not only our loss, it belongs to everyone. I describe how her showers went on forever. "Our bathtub was not a shower stall; it was her time machine." It draws smiles from the assembled mourners, but that dissipates quickly.

Michele and I step aside and let Dick speak my words written hours ago.

I cannot believe we are here.

We return to the black limousine to make one final stop.

Kristin is being driven to her final resting place so close to her starting place. A quarter of a mile from Leighton Park Cemetery stands the hospital where she was born twenty-one years ago. She has come full circle, decades too early.

The last few moments before Kristin is lowered into the ground.

After prayers, there are holy water, a lot of tears, and then total silence. We remain seated while Kristin is lowered into her grave. Everyone waits until this is completed.

As we leave, I point to dates on nearby gravestones. One woman lived to be 101. That is eighty years more than our child.

Further evidence that life is not fair.

What Is Wrong with You?

We arrive home following the funeral and burial. Friends, family, and coworkers move in and out of the house freely. In the backyard, the white tents make an unforgiving June sun somewhat bearable. Food, drink, and conversations about anything but *why we are here* make good distractions.

A few ask what the police have to say about the case. Others want to know how our family is doing. Many avoid talking about it. And that is okay. I would find it nearly impossible to say anything if this had happened to someone else. I have no expectations of what others will do or say. I'm simply going through the motions.

One coworker, Ann, with whom I've never had the smoothest relationship clotheslines me. "You know, I was thinking. Do you realize you could *do anything at work* between now and the end of the year, and the owners *wouldn't say a word to you?*"

I guess she was making a point, but maybe I missed it.

I stumble to find a response. "Huh? *What?*"

She explains that I could make any kind of mistake or do anything I wanted, and nobody would call me on it. As if I could take advantage of this rare opportunity. I would have a free pass the remainder of the year.

All I can manage is, *"Oh my God. What is wrong with you?"*

Who thinks like this? Or says this? How could anyone pick this moment and act so insensitively? So *odd?* This will repeat itself in my mind for years to come. Maybe it was a clumsy attempt at irony, but it felt appalling to me.

This long, hot day continues with a profusion of words of encouragement and comforting thoughts. I never knew we had so many allies prepared to pick us up on such short notice.

Tents are lowered, tables and chairs are folded, and people wish us well in our altered state.

We have a lot of adjustments to make.

Four Minus One

It reaches midnight on this day of the funeral. The house is empty except for the remaining three. Michele, David, and me.

This evening we ask ourselves how we made it through the past week. Adrenaline? Maybe. We had no alternative but to meet every deadline. Maybe it had to do with those prayers we fit into every open moment.

Yes, very possibly, it was those prayers.

We could not have done this without outside help.

Starting tomorrow, David begins a weeklong volunteer trip somewhere in South Dakota. He will work alongside his high school's group of volunteers on a housing construction project within a Sioux reservation.

Even under these circumstances, David still has an interest in going there. The three of us talk it through and come to the same conclusion; there is no upside in staying home now. In some ways, he might feel worse missing this trip with his friends. The decision to go is with the hope he will have a positive experience to add some color and perspective to his life during this dark time.

Michele and I do not like putting David on a jet. Airliners crash. And after "the thing that could never happen" happened, we feel nothing is off the list of the possible.

So, David flies to South Dakota.

Then we are back in the reality of Kristin's tragedy. We prepare for a memorial service at our daughter's alma mater, Saint Joseph's University, which is set for Sunday afternoon.

What will it be like to return there?

Memorial Service

Attending Kristin's memorial service at Saint Joseph's University means we will drive the same highways and tree-lined streets that took us to her graduation four weeks ago. The weather is identical to the day she hugged classmates and bid them farewell. We had been happy to see our investments in time, patience, and tuition paid off.

There's a spot reserved on the same lot where we met Kristin's boyfriend. We park close to where the white graduation tent stood the last day we saw her alive, the first time we met him.

I think about time machines. My mind goes there even though it's cruel.

What is time, anyway? Do then and now exist side by side?

This impromptu memorial service in the Smith Chapel feels correct. Jesuit priests offer readings specifically relevant to the loss of a child. These are followed by Kristin's professors sharing excerpts from Kristin's final semester papers. Hearing Kristin's words was an inspired idea. Everything fits perfectly within the charisma of the chapel. Their combined efforts call to mind what a warm and irresistible person she was.

Kristin's classmates tearfully recollect memories now frozen in the past. A slideshow set against songs like "Forever Young" by Rod Stewart sums up friendships that ended too soon. Every tune takes on a different meaning today.

People introducing themselves on this day will play an integral part in our lives and in our healing. That comes later.

We leave the chapel sad and silent. I wonder if we will ever walk across this campus again.

Kristin's Apartment

Our next stop is unfathomable. We are driving to the apartment in Conshohocken, Pennsylvania, *where it happened.*

Ed is a corporate lawyer with Riverwalk at Millennium Apartments in Conshohocken, Pennsylvania—where Kristin's murder took place. In his last job, Ed worked for the district attorney's office in Norristown. He knows everyone on the prosecution team assigned to Kristin's case. He can explain the entire process of moving a case from a crime scene to a prison cell.

What an advantage to have access to him.

In the Riverwalk offices, I meet Ed for the first time. Having him with me while I walk into Kristin's apartment should bring a measure of comfort. I don't know how I am going to handle this.

Michele remains in the car when I go into the apartment building. I will try to get this done quickly, but I also want to look around and not miss anything.

Ed unlocks the apartment door, and I step into the kitchen. What steals my breath away is directly in front of me. A large section of living room carpet is missing along with its padding. I'm looking at bare concrete. The crime scene people removed this flooring as evidence.

On the kitchen counter, I see a pad of tan-colored Post-Its. In Kristin's writing, I study a list reminding her to finish sending thank you notes out for graduation gifts. Some names are crossed off. "Mom and Dad" are uncrossed, but she had thanked us thoroughly on graduation day.

This entire apartment was a crime scene, and it surprises me to see a pan holding brownies and another with muffins still remaining. One has been removed from each container. I can imagine the peaceful setting in which these were baked, and the pure hell that ensued afterward.

Here, in this kitchen, is where a man lost all control and humanity, and savagely stabbed and slashed my daughter to death. Directly in front of me is the place where it started.

The medical examiner figured the wounds to her back came from her trying to escape from this murderer. She was probably trying to open the door leading to the hallway. It was her last chance at freedom. Her hands were injured trying to fend him off. All of her wounds were considered defensive.

This is no longer someone's apartment; it is a tomb, especially when I go into Kristin's bedroom. A living person, my own flesh and blood, died precisely where I am standing. Her bed was removed just days ago. Today, in this room, all that remains is a feeling of emptiness and silence.

No matter where she had gone in her short life, I know this is where it came to an end.

I cannot help but picture the struggle in this place that fateful last night. I cannot imagine how savage it must have been. I wish I'd been there to intercept the rage that man inflicted on my child. No matter where it took me, it would have ended better than this. But I did not get that choice.

Twenty-one years prior, I was an excited delivery-room dad at Kristin's birth. I was there when she took her first breath. Today, I stand where she died. The beginning and the end.

I snap out of the flashbacks, and my mind switches to a couple of stuffed animals Kristin had loved since she was small. She always kept them on her bed. But her bed is gone.

Were they taken away, too? Were they destroyed?

Because of what happened here, anything could have been removed as potential evidence. Anything could have been disposed of because of its condition.

One irreplaceable item is Kristin's Popple doll. Popple had white fur, yellow hair, orange cheeks, and contrasting blue and magenta ears. As a child, Kristin loved her Popple and never went to sleep without it. So, where is it?

Equally precious is a Curious George doll bought in Washington, D.C. in the Smithsonian Natural History Museum. Every Curious George on the store's shelf had several felt letters missing from his name on his red hat. I asked the salesperson to take a look in the back room for one with his full name. She doubted she would find one but returned holding it up high with all letters in place. Seventeen years later, all letters remained.

Once, on a beach vacation, George's left eye became lost. Kristin was quite young at the time, and this really bothered her. We had a needle and thread, so Michele and I stitched in an eye that was not perfect but pretty close to a match. Kristin was overjoyed to have George back with both eyes.

Small victory. Popple and George were untouched.

Looking into the bedroom closet, I can just make out Popple and George sitting high on a shelf. Thank God. What a relief to rescue something with meaning from this apartment. These are the only items I later carry to Michele who is still waiting patiently in the car.

I've seen all I need. I had to come here.

As Ed and I return to the kitchen, I stop short of the door. This was the entrance to Kristin's first home she could call her own. It's where her killer ex-boyfriend entered and exited after stealing her most precious possession—her life.

Above the door, I notice a wooden crucifix for the first time. Not intending to be sacrilegious, aloud I say, "It would have been better had this been a horseshoe."

Ed doesn't react.

I walk out of this hallowed place where an event hellishly beyond belief took place. In our daughter's apartment, she was attacked; she was murdered; she died. I had never known anyone who had been murdered. I do now.

It happened here.

With Samantha

Next on this marathon Sunday, Michele and I join Kristin's close friend Samantha at a tiny restaurant near a Hampton Inn where we are staying. This is the first time we speak with someone who knew Kristin as a best friend since the tragedy. Samantha also knows Kristin's killer.

This young woman is in disbelief about what happened and tells us this over and over. She cannot believe what he actually did. She had been on double dates with her boyfriend, Kristin, and the killer.

Samantha tries to humanize him, but I have no interest in understanding him as a real person. To me, he is a merciless murderer. I don't need to hear about how kind or generous he was. None of this has value to me.

I want him to pay for what he did. Big time. My feelings of anger are colliding head-on with my feelings of positivity about God and Jesus, right and wrong, forgiveness, and the afterlife. It's one big crucible that mixes reprisals, forgiveness, and damnation for this guy.

Forgiveness? How would I forgive someone who has performed this heinous act? Forgiveness? Forgiveness doesn't fit. Let that be God's domain.

Speaking with Samantha also includes the first instance when I am jolted hearing words like, "My mother would kill me if she knew I ... " I immediately create that scene in my head no matter how innocently she said it. I will later flinch when anyone says, "That guy was a backstabber," or anything similar to it.

With Samantha's help, we hope to learn what went down the days before the murder. But we're not going to learn enough from her. Samantha was not in communication with Kristin those final days. They had a huge blowup over Kristin's boyfriend's consistently controlling behavior and how Kristin accepted it.

Samantha pushed Kristin to get some space from this guy. His constant attention was suffocating her; all he wanted was

Kristin all for himself. In fact, Kristin and Samantha set up the entire Memorial Day weekend at the Jersey shore to allow Kristin time away from him.

Samantha and Kristin drove to a shore home, but this soon-to-be killer broke up the weekend by preying upon Kristin's emotions and guilting her out of there. The two women were to spend four days together. It was reduced to twenty-four hours when he drove there to take Kristin away.

The day after the weekend was ruined, on a Sunday evening, Kristin had her final conversation with Samantha. Things became tense again on the subject of "getting some space." One of them hung up the phone; Samantha doesn't remember who. They never saw each other again. Kristin's murder saw to that.

The Prosecution Team

It's Monday. Michele and I will attend a meeting as impossible to envision as any we have endured the past ten days.

Today, we introduce ourselves to the prosecution team working our daughter's case. Renowned on this team is Risa Vetri Ferman, the First Assistant District Attorney. She's second-in-command to District Attorney Bruce Castor. Ms. Ferman directs the county's detective bureau and oversees all homicide cases.

The prosecutor working our case is enjoying a rare vacation. After meeting with Charlotte Stark weeks later, nobody could ask for anyone better than her. Charlotte's experience was earned by handling hundreds of domestic violence cases. Those who assigned her to our case know it will be handled mightily. Charlotte is an active fighter; domestic violence cases are her passion.

Several assistant prosecutors and a couple of detectives take seats at the table on either side of Risa Vetri Ferman. There isn't time to get to know anyone, but one detective stands out for being sensitive to our situation.

In the weeks and months to come, we connect with Sam Gallen. He's married with two daughters and a son. We feel he identifies with us, starting with Kristin. Under different circumstances, Sam knows she could have been his daughter. Most cases he handles involve common, everyday criminals; not this one.

The prosecution team explains the steps already taken to get this killer into lockup. Coming next is a preliminary hearing where a judge will decide the merits of this case going to court. No date is set for this as of yet. Maybe a month afterwards, there will be a formal arraignment where the killer will hear all charges against him. What will follow are potential motions by both sides, more court dates, and—we hope—final sentencing.

One detective hands Michele a clear plastic bag with the jewelry Kristin wore the night she was attacked. Holding her rings, earrings, and necklace makes the truth real. If I were still in denial, this moment slaps me into believing.

With so much condemnatory evidence, plus an interview with the murderer taken that morning, the prosecutors say this case is airtight. This is the first we learn the killer literally admitted to doing this, the first welcome surprise.

The second welcome surprise is hearing about Montgomery County's ninety-eight-percent conviction rate. This means ninety-eight percent of the time an offender is found guilty. It could be from a successful trial or from a guilty plea. Either way, their success rate is very high, in fact, especially high compared with surrounding areas of Philadelphia.

They credit it to the level of professionalism they put into working cases. That includes collecting and protecting strong evidence and gaining confessions that hold up under fire in courtrooms. They simply don't drop the ball.

The murderer's 11-page interview, taken the morning of June 3 by Jim McGowan, is laced with the killer's amateurish lies trying to make his actions look like self-defense. The killer knew our daughter wasn't going to have an opportunity to give her version of that night in court, so he portrayed her as the aggressor. Those familiar with Kristin said this is the last thing they would believe. He was over six feet tall and built like an athlete. She was five foot three and demure. She never had a prayer.

Before leaving the prosecution team's office, there is one more piece of business. This one is pleasant and a complete contrast to the subject covered in our meeting. A detective hands us a cage containing Oliver, Kristin's hamster. They took care of this little guy after charging into Kristin's apartment that fatal morning. Oliver could have seen everything that happened. His cage was on a washer/dryer steps away from the kitchen.

Kristin's little hamster, Oliver

Michele and I exit the building carrying Oliver's cage. Our sights are set on a tiny beach house we own on Maryland's Eastern Shore. It was intended as an oasis of sanity for our family of four a couple of years ago. We hope it will be especially helpful today.

Our emotions have been running high, and we feel so drained that halfway through the drive we practically fall asleep. A stop at a small sandwich shop for a bite and a cup of coffee might do the trick. The place is empty except for Maggie, a tired waitress who's around forty-five. Maggie spots us carrying in a hamster cage and interrupts the quiet with, "No. He's gotta go. That is a health violation."

I set Oliver's cage on the floor and walk toward the counter, close enough to say to Maggie, "Tell you what, if he has to leave, we leave with him." This doesn't seem to bother her.

I explain the reason Oliver is here. After the briefest version of what we've been through, she backs down from her health-violation high horse and matches my sad story with her own.

About a year ago, Maggie's Saturday nights involved playing cards with her mother, brother, and a best friend. Today, not one of them is living. Her mother died from cancer; her friend had a fatal disease Maggie didn't want to talk about; and her brother killed himself after their mother's death.

Scratch the surface, and you'll find that everyone has pains to live through. Nobody gets out without suffering a little or a lot.

Maggie asks us to keep Oliver under the table in case someone from the health inspector's office walks in. The likelihood of that seems slight, but we grant Maggie's wish and Oliver stays with us where he belongs.

Later, Michele, Oliver, and I arrive safely at our precious little rancher.

Retiring Kristin's Cell Phone Number

This morning, we will paint the front porch I scraped and primed weeks before the tragedy. Finally, something positive is coming together. All we've had to think about lately has been destruction. This work will be therapeutic.

We paint for a while, then stop to focus on voicemails that remain on Kristin's cell phone line. We hold our breath listening to each one. After we get through them, we question whether detectives combed anything offensive since nothing disturbing is from Kristin's killer. The last voicemail is David demanding Kristin call him back the night of June 3. It's heartbreaking.

Sitting outside of the beach house, the sun feels soothing. Such a pleasant contrast to the turbulence pitching around in our minds.

Next, we call Verizon Wireless to retire Kristin's cell phone number. With this, we take another step toward putting our daughter's life into the past. I ask what happens when a cell phone number is retired like this. They take it out of service for two months; then it is reassigned randomly to someone at that time.

Kristin's cell phone number could go to whoever needs a number at that time. When our call ends, Kristin's number is immediately taken down. I think about all the other parts of her life we will soon be shutting down. We are clicking off circuits of a life. Everything will eventually go silent and dark.

Michele and I finish painting the porch. For most people, maintenance is an undesirable part of homeownership. If anything, this painting project feels like it has ended too soon. This porch looks pristine, and for a moment I feel quasi-good.

It doesn't take much when a person feels this bad.

Where is David?

David is worlds apart from us. We know he's in South Dakota on his high school's voluntary service learning trip to a Sioux reservation where they're building affordable housing. He's been there five days with only a few days remaining before he returns home.

He does an excellent job of staying in touch. He knows how important his calls are, especially during this time.

At sixteen, he understands the circumstances he and his parents are living through, so he called from the airport after he landed in the West. He called from the van carrying teachers and his high school pals. He called from the place he was staying.

But this afternoon, there is only silence. We call David and leave voicemails. Maybe his cell phone battery died. Maybe the cellular network on the reservation is spotty. Why didn't we have a backup plan? Why didn't we think to get someone else's cell phone number too? In the midst of all we were dealing with, did we misplace any emergency contact numbers we were given? But why doesn't David borrow someone's phone and call us?

"Come on, David, call us back!"

Only silence.

I become increasingly distracted when we reach the evening. Michele and I take turns worrying aloud, then offer each other credible explanations.

When we finally turn in, there's still no response, and we're 100 percent worried. We try to talk ourselves out of it, but just two weeks ago, we lost Kristin. So where is David?

At one a.m., my cell phone rings. It's David. He's full of apologies at his end. We're full of relief at ours.

Earlier that day, his group was at a site working on a house. It must have been time for high school boys to be high school boys. David found some kind of a squirter toy and figured out how to shoot water at a friend. In retaliation, the other guy grabbed a rubber mallet and chucked it toward David. End over end it went. Rubber end, wooden handle, rubber end, wooden handle. Bang. The wooden handle is what David took right in the teeth.

Broken front tooth.

The remainder of that day was spent on the reservation calling around to find any dentist who could help. Calls to dentists drained David's cell phone battery. Nobody thought to bring a cell phone car charger. Sioux dentists weren't prepared to assist someone from outside of the reservation because of federal Native American healthcare-related laws that made it unclear if this was permitted. So, David was turned down a few times.

Mr. Stanton, an administrator from David's high school, told one dentist, "Look, we've come here from the East. We're working on housing on this reservation for your people. Come on and help this guy."

A temporary tooth went in. David tells us it's not a perfect match, but it's not Jim Carrey in *Dumb and Dumber*, either.

Between calls to dentists and spotty cell reception, David was unable to call until late. But Michele and I can breathe again. A broken front tooth is not life-threatening.

We wanted to yell, "David, don't scare us like that!" But he knows how we feel.

"Sorry, Mom and Dad. Love you. Good night."

A couple of days later, David and his temporary front tooth arrive home from the West. We have never been so happy to see anyone in our lives.

We are three again.

Kristin Mitchell
BROTHER DAVID

When David was born, he arrived home to be loved by his nearly four-year-old sister. She waited for him with open arms. Fully prepared, Kristin adored David with her whole being, sometimes more like a third parent. She comforted him when he was afraid, read to him regularly, and invited him into whatever she was doing with friends.

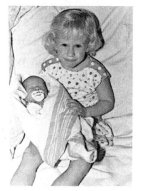

In the hospital the day David was born.

There was never a moment of sibling rivalry. Her deep love never changed throughout her life. We knew this was rare, but it was real.

She was tested at times, like when David was two and he took a black permanent marker and enhanced the faces of Kristin's Barbie dolls. It seemed like a good idea to him but was an unspeakable mistake on his part. She managed to forgive him. She also did a better job of keeping their things separated after that.

They loved Disney and other children's movies. Sometimes, they would finish a movie, like *Aladdin*, and rewind the VHS tape and watch it again from the start. They loved *Willie Wonka* with Gene Wilder and could quote every word of dialogue.

When Kristin was in fifth grade, she taught David to read. He was still in kindergarten. She attempted to teach him algebra, but that found scant success. She treated him like her equal, and he responded well to it.

Michele and I loved that their facial characteristics were so similar. Their mouths and eyes were identical; only their noses were distinct. On most photos, if you covered over Kristin's hair, you could not tell if it was Kristin or David.

This was a comfort after she passed.

At Saint Joseph's University, Kristin wrote about David to a close friend.

"I feel David is the perfect person, and he puts the perfect amount of effort into things, gets the perfect grades, and lives the perfect life. I can't help but love him for this because he is such an incredibly good person. I have problems finding a flaw in him. This is the honest truth. He is like a saint.

"When he grows up, he wants to do a job that involves some type of research and analysis as well as hands-on work. He will probably get a full college scholarship and go to the perfect college. He deserves it."

Kristin and David were always great together.

Kristin adored David. She accepted him as the good and honest person he is. Her love was unconditional. And he loved her just as much.

Before Kristin and David were born, Halloween, Thanksgiving, and even Christmas had lost some of the fun. They had become repetitive. Michele and I would go into the attic, bring down dusty boxes filled with decorations, put them in place, and put them away like somewhat of a chore. Kristin and David brought back the joy to our home.

Truly, thank God.

They made our hearts dance again. They seemed happier giving presents rather than receiving them.

When Kristin was about seven, on Christmas Day, after all of the presents had been opened and the room looked like a whirlwind had torn through it, she worked like a window dresser at Nordstrom taking it upon herself to arrange every open present artfully under the tree. It was her display; she preferred to do it all by herself.

The home videos recorded during those years captured the magic beginning with Kristin's first Christmas morning. I remember how much fun it was recording these scenes.

Too bad we cannot bear to watch them now.

Now What?

The timeout we took at the beach house was a good move, but now we are back to real life.

Sympathy cards take over our kitchen counter. The majority of inscriptions begin with, "Words cannot express … " Had this happened to someone else, I would have struggled to write anything better. There are just no words when something this horrific happens.

"I am so sorry … "

Everyone is.

We will deal with this loss of our child. Is there a choice? Besides how we feel, there are specific calendar dates coming when there's a murder case looming. It starts in five weeks with a preliminary hearing, when a judge decides if there is a case to be heard. This is standard procedure. When someone is murdered, of course, there is a case, but the system has to go through the motions anyway.

At the preliminary, Charlotte tells us the killer will be led in and will sit at the defendant's table with his court-appointed attorney. The prosecution summons a few witnesses who testify. The procedure takes only a few minutes. Pro forma.

We're also told there's no need to drive to Philadelphia and attend this hearing. But we will. We will attend every single stage of this, no matter how formulaic, trivial, or seemingly insignificant it sounds.

This is our child. This will always be our child.

Back to Work

Too soon, it's a work Monday. For two weeks, I've been away from my position as a creative director in the advertising business. It feels like two months.

As the manager of a department of talented creative people, I am expected to lead the team from client input to strong strategies and superior creative ideas. It feels like a lot in my present state.

In a brief conversation with a mid-level manager on the account services team, he confides, "Some people thought you'd never return."

Really? They don't know me well. I'm more resilient than that. Did they think I'd stay home and wait for my life to end?

Coming up with ideas and helping to sell them is why I was put on this earth. I have a reputation for being intractable when I want something badly enough. My job as the creative director is clear: take whatever product or service we have to sell and make it worthwhile to buy. That's what they pay me to do.

Besides that, right now, being at work represents a few steps away from real life. My work friends ask how our family is handling this. They also want to know what is happening with the case. I'm pleased to see they care.

Some at work act like nothing happened. Life goes on.

One unexpected aspect emerges. My patience with people is super high sometimes, but at other times, quite low. When someone acts out abusively, which, in an ad agency happens too often, I feel the need to retaliate. I know this might not be good for me, but I have seen what people can do to other people.

I begin to lose it when someone bullies a person I care about. I pledge I will leave the immediate area if I feel an inner fury coming on, and I pray I don't act out. I don't want to become anything like the abusers I detest—even though I would be acting out to rescue someone else. It's complicated.

Is abusing an abuser permissible? Is it "two wrongs trying to make a right"? Maybe so.

Bearsie

Still on my first day back in the office, at eleven a.m., there's a call from Michele. A high-pitched animal is wailing like a baby pig in the background.

"Sounds like you're calling from a farm," I say.

Not quite.

Michele stopped by the school where she teaches to pick up several educational materials. A school worker had brought in a cardboard box containing three feral kittens found under a bush. A female calico, mostly white with splashes of brown, orange, and black, cannot take her cute little eyes off Michele.

A little background before we continue ...

Six years earlier, in the summer of 1999, Michele's mother passed away. On the first anniversary of her mother's death, just three blocks from our home, Michele was jogging when a common city pigeon flew by and landed next to her. It followed her home. At our front door, the pigeon was intent on coming in.

Bearsie. A tiny cat with a huge appetite.

Michele hurried into the house while the pigeon repeatedly flew up and bashed its beak into our front door. Then it went around to the back of the house and started hitting a kitchen window with Michele inside.

I saw the pigeon for myself. We conjectured maybe Michele's mother's spirit took over the pigeon that afternoon. We dubbed the bird "Pigeon Mom." It came into the garage where David and I were working on his bike. It spent the entire day with us. At dusk, Pigeon Mom disappeared and was never seen again. She made it only for the anniversary.

Days before these feral kittens were found at Michele's school, Michele remembered "Pigeon Mom." She proclaimed, "If a baby cat wanders into our lives, or shows up at our front door, *we have to take it in*. It could be Kristin's spirit brought back as a cat." I doubted that would happen.

So, seventeen days after Kristin died, a baby kitten is living with us. She's christened "Bear" after Kristin's baby nickname. "Bearsie" is what we later call our newest family member.

Bearsie makes four cats in this house starting with Gatsby, the nineteen-year-old Siamese who's hanging on with kidney failure. A class act, Gatsby was always Kristin's favorite directly from kittenhood. They grew up together.

Bearsie came into our lives as a welcome addition.

Sophie, our fourteen-year-old Siamese beauty, is always at Gatsby's side, akin to a miniature married couple. Her four-year-old half-brother, Nemo, is a smallish snowshoe Siamese, incredibly intelligent, and a loving pal. When David was a thirteen-year old, Nemo became his kitten.

Bearsie tries her best to fit in with her three more-sophisticated and sometimes territorial Siamese housemates. She is so full of energy they don't know what to do with her.

Our vet estimates Bearsie to be roughly four weeks old. It's too early to be away from her mother, so we feed her milk with a doll's baby bottle. Although she weighs a very light thirteen ounces, this girl is strong. And she is hungry. Feeding her with her needlelike claws is excruciating, but the circumstances of how she arrived with us make up for everything.

We have not accepted the concept of reincarnation, but we are not taking any chances with this cat.

She is our miracle cat.

Removing Kristin's Belongings

I send an email to the lead detective of Kristin's case:

Hi Sam,

We wanted to let you know Michele and I will be clearing out Kristin's belongings (from her apartment) on Monday, June 27. We expect to be there sometime around noon.

Bill Mitchell

We're driving to Conshohocken, Pennsylvania, one last time. We're taking everything out of Kristin's apartment and bringing it home. We want this to be quick and unemotional.

Riverwalk at Millennium Apartments has a couple of young sales guys prepared to assist in lugging boxes and loading them into my Ford Explorer. For Michele, going into the building remains too much to endure, but we want this move accomplished.

There will be no decisions about what to take home or leave here; anything of value is going into the car. To match the mood of the day, it is raining, humid, and completely depressing.

The Riverwalk sales guys say little but are immensely helpful carrying overloaded containers through the rain to the car. They wear nicely pressed white shirts and ties today but are thoroughly soaked in no time. No complaints. All business.

I underestimated the space to stow everything. We need a second vehicle. I tell the sales guys, "We'll be okay. You can go. Thanks for all of your help."

We stop by a Hertz office and ask for an oversized soccer-mom van. Looks like we're too late. They just rented the last one to someone who's coming in later today. Just our bad luck.

When Michele retreats down a hallway toward the ladies' room, I lean back to the attendant behind the counter. "Did you hear about that Saint Joseph's female grad stabbed to death a couple of weeks ago?"

He did. "Yeah. It was on tv. Sad story."

I lean in. "Well, I'm her father. That woman in the ladies' room is her mother, and I need that van. Can you make it happen?"

He tells me, "We'll get it cleaned right away."

"Don't bother cleaning it. Just bring it around."

Michele returns, looking forlorn. "Now, what do we do?"

I smile. "Oh, that van just became available."

Soon, I am back on the third floor in Kristin's apartment. A few more trips and we should be finished. I hurriedly tape up the last few boxes. Since this is our last time in this location, when I get back to the Explorer, I ask Michele if she would come into Kristin's apartment and say a prayer with me.

I've walked this hallway dozens of times carrying boxes, but this is Michele's first entry into Kristin's apartment. She moves like someone expecting to see the worst.

Take your time. All we have is time.

We enter the apartment. For me, it feels like that first time I was in here. I know exactly what happened in this kitchen. Michele sees the living room carpet and padding removed. A few steps to our left is the bedroom. There is only a nightstand and a chest of drawers. The missing sections of carpet and padding need no explanation.

We stand together in this solemn place where our child met with death. We hug each other exactly where Kristin died. No words. Our hearts connect this place with that hospital room nearly twenty-two years ago when Kristin was born. We feel we are together as we used to be.

We know Kristin is watching. She is with us, and we stop and pray.

At home, we take everything out of the rental van and my car, and we place it all in the middle of the garage floor.

We got it done.

The Jeweler

Kevin Welsh is forty-one, handsome, powerfully built, and never married. In his comfortable high-end jewelry store this July afternoon, he awaits Donna, who is one of Michele's closest friends. Donna and Michele taught at the same elementary school three decades prior. They practically raised their babies together.

When Donna set up this appointment with Kevin, she told him, "I want to come in and talk with you about something. And I'm bringing a couple of friends with me for support."

He thought, "Who needs *support* buying jewelry? Didn't she mean, *for their opinions?*"

Kevin had no idea what he was in for, so he asked his assistant, Linda, to be there even though it was not during her regular hours.

Donna drives to Kevin's store with Gail and Teresa. Gail was Donna's roommate in college; they have never missed a beat all of these years later. She's known Teresa for over two decades. The car ride includes short eruptions into tears with all of their emotions coming out. Kristin's story makes any mother sob at the shear senselessness of losing a daughter in such a violent manner. The truth is, Kristin could have been one of their daughters, and no mother can contemplate a devastating tragedy like this.

Donna's intention is to choose the perfect gold locket and chain for Michele. This piece will display precious portraits of Kristin and Michele—with a window between them to hold a lock of Kristin's hair.

Donna tells Kevin that Kristin dated a man and was fatally attacked while breaking up with him a month ago. This disheartening story catches Kevin off guard. A quick wipe of a tear is unnoticed by Donna and her friends while they flip through catalogs.

Donna requests Michele's locket be completed by the end of August so she can make the presentation on Kristin's twenty-second birthday. There is more than ample time to identify locket styles, size the photos, and perform the final assembly.

Donna, Gail, and Teresa are pleased with today's progress.

Alone now, Kevin feels distressed. This locket assignment brings emphasis to a fear he can't shake. It's as if Kristin is telling him his life is not safe.

Kevin had been receiving threats, some not so veiled, from a woman he had been dating. She gave him warnings like, "Don't you *even think* about breaking up with me!" She meant it.

This woman seemed unbalanced. He saw a significant shift in her personality, as if she was experiencing manic and depressive episodes. For his safety, he was desperate to escape this relationship.

One specific concern was running through his mind. "If I tell her it's over, she might stab me." Her actions led him to believe her mindset would be: "If I can't have you, nobody will!" Her remarks had become more frequent and biting.

Kevin has a gun to protect his business from robbery. But today, his concern is not about someone breaking in; it's about this woman. He worries about his weapon falling into the hands of this woman who is extremely controlling—and openly hostile.

This much is clear: the tragic story he heard about Kristin is a warning for him. In Kevin's mind, Kristin is unquestionably his angel-protector. He needs to be on guard.

Meeting with Charlotte and Sam

An email from the lead detective of Kristin' case:

Mr. Mitchell:

As we discussed yesterday, Assistant District Attorney Charlotte Stark and I will be driving down to Maryland to see you on Wednesday, 07/20/2005.

I anticipate our arrival at around 11:00 a.m. If it's okay with you, and your wife, maybe I can interview you and ADA Stark can meet with Michele.

Please let me know if that works for you.

Thanks again.
Sam Gallen

Today, Michele and I receive two visitors. We thought they would arrive in a marked car. We breathe easier when they don't.

It's our first meeting with Charlotte Stark, the prosecutor assigned to Kristin's case. She's joined by Samuel J. Gallen, the lead detective we met weeks ago. They drove from Philadelphia and want to get to know us before things get rolling.

Stepping into our foyer before we settle into a discussion, Charlotte asks me, "Do you mind if I walk around a bit?"

She notices an antique display cabinet filled with charming Madame Alexander dolls given to Kristin by Gaga and Poppy Mitchell. There are eighteen dolls, each representing a different country in appropriate dress.

Gazing through the cabinet glass, Charlotte thinks aloud, "I can feel a vibe, a real sensation just standing here ... "

She feels a vibe? Okay, that was unexpected.

Look, if she is connecting with Kristin in ways that pay off in a courtroom one day, let her roam.

For Charlotte, the vast amount of her caseload is tackling domestic violence cases. One day, she could be coming to the assistance of a wife who was beaten by a husband. The next day, there might be someone shot and killed by a husband or boyfriend. Charlotte is fully prepared to do battle and see justice served. She has no fear.

This woman is a tall, clearheaded, and dignified woman. I immediately understand why she will be representing both the Commonwealth of Pennsylvania and our daughter. Her presence is imposing. She does not appear to wear makeup which, when we get to know her better, I will surmise is something she simply doesn't feel she requires. She has more pressing matters. This is purely my opinion. She looks the part of a prosecutor who will bring the full power of the law and use it for those who need it.

Before settling into today's discussion, Charlotte smiles and professes, "I love my job. I just love my job. I go into that courtroom and fight for people who cannot represent themselves."

It's true. Kristin cannot tell of the struggles she endured and the harm done to her. Charlotte will communicate for her.

"I get the domestic violence cases. Could be an assault, could be attempted murder, and sometimes, it's homicide." Charlotte gets more than her share of domestic violence cases. At any time, as many as eighty cases are active.

She tells us she received a strong sense of who Kristin was by the pans of brownies and muffins left on her apartment's kitchen counter. "It said a lot about her. This wasn't some woman with tattoos and a rough lifestyle. She wasn't a druggie. This was someone who baked brownies for her friends coming over. Who does that at twenty-one these days?"

Participating in a murder case wasn't on my bucket list, but I'm open to anything that brings justice for Kristin. If humanizing our daughter gets the desired result—putting this murderer in prison for a long time—today is our launching pad.

Sam, the lead detective, fits a type that matches other detectives we will meet: a solid citizen who goes hard all day pursuing indisputable evidence. He was born to put bad guys away. We immediately like him.

At this moment, he is here to meet a victim's parents. But later, when we get to know Sam better, we learn he is a devoted husband and father who coaches his son's winning hockey team.

He is a real-life hero. Not a slick TV cop with snappy dialogue.

As one part of their jobs, Charlotte and Sam are called to walk into and study active crime scenes. What would give most people life-altering nightmares is what they do when investigating cases. Nothing could prepare most of us for that.

They stay about two hours. We presume Charlotte wanted to get to know Kristin by seeing what kind of people her parents were. Michele and I feel as confident as a couple could in our position.

Charlotte and Sam are kind, professional, honest, and determined to bring justice to our daughter's case. The truth is: this is not our case anyway. It is between the Commonwealth of Pennsylvania and the guy who did it. All decisions belong to Pennsylvania, but they will consistently check in with our family before the most critical decisions are made.

A note from Charlotte Stark:

Bill,

Thank you for your email. I am sorry I had to meet Michele and you under such sad circumstances. Life can be very painful. The detectives and the District Attorney's Office operate as a team.
If you need anything, we are all here for you. If David wants to talk to me, please let him know he can call.

Charlotte

I follow up with a note to Risa Vetri Ferman, who supervises county detectives and oversees all facets of homicide cases.

Hi Risa,

We had a visit today here at home (in
Maryland) with Charlotte and Sam.
What great people. They are so thorough
and careful, and are just enjoyable to be
with. Whatever happens with Kristin's case,
I'm sure she would say she had the best
people working on it. I hope this email
finds you well.

Bill Mitchell (Kristin's dad)

Don't Think About Me

Because of our tragedy, I hear and react to things I might have otherwise overlooked. Everything I feel is on the surface.

At work, after a Monday morning status meeting, one of our sales people reaches across the conference room table and shakes hands with his boss.

"Hey, just heard some great news. Congratulations!"

"Well, you know, we prayed she'd find a great guy, and yeah, they're engaged. Couldn't be happier."

He grins from ear to ear.

I hear this and couldn't feel worse. It hurts even though it has nothing to do with me. I get that.

I would have been out of that room had they waited a few short seconds. Nobody is thinking about me. Why should they? But my daughter's funeral was a month ago. Show some mercy, guys.

A month later, that same proud father stopped by my office. He felt the need to chat about his latest good turns in life. He had this recurring habit of thinking if something went well in his life that everyone would feel just as good about it.

In my office, he forges ahead and says, "I was thinking how great things are for our daughters ... "

Our daughters? I could use clarification. "I'm sorry. What did you say?" I must have misheard him.

He keeps it coming.

"Our daughters. I was saying how great it is for our daughters. You know—"

How does that make sense? What kind of convoluted concept is this? Is he comparing his engaged daughter to my daughter who was buried two months ago?

I shoot back, "What are you talking about? My daughter's dead and buried, and yours is alive. Living. You see a comparison here?"

He looks at me dumbfounded.

As if I didn't embrace the magical connection these two young women share. I guess he meant *my daughter* is in Heaven—all taken care of—and *his daughter* is all set with an engagement to some great guy.

He stares at me, bereft of anything to say. Clearly, he hadn't planned on me being unhappy with this discussion. He looks at me as if I will suddenly smile and agree.

I don't relent.

"Honestly, there's no comparison between *my* daughter's state and *your* daughter's. I don't appreciate you making a comparison or contrast, or whatever it is."

He's disappointed I didn't appreciate this *thoughtful gift* he brought me. Maybe he meant to make me feel *all better* about losing my daughter.

It didn't work.

Weeks later, there's a birthday bash at work for everyone who was born in that month.

I walk into the company's cramped kitchenette. From the back, I cannot tell the person in front of me is holding a long, serrated bread knife in her hand and is about to slice a sheet cake. I excuse myself to step around her when she quickly turns and holds the knife directly up to my face.

"Mitchell, stand back! I've got this; I know how to use it!"

It wasn't meant to give me PTSD, but it was shocking. She catches herself immediately with, "Oh, I'm so sorry about that. Forgive me."

I'm sorry too. Nothing personal. These things happen. I guess I'm touchy.

Sometimes, what was meant to be nice isn't nice anymore. What was funny is no longer funny.

The Locket

Kevin runs his jewelry business while balancing the potentially dangerous situation with the woman he had been dating. She continues to antagonize him. This is becoming his *Fatal Attraction*. One tactic he uses to gently dial down this relationship is making it impossible for them to get together. He fills his calendar with commitments with his mother and nephews. He finds reasons to make business trips to New York City. Kevin expects that dropping her abruptly could put her on the offensive. He hopes she will give up and move on.

She peppers his days with distasteful calls and texts about *when are we going to get together?* And *what the hell's wrong with you?* He doesn't know this kind of abuse rarely ends smoothly. People who become like her don't give up easily.

Kevin makes an appointment with Michele's friend, Donna, to come by and evaluate several lockets that arrived. Each could fit her purposes, but one stands out. When Donna sees it, she agrees this is the one.

Kevin sizes and prints photos of Kristin and Michele. He places the two photos side by side. Mother and daughter. Could this story possibly be more tragic? He holds Michele's picture, and sadness fills his heart. Here is a woman whose daughter was viciously ripped from her life. All those years of preparing this girl from baby to young woman to adult, and with one man's vicious act, it is gone.

Maybe this locket will bring a few minutes of happiness back into this mother's life. Perhaps Kevin's ability to empathize was the reason Michele's locket was placed in his gentle hands.

The envelope with locks of Kristin's precious hair is the last trace of her physical existence not buried. Kevin keeps it secured until the locket goes in for final assembly. This locket is beyond mere jewelry. It carries greater responsibility than any project he has ever touched in his shop. This one is coming from a higher plane of existence.

Kevin replays Kristin's story and senses a deep connection. While studying her picture, he would give anything to hear her voice just once. He knows this young woman is urging him to be on guard. Her story and his exist side by side.

This is not imagination.

Underscoring his concerns, his cell phone continues to receive threatening texts and calls he doesn't want.

This cannot continue.

Farewell, Gatsby

Kristin's soulmate and forever favorite cat, Gatsby, has been experiencing a slow decline the past year. At nineteen, his kidneys are worn out. He is weak and his life will end soon. We set up a vet appointment for Wednesday at five-thirty p.m. This is when we will have him put to sleep.

August 3 is precisely two months after Kristin's death.

That day, I leave work and arrive home at four-thirty. Gatsby has been lying on a towel all day and hasn't taken water or food. He's been a brave fighter all of this life, but there is no more fight left in him.

The plan: take him to the vet, and they will euthanize him. Afterward, we will drive to the gravesite where Kristin was buried and bury him as close to Kristin as possible. Burying an animal in a cemetery for humans is not allowed, so we bring two tiny bushes as decoys. It will look as if we are planting them. We are not.

Gatsby very near the end of his wonderful life.

Michele and David are upstairs changing into clothing suitable for digging. In the kitchen, I'm cradling Gatsby and thinking about what will happen next. At the vet, we will watch this precious little family member lie on a cold metal table and have poison injected into him. How horrible. I cannot stand this.

Anger rises within me. Gatsby doesn't deserve this ending. He should go out gloriously. Or, at least with dignity.

I pray aloud, "God, if you *REALLY ARE* out there and paying any attention to our family this summer—and *ALL WE'VE BEEN THROUGH* already ... If you really *ARE* all-powerful, let this little boy die here in his home, with his family. I'm asking you to take him here. Now."

Do I feel better? Maybe a little.

Less than thirty seconds later, Gatsby is struggling to breathe. It is happening; he is taking his last breaths. I call upstairs to Michele and David, *"Come down. He's dying in my arms!"*

David, like his mother and me, isn't sure what to do. Has Gatsby died? This is unexpected. Is he suffering? We don't want our dear cat to suffer.

See how confusing a little miracle can be?

Gatsby has died. With the three of us holding him.

We carry him to the car packed with our diversionary bushes and other items we will bury with Gatsby.

The Lord does work in mysterious ways.

We stop at our veterinarian to be certain Gatsby has indeed passed. He has. God bless him. He was the best cat and friend.

At the cemetery, I begin to dig directly over where Kristin is buried. This is so strange. I am digging in a graveyard. David is standing by keeping watch, ready to pitch in. Only a few minutes into this, my shovel hits something hard. It is the sound of metal hitting concrete. I immediately look at David.

"I hit Kristin's vault ... don't tell your mom right now."

His eyes get big. This is so off the wall. I'm not sure what this is teaching my son. Fortunately, Michele is at the car about to bring Gatsby to be buried. I'm relived she missed this.

Into his final resting place, we lay Gatsby. With a few prayers and plenty of tears, his beautiful Siamese body is inches away from Kristin's. So close. We believe their souls are united. They are forever together. Just how it should be.

Once home, I call my parents and tell them about our day: Gatsby, a prayer, God's intervention, going to the vet, and the burial. While I am talking to them, Michele urges me to come upstairs and see something.

What is This?

I enter our master bedroom. It's dark. The ceiling fan is on.

This fan was installed when our house was built seventeen years ago. The fan's tiny red and amber lights once indicated fan speeds but haven't worked in years. They must have wiggled loose. We know what speed the fan is running by the number of chain pulls we make.

Michele asks me to lie across the bed and look toward the fan. There are no lights on. I can hear the fan but cannot see it. Michele goes into the bathroom. With the bathroom door closed, she switches on a light and says, "Okay, just watch the fan."

As she slowly opens the bathroom door, the light spills out across the bedroom. When it does, the tiny red and amber fan lights begin to flicker then light up.

They have not worked in years. Tonight, they're working?

The wider Michele opens the bathroom door, the more light comes into the room, and the greater the red and amber lights light up—until they are fully on. This makes no sense.

Never in seventeen years had the red and amber fan lights shown any sensitivity to light in the room.

Michele turns off the bathroom light, and the fan's red and amber lights go out. Next, she goes into a

The arrow points to location of the fan's small amber light.

bedroom closet, reaches out and flicks on the closet's light. She slowly opens the closet door which lets light out into the room. Again, the fan's lights react the same way, going from flickering to full on.

I have an idea: turn off all of the lights, then turn on a flashlight and aim it at the fan.

Whoa, that works too.

The more light from the flashlight, the more the red and amber fan lights brighten. There is no explanation for what is happening.

All of this started tonight with our arrival home after burying Gatsby. Are we having another "God Moment" since Gatsby has died? Because we definitely have another electrical occurrence.

The red and amber fan light phenomenon lasted for many years. About eight years after it started, we had a professional electrician in our house to replace smoke alarms. We asked him to look at our bedroom fan. We told him we had questions about the red and amber lights.

After seeing the fan lights, he said, "The fan probably has light sensors built into it." But then he stopped himself.

"Wait, this was installed in 1988? They didn't have light sensors on fans back then."

I asked how he would explain it.

He came back and said, "I don't know ... ghosts?"

Charlotte's Call

During an afternoon call, Charlotte tells me, "I've been reviewing Kristin's crime scene photos today. Afterward, I felt as if all the air in me had been let out. The lovely apartment. The brownies on the stove."

She characterizes what a good person Kristin seemed to be.

"No drugs in her system, no *stuff* in the apartment. Beautiful girl dating the wrong guy." She collects herself. "The photographs are rough for any parent. I would think you just wouldn't want to see her like that, but that's your call. If this comes to trial, if this were me, I'd want to leave the room."

Charlotte focuses on who will be testifying on the Commonwealth's behalf at the preliminary hearing and what that will be like with the district justice who will be running this.

"I don't know if this is going to trial. I would doubt it. But you never know. We have to act like it will."

She slides off of that and asks how our son, David, is doing. I need to give Charlotte credit for treating Michele, David, and me like more than the parents and the brother of a victim. She treats us like people with ongoing lives. She sees our situation holistically and knows *Kristin's tragedy* is *our life tragedy*. It is all interconnected.

After the preliminary hearing, she wants to huddle somewhere near the district justice. Maybe get coffee some place.

She leaves me with, "This case is an obsession with me. This case … it overrides everything. This is a serious case as hard as it is and as draining emotionally. I mean, yours is just the most draining. It's a hell of a responsibility."

She reassures me they have excellent detectives, and they have time to focus on cases like this. Top priority. Top drawer.

The Preliminary Hearing

Mr. Mitchell,

The preliminary hearing has been rescheduled for
Monday, August 8, 2005 at 9:30 a.m.

The hearing will be held before
District Judge Deborah Lukens
Her office is located at:
4002 Center Avenue,
Lafayette Hill, PA

From the main road, the Whitemarsh Beverage liquor store, with its weather-beaten Coors Light, Miller Lite, Bud Light, and Pennsylvania Lottery posters, blocks the view of our destination.

With some difficulty, Michele and I locate the Montgomery County District Court Building in Lafayette Hill, Pennsylvania. A  sun-bleached red and yellow sign indicates we have arrived at the location of the preliminary hearing. This will be the first time since Kristin's graduation we see this man who killed our daughter.

The building could pass for a library in a very small town. Upon entry, I don't see any metal detectors or screening devices. If I'm not mistaken, anyone could carry a weapon in here and do some real damage. I don't need thoughts like this, but they appear. Under these circumstances, my mind goes where it wants to go.

Before the hearing commences, Charlotte Stark suggests Michele and I join her for a quick chat. In a room approximately the size of a broom closet, she explains that Judge Deborah A. Lukens will hear the complaint. Then, Charlotte will bring two or three witnesses to the stand. The first is Detective Jim McGowan who intercepted Nick at the hospital and conducted an interview with him the day of the murder. McGowan is the detective I spoke with by phone that first fateful evening.

In movies, interviews are called "confessions," but in the real world, law enforcement calls them interviews. That June 3 morning, our daughter's murderer waived his right to have an attorney present and gave his interview. I guess he wanted to give the impression he was not guilty and he acted in self-defense. So, since he was "innocent," he felt he didn't need a lawyer.

Before leaving our huddle with Charlotte, she says Kristin's killer—and his court-appointed attorney—are seeking a voluntary manslaughter result. If that is successful, Nick would likely receive a four-to-seven-year prison sentence. With good behavior, he could be out on parole in three years. Free and clear.

This is shocking, but what follows shocks us even more.

Charlotte Stark complains, "Yeah, he stabs and slashes your daughter fifty-five times, and they think they can make that into a manslaughter plea? Ridiculous ... "

We were aware Kristin had been stabbed multiple times but had not heard a specific number.

Fifty-five times? Oh. My. God.

This abhorrent graphic doesn't have time to settle. We follow Charlotte into a courtroom which is unpleasantly warm from the strong August sun pouring through large windows. We are pleasantly distracted to see Kristin's close friend, Samantha, seated behind us. We give her a look implying our sadness at being in this place. She nods in agreement.

A dark van arrives in front of the building. Through the sun-filled window blinds, I can see the murderer who sent our lives off course. He is outfitted in a navy-blue jumpsuit and heavily restrained by manacles, handcuffs, and chains that connect everything together. With a couple of guards at his sides, he enters the room from our left and walks in front of the prosecutor's table where Charlotte, Michele, and I sit.

He doesn't look our way. Good.

He takes a seat only fifteen feet away. So close. Having just heard the fifty-five wounds number from Charlotte, I contemplate how a person could sneak a gun in here. My job as a father had been to protect my family. I failed, so now revenge comes to mind.

I fight off that thought, too. That will not happen.

The proceedings start.

Assistant District Attorney Charlotte Stark states she is not going after the death penalty because there are not sufficient circumstances to qualify in this case. But she will be seeking a first-degree murder conviction which carries a life sentence.

Through his court-appointed lawyer, Nick pleads not guilty to charges of first- and third-degree murder. He also pleads not guilty to the possession of an instrument of crime. Voluntary manslaughter is not mentioned. That's the charge Charlotte called "Ridiculous."

Charlotte Stark tells the court, "We do not believe this is a manslaughter case, Your Honor. We believe this killing was intentional."

Charlotte calls Detective Jim McGowan to the stand. Jim intercepted Nick at the hospital while he was seeking medical attention for wounds to his neck and arms. Later, the medical examiner reported Nick's wounds were consistent with self-inflicted injuries. Detective McGowan's opinion was that Nick created physical evidence to make it appear he was attacked and wounded, and therefore, he needed to defend himself.

Detective McGowan describes the contents of the eleven-page interview he wrote by hand that June 3 morning when he caught up with Nick at Riddle Hospital's emergency room. This detective is famous in local detective and prosecutor circles for his invaluable ability to collect "textbook, airtight verbal evidence that sticks in a courtroom." He impresses everyone this morning with his ability to explain clearly and simply the content of information he gathered. Jim is a pro.

While our daughter's name was on the apartment lease, Nick's name was listed as "occupant." We know very little about Nick and have nobody we can ask. Kristin first met him at an

Ardmore, Pennsylvania, restaurant where each was employed part time. This killer also told her he had a job with his brother's web-based résumé and profile company that placed high school athletes in colleges. How successful this was is not known and, honestly, not the least bit interesting to me.

Detective McGowan said that in the interview Nick explained how a fight broke out between himself and Kristin after she ordered him out of her apartment. He said the dispute got out of hand, and Kristin slashed at him with a kitchen knife at around three a.m. But Michele and I know Kristin. Portraying her as aggressively attacking anyone was a lie. She was not that person.

From the stand, McGowan explains that authorities first learned of a possible problem on June 3 at about nine a.m. Emergency room personnel at Riddle Hospital in Delaware County, Pennsylvania, contacted state police and told them they were treating Nick for knife wounds.

Nick told the ER staff his girlfriend had stabbed him during a fight. When asked about Kristin, he said he didn't know if she was still alive. Conshohocken police raced to Kristin's apartment and discovered her lifeless body, lying on her bed under a comforter. She had bled to death from multiple knife wounds, according to the report. That is all they need from Jim McGowan at this hearing.

The next witness is Detective Jim Carbo, the first detective to arrive at our daughter's apartment. He said he kicked the bedroom door open to get in. He testifies about what he found that morning in the room.

My God, this is hard.

This case will be going to a formal arraignment in a month.

For his safety, everyone is asked to remain seated until Nick is returned to the prison van. We are free to leave.

After a short chat with Charlotte and Detective Sam Gallen about what happened today and what's coming next, we drive home.

The following is a recollection from the preliminary hearing. This was written in 2017 by Kristin's close friend, Samantha.

"As I headed over to the courtroom in a tiny town just outside of Conshohocken, I was in good spirits and felt in control of my emotions, and the pain from the horseshoe tattoo I had gotten just weeks earlier in Kristin's memory was finally dissipating.

"Things had been incredibly surreal ever since I had received that concerned text from her college friends asking if I had heard from her. A text message that opened a world of horror and reality I could never have imagined just three months earlier.

"I parked in the lot just out front and greeted the many people I knew who were there for the same reason. First and foremost, I was a representative for our friend, our sister, who as a result of this heinous crime could not be there to represent herself; as support for her family who were living a nightmare that no family should ever endure; as a mouthpiece should the acting prosecutor or any individuals fighting for Kristin need additional information of any sort; out of pure morbid curiosity and confusion as to what in the world was happening; and lastly, in the hopes that the outcome of this trial would bring some measure of comfort and closure during a bleak, painful time for all. While hindsight has made those motivations apparent, at the moment, I was just a twenty-one-year-old college student who was emotionally distant from the reality that this guy I had known, this guy I had had heart-to-hearts with, this guy I had spent significant time with over the previous few months and had entrusted with Kristin's heart had snapped and brutally murdered my closest friend in the most violent, gruesome way imaginable.

"I sat in the courtroom pews nonchalantly chatting with Kristin's parents and a few others, waiting for the hearing to begin. I almost felt like I was watching a movie of the beginning stages of a murder trial from afar, with interest but without real emotion. Because of this, I was horribly unprepared for the emotional reaction to come.

"The room got quiet as a haggard, scruffy, angry-looking guy in a jumpsuit was escorted in by two guards. His hands were cuffed; his feet were shackled. While everyone else stared quietly, I looked up at this guy I thought I had known, the guy who had stabbed my friend more than fifty times with a kitchen knife and left her in bed to bleed to death. As reality hit me that this was not a nightmare nor a movie but an unfathomable reality playing out in front of my eyes, I started sobbing. Hysterically and uncontrollably. I covered my face to muffle my reaction, jumped out of my seat, and rushed to the small door out of embarrassment and an attempt to cause as minimal disruption as possible. Though I knew the feelings were justified, I couldn't handle the sad looks my way and the attempts of others to comfort me. I just needed to breathe and process.

"On my way out the door, I nearly ran straight into a tall, handsome, well-dressed guy. Oh my God, I thought. That's his brother. I had just met him weeks earlier as Kristin, Nick, and I met him and his wife at Olive Garden downtown for an impromptu lunch. He looked exhausted and saddened by the future that lay ahead.

"Aren't we all? I thought to myself. Aren't we all?"

Opening Boxes

Michele and I open another box recovered from Kristin's apartment and search for glimpses of our daughter's recent past. We want to find any clue that leads to understanding what happened, but we don't expect to find any.

Mostly, we remove thick business school textbooks, test papers, pencils, pens, a Texas Instruments calculator, computer software disks, CDs from classes, and notebooks. We survey every single page of every single book, looking for anything Kristin might have written. Nothing is too trivial to read, remove, and save.

At first, I cannot bear the thought of throwing away anything with her handwriting on it but decide I am being ridiculous. Keeping thick textbooks is impractical. I remove every Kristin Mitchell signature I find, and there are many. Every test paper means another priceless autograph.

At the bottom of one nondescript corrugated box, there are several light-green 3x5 inch pieces of lined paper. They had been torn from a small notebook, the kind someone would use for a grocery list.

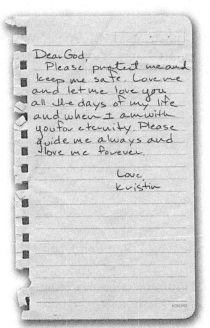

I would have thrown these papers out had I not been studying everything I found so carefully.

One piece of paper holds a Kristin-made prayer. I read it as if I have disinterred a holy relic. Maybe I have.

What was going on when this was written? With this precious object in hand, everything I was doing and everything I might do comes to a halt. This is my entire focus. I cannot believe what I am reading.

Where is Michele? She needs to see this.

Michele reads with intensity, her eyes filling with tears.

This is treasure. We were tuned in to Kristin's spirituality when she lived with us at home. But this note, probably written within months of our reading it, underscores she found comfort knowing God was with her.

Michele and I share this with Charlotte Stark. Her reply gets right to the point.

Mon 8/29/2005, 5:40 p.m.

Bill,

Thank you for your email. That is quite a lovely note. But it is almost a premonition. Kristin was obviously religious.

Charlotte

Weeks later, in another box, I locate a second note. Nothing about its look cries out for attention. This time it's a little piece of pink paper, with torn edges. It could easily have been crumpled up and tossed out. It is written with red ink.

I deliver this second prayer to Michele. She says, "I wonder what was going on when she wrote this?"

> Dear God,
> Please show me who you want me to be. Please let me do your will and serve you. Do not let me be selfish, but instead be a woman for others. Allow me to live the life that you know is best for me.

I have no idea. We get the first Dear God note and compare the two. I scan them, print them out, and we frame both copies.

As Charlotte aptly put it, "It is almost a premonition."

It is comforting that no matter what the circumstances, Kristin was staying in touch with her Maker.

This is a positive sign.

I think about the last events Kristin experienced in her short life. I imagine at the end, if she had any opportunity at all, she would be praying to God all the way out to eternity.

RECOLLECTION

Religion Class

Exactly four years after Kristin's death, a female high school friend named Julian emailed me a story about Kristin.

"Years ago, in religion class, we were discussing death. I was saying how if I died, I'd want some sort of huge hoopla.

"The nun who was the teacher was talking about grief and mourning, and she made some kind of comment directed toward Kristin regarding loss.

"The sister then asked Kristin, 'You wouldn't want people to cry?'

"Kristin said, 'No, I'd want you to cry ... *but not forever.*'

"Everyone laughed at the way she said it.

"Sister said something a little snippy back to her after that, but it really made no difference. I distinctly remember looking at Kristin and smiling.

"I remember Kristin shaking her head. (I think she was annoyed with the religious logic that the teacher's argument was based upon.)

"Gathering up her stuff and going off when the class was over, it made me smile because Kristin didn't speak a whole lot in class, and I admired her bravery.

"I just remember that the context of her statement was rebellious because the nun didn't like it! :)

"I'm sorry I can't remember more."

"I'd want you to cry but not forever..."
I love that Kristin said that. It was good advice for us in that moment. It had become normal to feel sad most of the time.

The Locket Is Ready

It is the third week of August. The locket is finished. It's utterly perfect for its purpose.

This piece represents everything Donna imagined it could be. Kevin Welsh has transformed this oval jewelry—with its unique contents and melt-your-heart story—into the greatest gift a friend could bestow. It will be the most precious gift Michele will ever receive in her life.

Kevin contacts Donna.

"The locket's ready. I know you'll be pleased."

She says her husband, Brad, will swing by around noon if that time is good. Kevin insists, "Look. I need to stop by Verizon on Route 40. Ask Brad to meet me there around noon, okay?"

Sitting in his car outside of Verizon, Brad admires the locket. After shaking hands, Brad exits the lot, and Kevin walks into the store.

Kevin asks a sales associate how he can change his cell phone number. He dislikes having to change his number because it is used for all of his personal and business calls, but harassment from his ex-girlfriend makes a change his only resort.

The associate hands Kevin a card. "Sir, we don't change numbers in the store. But call this number. They'll take care of it."

After parking his gray Toyota Land Cruiser in front of his jewelry store, Kevin calls Verizon and explains someone's been harassing him with abusive calls and texts.

"Okay, so there is usually a twenty-five-dollar charge for this. But since this is a matter of safety, we will waive that charge for you."

Kevin writes down his new number.

August 24

It's Kristin's birthday and the first time without her to celebrate with friends and family. Roses arrive from a young man she dated at Saint Joseph's University during freshman year.

If only that had worked out.

More flowers arrive.

Gaga and Poppy Mitchell also send roses. Friends send bouquets we accept at our front door. We appreciate the effort and thoughtfulness, but every arrangement underscores our punishing loss. Kristin's Facebook page fills with friends sending love and telling her how much she is missed.

Donna plans to visit Michele at our home today. She will present a most significant gift. More than *significant*; it will be life-changing.

Arriving early, Donna wants to see how her friend is coping with life, but she is also keeping one eye on the clock. Donna had learned on the night of Kristin's viewing that Patricia received her lockets one at a time on her daughter's birthdays. Donna will present Kristin's locket at precisely 4:17 p.m., the exact time Kristin was born on August 24, 1983.

The locket at the center of the most amazing story.

From first glimpse, the invaluable gold locket is received with profound joy, sadness, and love intertwined. It's nothing short of overwhelming to behold. This object directly connects Michele with happier memories.

Nearly three months after Kristin's death, this one piece of jewelry commemorates her entire life. During a time when everyone is so heavily consumed with grief, the locket brings to the present how Kristin brought happiness to people's lives.

The locket's photos of Kristin and Michele were taken when our family celebrated the Fourth of July with Donna and Brad's family aboard their boat on the Chesapeake Bay. The lock of Kristin's hair, lovingly displayed between two thin windows, connects to a real person. Not a memory of her.

A life is reconnected through this gold locket on its long gold chain. Taking it to her heart, Michele caresses it and puts it on. She and Kristin are united once more.

From this moment on, Michele's locket becomes the focal point when telling what will emerge as a most incredible story. Some will say it's a miracle.

David's Senior Year

With his summer ending soon, David will return to high school for his senior year. His entire summer was more about tragedy than fun and relaxation.

It seemed like only a few weeks ago, David received his senior ring. At about the same time, his high school JV tennis team triumphantly beat their school rival and won the league championship. David received the Unsung Hero award. That awards ceremony was only two weeks before Kristin was killed. We felt so good but, soon, so bad.

Further proof that summer is ending: David is having his senior photo taken. A few days later, he is back at school.

David has vastly matured after seeing what life can do. We are not masters of our fates, but he believes we have a good influence over how things turn out. He decided this while sitting on that bench outside of the funeral home the day after Kristin was killed. If life can be so random, he wants to call the shots in his life.

Not such a bad outlook.

This year is the first year David will drive the twenty-three miles to school. He welcomes the freedom. Life is forcing him to grow up; he's doing it the hard way.

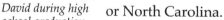
David during high school graduation.

Looking ahead to college, there is something about the South calling him. The pace will be slower; the weather is warmer; the people more relaxed. This is his perception. He is focused on attending a college in either Virginia or North Carolina.

Kristin's passing has emboldened David on what is important. He hopes the South will be the right environment to reflect on what matters most in life and a place to decide what he wants going forward.

The Formal Arraignment

It's late September. We're in Norristown, Pennsylvania, at the Montgomery County Courthouse, an immense marble building considered one of the most beautiful buildings in the entire county. It has multiple courtrooms on every floor.

The formal arraignment will be held today. Such a huge step toward putting this murderer away.

Nick, the man who destroyed my daughter and possibly our lives, will hear a list of charges against him. Prosecutors are hoping to convict him on as many as possible. They want to put him away for as long as they can.

We agree on that.

At the top of the list are first- and third-degree murder. Prosecutors will also charge him with possession of an instrument of crime. Whatever happens, we hope he goes away, as they say, in perpetuity.

Before these proceedings commence, Michele and I sit, stand, and wander around a large hallway. We are soon joined by Kristin's friend, Samantha. She has attended every critical step.

Michele and Samantha chat about what we expect to happen today while I am walking in circles with my thoughts. I want to listen to Kristin's last two voicemails which I have saved for nearly four months. I haven't heard them in a while, which surprises me since I previously listened daily. The first was sent to me a couple of days after Kristin's college graduation. She mentions her new digital camera.

> Kristin: "Hi, Dad, it's me again. I'm calling you back. I figured out the answer to my own question because I finished up that first tiny little memory card. Then I took it out and put it back in, and the pictures are still there. Anyway, I just wanted to also thank you for everything this weekend, as far as graduation day and the gifts.

"The camera is awesome. It's perfect. Believe it or not, I already figured out how to take some pictures, and I've been taking them since yesterday. Which I can, hopefully, download later this evening and send to you. Anyway, thank you very much, and I will hopefully talk with you soon. I'm not sure if you talked with Gaga and Poppy regarding the fact that I spoke to them but maybe you have. Talk to you later, Dad. Love you. Bye."

Then I listen to the second voicemail from Kristin. It was from forty hours before she was murdered.

Kristin: "Hey, Dad, it's Kristin. I got your message. It's about 10:20 on Wednesday morning. I'm at the new apartment. It's beautiful. There's a lot of stuff to be put away and a lot of stuff to be gotten, but I did get your message last night, and obviously things were a little bit hectic, like I was really tired and trying to put stuff away and whatnot.

"So, give me a call back when you get this, and I wanted to thank you for helping me out and putting that money in there so that I could pay all of my rent today and still be able to live and pay the bills that are going to come from activating the phone and internet and whatnot. I love you. I guess you're at work. I'll talk to you later, Dad."

Six months before those messages were recorded, I read my new cell phone's instruction booklet cover-to-cover. I learned how to access the names and numbers of people who left me voicemails. These features are standard on today's smartphones but weren't available without some effort back then. I also learned how to identify the dates and times voicemail messages were made.

While listening to Kristin's voicemails, I hit "#5" key to check whose phone was used to make those messages. It didn't say Kristin's phone, as I thought previously. This time it says Kevin

Welsh. I don't know Kevin Welsh, but I know the "#8" key will call back the phone from where the voicemails originated.

I leave a message on voicemail.

"Hi, Mr. Welsh? I'm Bill Mitchell. I know we don't know each other, but you might know my daughter, Kristin Mitchell. I think she may have left messages from your phone at some time. If you don't mind, please call me back when you have a chance."

I also leave my cell phone number.

Time for court. This courtroom is nothing like the one last month at the preliminary hearing. It is a large auditorium with audience seating shaped in an arc. There is a stage and two long desks and chairs. Of course, there is also a raised judge's bench.

Nick is led in. As we saw before, he is uniformed in a dark-blue jumpsuit with manacles at his hands and feet. The prosecution team and defense lawyers confer; none of it is understandable from our distant seats.

While I'm looking around this immense place, searching to see if Nick's brother might be in attendance, Michele becomes upset about something.

Samantha also complains to me. "Bill, I can't believe this. Nick was actually smiling at us."

Either Nick is feeling emboldened that his self-defense story will hold up, or Michele and Samantha misinterpret what they saw. But I missed it, and I trust it happened as they said.

I wonder if he will ever face my family, considering what he did. I also wonder how he is coping with his self-created misery.

Was Nick doing what Michele and Samantha thought?

Why would he be smiling? Was he? I missed it. Besides the look, this courtroom procedure is as anti-climactic as the prosecutors warned us it would be.

With this formal arraignment concluded, we drive home.

Kristin Calling?

Driving south, approaching Baltimore, my cell phone rings. A fright shoots up my back. It's a ringtone I haven't heard in four months.

I'm stunned. I can't answer. It rings again. Michele asks the obvious, "Are you going to answer that?"

It rings again. I whisper. "That ... is ... Kristin's ... ringtone."

It rings a third time. Before the call gets away, I answer sheepishly, "Hello ... ?"

"Mr. Mitchell? Hi, this is Kevin Welsh. You left a voicemail message for me. I don't think I know you, and I don't know your daughter, Kristin."

"That's okay, Kevin. She is no longer with us." Even though her ringtone brought her back for a moment.

Kevin says sadly, "Oh my God. I'm so sorry to hear that. If I was in front of you right now, I'd hug you."

"You'd hug me? A total stranger?"

"I would." This Kevin guy sounds like he means it.

"Mr. Mitchell, I've only had this number for a month. Maybe some things got crossed up."

"Well, I appreciate you calling." Apparently, our call was not going anywhere.

Kevin adds, "I'm just a jeweler in Catonsville. I've been racking my brain on how I would have known her."

So why is his name stamped on my daughter's last two voicemails? I try to figure it out without losing him. Nothing is registering.

Hold on. Wait.

There was a jeweler Michele and I saw years ago about alterations to Michele's engagement ring. I begin to remember his shop. It had great cases of high-end rings in gold, silver, and platinum. And diamonds and bracelets and mirrors all the way around.

I think I remember Kevin Welsh.

"Wait. You're a jeweler in Catonsville ... Do you know Donna Watkins?"

Kevin says, "Yes, sir."

I recall him now. He competed with the largest jewelry stores in the area and beat them at their own game: superior work at attractive prices. He was a perfectionist who allowed only one client into his store at a time so he could give customers his complete focus.

But what is happening today?

Now, it hits me...

A jeweler created a locket for Donna, Michele's dearest friend. The locket, with photos of Kristin and Michele—and an oval window that holds a lock of Kristin's hair—captured our hearts and minds.

"Oh my God, Kevin! You made a locket for my daughter who passed away. It holds a lock of her hair. You now have her phone number!"

That is why Kristin's ringtone was ringing. Kevin Welsh has Kristin's old cell phone number. The number we retired in June.

Meeting Kevin

As if turning a page to a new chapter in our lives, Michele and I meet Kevin at a restaurant several blocks from his store. We don't know where this relationship will lead, but something or someone must have predetermined it. Once we settle into our seats and order a drink, Kevin shares shocking details of the story behind his cell phone number change a month earlier.

It appears that Kristin, our daughter and Kevin's protector-angel, came through with a kind of miracle.

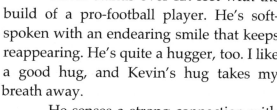

Not wanting to gather false hope, it's a lot to believe.

Kevin stands over six feet with the build of a pro-football player. He's soft-spoken with an endearing smile that keeps reappearing. He's quite a hugger, too. I like a good hug, and Kevin's hug takes my breath away.

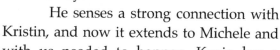

Kevin and Michele. At the center of the locket and cell phone number story.

He senses a strong connection with Kristin, and now it extends to Michele and me. This association with us needed to happen. Kevin has a welcome suggestion.

"I call my closest friends 'brother.' I mean, the friends most precious to me. Can I call you, Brother Bill? Is that okay?"

I jump at his proposal. "Yes, Brother Kevin."

Attempting to include Michele in our new monikers, I ask, "So, should we call Michele, Sister Michele?"

It sounds like a nun's name. Better not.

Brother Kevin provides an unfiltered version of his ex-girlfriend, including his concerns about how abusive this woman was and how his attempts to exclude her from his life have failed. He warned her he would call her managers at work and say she was stalking him. That threat did not stop her, so he called her place of employment and did just as he warned. Only then did she discontinue her campaign, but Kevin remains on guard.

I lost a daughter, but have found a brother.

We suggest Brother Kevin should retain the remaining hair given to him by Donna when he made the locket. Maybe, somehow, Kristin will keep him protected.

He creates four wallet-sized cards with Kristin's photo on one side and her *Dear God* prayer on the other. On the prayer side, he also adds a lock of her hair. He laminates them and gives one to Michele, one to David, and one to me. He keeps the fourth. I will keep mine close at all times.

A year later, David lost his wallet and didn't realize it until the next morning. He was torn apart at the thought of losing the Kristin prayer card Kevin gave him. David returned to the parking lot where he thought he might have dropped the wallet. At a nearby fast food restaurant, he learned someone had turned it in.

Everything in his wallet was untouched.

Go Consolidate Yourself

Another Monday at work.

Michele and I might have uncovered a life-changing miracle with Kristin's cell phone number going to Kevin, but this is just another week in advertising for everyone else. Many would prefer I keep my "life interruption" to myself. Although there is a murder case looming like a life-threatening storm over me, the owner of this agency wants my concentration fully on his business. I don't feel I've missed a beat, but he and I disagree on that.

The reality is, I can receive a call from the prosecutor of our case at any moment. I cannot control what is happening in Philadelphia—125 miles away. Very little of this evolving murder case fits neatly within my workweek.

The owner complains, "Can't you find a way to consolidate all of this into one day a week so it doesn't interrupt your work? Maybe take Wednesdays and address it all that day?"

I shoot back. "Do you really think I can control this? Do you think I can plan when I get calls from a prosecutor's office in Philadelphia? I don't think anyone could do that."

I can't believe this guy.

I ask myself how he would handle this atomic life-bomb had it struck his home and family or, specifically, his daughter. I wish he would let me juggle my life without suggesting the impossible. It only makes matters worse.

My concentration is on the work when I'm there, just as much as the next person. If something is missed, or the work isn't there, let's talk about it then.

We're Going to Court?

We have been counting on Kristin's case not going to trial. The district attorney's office in Montgomery County, Pennsylvania wins ninety-eight percent of its cases. Odds are, there will be no trial. We have been told multiple times that not many have the nerve to test these prosecutors in court.

They win nearly every case because Montgomery is a well-to-do county and well-to-do counties can afford the best criminal law and prosecution teams. Most cases go to pleas. Kristin's murderer admitted to participating in this crime, so we feel it is only a matter of time before he wants a plea. Afterward, we hope he will enter into a lengthy prison sentence.

"It's different here in Montgomery County." That's what we've heard, and we believe it. I guess we should consider ourselves lucky, but with Kristin gone, we don't feel so lucky.

Charlotte Stark, our prosecutor, tells us it was better this tragedy didn't happen within the city limits of Philadelphia. They are crazy-busy there, and we will get more attention in Montgomery County. Unlike Philly, our prosecutors have time to communicate with victims' families and keep them informed about what is going on with cases.

So, here we are, four months after Kristin's murder, waiting for word of a plea, and one afternoon I get a call from Charlotte.

Her tone is grim.

"We're going to court. He wants to take this to trial."

I'm confused.

"What? He? Who wants to … ? You mean Nick?"

Charlotte doesn't sound much like Charlotte.

"That's what he wants to do. Must be holding out to see if this can be voluntary manslaughter. Maybe even self-defense … "

"Oh," is all I can say.

"The trial date's set for Monday, December fifth."

Michele and I were prepared for a plea, but Nick and his court-appointed attorney want to try this case before a jury. Better put the date on the calendar.

We never saw this twist coming. What happened?

Merry Christmas, everyone. This case will run right up to Christmas. Apparently, Nick expects to get this murder reduced to a manslaughter or walk out a free man with self-defense. The overwhelming evidence against him should prevent him from walking. That's what I'm thinking. His interview puts him there, and it was an admission. But anything can happen with a trial. We don't need to be reminded of famous cases where the evidence was there, and the defendant walked away a free man.

A trial would be a test of endurance and horror, but Michele, David, and I will get through it. Look what we have endured thus far.

That which would never happen has a date, and it will happen.

We are going to court. I have been in court for a couple of traffic tickets, but nothing will prepare us for this.

More than ever, our fingers are crossed, hoping this somehow ends in a plea. As long as there is time, there is hope.

Emotional Impact

    A trial is coming. We knew it was possible but heavily relied on the prosecution's reinforcement that under this case's circumstances, a trial was extremely unlikely. It would be too risky for the perpetrator; he could spend the remainder of his life in prison if he lost in court. A trial is no longer simply a possibility; it's inked on the calendar. It's just another bombardment we will need to withstand.

    Michele faces panic attacks. It's understandable. Each of us has been carrying on the best as we have been able with the impact of a murder on our minds every day for five months. David and I are able to keep our disappointment at surface level. It hasn't gotten to us yet. But for Kristin's mother, it's wholly different.

    Michele was (is) a great mother to Kristin. I need to include the nine months before Kristin was born—when Michele was continuously vigilant about what she ate or drank. She never took chances with her unborn baby. She attended every class and read every book she could find that would give her baby the best beginning in life. She clipped, read, and saved every informative baby magazine article she found. Nothing was too much of a sacrifice. And when Kristin was born, she was everything a mom ever hoped for in a newborn. Kristin was Michele's reward.

    A murder trial is no reward. Nothing led up to this.

    No matter how this case proceeds, whether if it goes to court or is handled with a plea, the sad truth is our daughter had no choice. She had no say in her fate—but her killer gets the royal treatment compared with Kristin.

    For us, this latest news is a wellspring of sleepless nights. Having spent our parental years doing what seemed best to keep our children safe from harm, murder is the worst outcome. We will now see an entire massacre played out in a public courtroom.

The Candlelight Vigil Video

Coming our way in early November is a candlelight vigil in Kristin's name at Saint Joseph's University.

The announcement reads:

Save the date:
November the 14th! 7:30 p.m.
Night of remembrance and Protest!

Walking candlelight vigil in honor of Kristin Mitchell '05 Graduate of SJU who was violently stabbed and murdered by her "boyfriend" two weeks after graduating from SJU. The perpetrator has decided to go to trial instead of pleading guilty and sparing this community and the family needless pain and hurt. The Office of Mission in conjunction with the Women's Group of SJU, and the Mitchell family will walk from the Haub School of Business in candlelight protest of this terrible loss and memory of all the victims of domestic violence killed in our homes every year. National Director of the Child Abuse and Neglect Division of Health and Human Services Department in Washington D.C., Catherine Nolan, MSW will be the Keynote speaker after the "March for Kristin" concludes in the SJU Chapel.

JOIN US IN MEMORY AND STAND UP
AGAINST THE VIOLENCE!

Leading to this heartfelt observance, I create a video tribute to Kristin. It is intended to give the audience the real person behind the tragedy, and what a beautiful soul she was (is).

Without glossy production, using slight camera moves on still photos, I plan to honor Kristin's life through a portrayal of her innocence, beauty, and womanliness. The audience will see aspects of a life that could have become forgotten when the focus of late has been on the manner in which she died. I want people to know and remember a young adult who had a good life, was full of fun, played the flute beautifully, bravely rode horses, and loved her family, friends, and cats completely. They need to see Kristin as a living, loving person. The real Kristin.

Underneath the scenes that move across the screen, Faith Hill's tune, "There You'll Be," from the *Pearl Harbor* film accomplishes the mood.

The Night of the Candlelight Vigil

It's a late Monday afternoon in November. We borrowed a van so Michele and I could bring David, Gaga and Poppy Mitchell, and Donna to a ceremony at Saint Joseph's University.

In the atrium of the Haub School of Business, where Kristin took the majority of her business classes, an easel holds a two-by-three-foot portrait of Kristin. Gaga and Poppy Mitchell chat with David, Donna, and me while we wait for this event to commence.

Here is where Kristin spent four years preparing for the next steps in her life. A launching pad for a bright future.

A few steps from us, Michele studies Kristin's portrait. A mother's child is lost, and there will be no bringing her back. This moment in this building is another echo of her past. Seeing Michele and her daughter's picture underscores how the grieving process takes time.

A very long time.

Just past seven p.m., marchers light candles, and Father Gerald McGlone, a Jesuit priest, begins prayers. We are about to walk in Kristin's footsteps.

Kristin's portrait at the Haub School of Business.

We leave the building and progress along paths through the campus asking *why* this happened to Kristin. *Why* is our daughter, who graduated from this institution only months ago, no longer alive?

Along the route, several marchers whisper to me, "Mr. Mitchell, how is your family?" And, "Will that guy be going to prison?" I appreciate their interest.

With a trial commencing in three weeks, I know it will bring vast challenges to our souls and equilibrium.

The defense attorney our prosecution team will face is reputed to be an intimidating force. He is highly experienced and will do all he knows to keep our daughter's killer from going where he belongs. That's his job. Honestly, it feels like Kristin will be on trial rather than her murderer. The defense will probably create ways to drag her down while portraying her killer as this poor soul who made only this one big mistake in his life. As if he only had one bad day. Walking in this procession, I am trying hard not to think about what is coming.

Upon reaching Smith Chapel, there will be prayers followed by a few short speeches. I will run Kristin's video, then Michele, David, and I will speak. We each have found our voices and intend to give listeners insights we have gathered since June. We want everyone to think about what happened to Kristin and see how it applies to their own lives.

Father McGlone begins with an invocation about violence but also the subject of hope. "Father Jerry" is outspoken about women's issues, and he adds extra emphasis on what happened with Kristin. He is troubled that today's women do not know the prevalence of danger surrounding them.

Months earlier, Father McGlone suggested the creation of a women's center at this university so women could come and privately discuss whatever issues they were facing in life. I picture the center here soon.

Our procession flows into the chapel. We spot Charlotte Stark. I had mentioned this vigil to her but doubted she would show on a worknight. With such a demanding caseload, how did she fit this in? Charlotte is a force.

In dimly lit Smith Chapel, marchers solemnly walk to a container of sand near the altar and extinguish their candles. When the blend of friends, students, and faculty are seated, the chapel becomes hushed. Father McGlone quietly walks to the podium and reminds us why we are here. We will pray about violence against women; pray for victims and survivors; pray for the dead. And, specifically, we will pray for Kristin Mitchell.

It hurts to think of her as dead.

The National Director of the Child Abuse and Neglect Division of the Department of Health and Human Services in

Washington, D.C. is our keynote. She is scheduled to speak fifteen minutes and has brought an abundance of information. The director describes violence against women with facts and statistics, both current and historical. "The violence is getting worse" is her message. She reports how prevalence of intimate partner violence is overwhelming both in impact and inundation.

At the half-hour mark, the director lists a few topics she will cover *later in this speech*. Websites, phone numbers, and addresses are also yet to come.

I thought she was speaking fifteen minutes.

Our audience does not know the Mitchells are going to be speaking tonight. What if everyone leaves before Kristin's video plays and my family speaks? This opportunity will be lost.

A new distraction is a light high on the back wall behind the altar. It flickers a bit as if the bulb is about to blow, then it shuts off. Under different circumstances, I wouldn't put any significance on this. But lately, electricity seems to be affected when the prevailing subject is Kristin.

For a few minutes, the light is out. But it then it flickers and comes back to life.

Samantha, Kristin's friend who is sitting behind me, taps my right shoulder. "Mr. Mitchell, is Kristin doing that?"

"No," I smile at her. "When Kristin plays with lights, they go out for good." I say it as if I'm some kind of authority on how deceased people are able to touch the world of the living. I'm not.

At the podium, the national director finishes her fifteen-minute keynote at forty-five-minutes. I see people are remaining in the chapel.

Like a shot, I rush to the DVD player to hit play on Kristin's video. I turn up the sound, push buttons, hear music playing, and watch the assemblage transfix on the screen. Close one.

The audience sits captured by Kristin, who is brought to life in this video. Tissues out, many dab tears away.

There is power in her short, but sad, story. It's a Greek tragedy of evil triumphing over good. It's so wrong. But gaining people's attention is the first step in influencing them to care about Kristin, and I hope, beginning to care more about their own safety.

As the video fades at an end, Michele takes the podium. For me, it is surreal to see my wife speaking about our daughter in this place. She is talking about what it's like to tragically lose someone you love.

Michele dislikes being in the public eye but handles this moment so well. With poise, she is such a model mother. I would be impressed with anyone in her position tonight, had she been someone I didn't know.

I am proud. I see her, and I see Kristin in her.

Michele describes how Kristin wanted to accomplish two primary goals in her young life. "Graduating from an outstanding college and landing a position with a good company. She did precisely that. She graduated with a degree in food marketing from Saint Joseph's, and she won her job with General Mills ... "

Michele gives us insights into how Kristin wrote the most loving cards, picked out the most meaningful presents, and kept in touch with her family. Michele spoke about her daughter's work ethic and kind character.

Kristin loved her freshman year, English especially, because it doubled as a service learning class. She took pleasure in working with a woman she called Miss Betty, who lived in a low-income section of Philadelphia. Miss Betty was about fifty but could read only on a third-grade level.

Miss Betty and Kristin.

Michele says softly, "Kristin would put together lesson plans for Miss Betty. She admired this woman for trying so hard to obtain her GED." They were good for each other. Miss Betty would be crushed if she knew what happened to her friend, Kristin.

Next, David comes to the podium.

Earlier today, our high school senior took his time getting his thoughts lined up perfectly. Once David was thoroughly organized, he went into hyperdrive at the keyboard. He still holds his high school's record for most words typed per minute. His hands become a blur.

We did not review each other's speeches before this evening, but David hits home runs with his concepts and unique choices in words. I am in awe of the way he expresses himself.

Tonight, it's beyond a homerun, it's a moon shot.

He recalls vacations when our family drove long hours from Baltimore to Hilton Head, South Carolina. In the backseat, he and Kristin would sometimes conspire to tease their mother. They playfully referred to her as *The Fun Police* when she tried to quiet them down. Michele was a mom being a mom. She loved the attention as much as everyone else.

David describes his family picking out and sawing down trees at a Christmas tree farm. He gets a rise from listeners with a story about Kristin attempting to teach him algebra when he was still in first grade. How she tried so hard, but he wasn't ready.

He breathes life into scenes of Kristin getting dressed for just about any occasion. "She always looked perfect. She was beautiful." He talks about her smile and hearing her laugh. About smelling her hair and feeling her embrace. He makes her real.

"When our family went out to eat, she would order the most expensive things on the menu but only eat half of them," and, "how it bothered our parents."

The chapel audience hangs on every word, picturing the moments and reacting with smiles or tears. He likens Kristin's current state like a burnt candle. The candle has gone out but the scent lingers and surrounds those around her. He says, "We suffer for a reason, and we all must face pain and try to keep our faith."

When he finishes, I expect the attendees want to applaud David for displaying his heart so openly, but this is not an evening for clapping. And now, it is quiet again.

I rise to the podium. As I begin, that same light on the wall behind the altar flickers and shuts off. It is impossible not to notice.

I stop, smile, and go off script.

"We have experienced many lights blowing out at our home. And we also had three cars that wouldn't start that first week after Kristin was gone. Our printer quit working while I was writing a eulogy, but then it worked the next day. I don't think tonight's light show is Kristin's work. Kristin tends to put lights out permanently."

"Parents want their children to be safe and happy, in that order. This is what we wanted for Kristin. Safe *and* happy." I know that when your child is not safe, everything else is secondary.

Never was this truer than now.

I quote from an email Kristin sent when she was a sophomore at this same university. She explains how much she misses us. It captures how I feel at this moment. I miss her. Being in this space makes me long for Kristin. It's just so painful.

I know the audience feels our tragedy tonight, but maybe what they did not expect to feel is a sense of hope. Dating violence tragedies will become fewer when each of us gains a basic level of education about the red flags that exist in every unhealthy relationship. Most of us lack fundamental knowledge of what dating violence is. So, it sneaks up and has us in its grip without our knowing it.

This evening will become the inception of dating violence speeches for me. I explain what it is like to be on the receiving end of this epidemic. For tonight, this is enough. I finish by thanking the staff for setting this up, and I thank those who attended.

One of Kristin's professors quickly takes to the podium microphone and asks if he could cover one more item. He and other professors had a version of Kristin's diploma framed to present to our family. This finished piece is two-feet wide and written in Latin. It is powerful. It reinforces the hard work Kristin put in but will not be able to take forward.

The only words I can understand on the diploma are Kristin Marie Mitchell. Ironically, Kristin had intended to pick up her diploma from Saint Joseph's on Friday, June 3—the day she died. In time, these same professors will populate my email contact list and become the dearest of friends. That will be a year from tonight.

Our family is sent home with sincere hugs and handshakes. We are wished the best outcome for the upcoming trial which is less than three weeks away.

The Next Day

I have a call with Charlotte Stark. Even as engaged as she is in active cases and court appearances, she managed to attend last evening's candlelight vigil.

She felt Kristin's presence just as she did in our home four months ago in July. "That was amazing. I came in this morning and raved about last night."

She asks about the buttons emblazoned with Kristin's portrait that people were wearing at the vigil. She wants to know who took the picture.

The fact is, I dislike that photo very much. Someone pulled it from her Facebook page and had buttons printed.

"Charlotte, that was taken by the guy who killed her."

Charlotte says, "Oh, you're kidding. What's the irony of that? You know, it's not my favorite photo of her. If you look at it, she doesn't seem as relaxed as she does in a lot of her other photos. Very posed. She just doesn't seem as comfortable as she appeared when she was with her family. That's my read on it. So, I kept wondering, *why that photo?* I could go on and on about that photo."

Charlotte shifts her focus to David. "Your son is remarkable for his age, very ... strong?"

I reinforce that. "He's what some refer to as an old spirit. When he was four or five, he was that little boy the grown-ups loved to talk with for an hour and a half. He's always been that way. He wrote what you heard last night in maybe forty-five minutes, and it's just so great. He gets his head together and nails it."

"It was fabulous," she remarks. "It was just amazing. All of you were so amazing. I don't know how you did it."

"We don't either," I say.

I really don't know.

Charlotte finishes. "Well, it's terribly sad, and I feel horrible for you people. As my husband used to say before he died, 'Charlotte, the world isn't fair.'"

"Yes. Life isn't fair, and death is more unfair."

Two days after the vigil, I receive a call from Angela Keeler, the administrative assistant who set up the event. Angela was in Smith Chapel the evening of the vigil. She was also in that same chapel the night before and the night after the vigil.

Only on the night of Kristin's candlelight vigil did that one light flicker and shut off. The other evenings, it worked fine.

Interesting.

Years later, some participants recalled the chapel lights playing an even greater part toward the end of the evening. Lights were said to be rising and falling, guided directly by the volume of the singing of "Amen," the traditional gospel song. There was a noticeable gasp at one point when the lights were almost completely out, and the chapel went dark.

RECOLLECTION

Remembering My Friend, Kristin

The following is from Kristin's college friend, Samantha:

It was a Wednesday morning, a couple of years back. I was in the shower watching my newborn boy through the glass as he sat peacefully in a chair. I was playing music on my phone. Life had changed so much—college and my twenties were a distant memory—and as every new mom knows, showers are a sacred place to relax and zone out.

All of a sudden, an old song came on. "We got winners, we got losers …. Chain smokers and boozers …" "I Love This Bar" by Toby Keith. I was instantly transported. I zoned out, standing under the hot water. I was taken back to our frequent car rides to Baltimore to visit friends at Johns Hopkins University. High school and 'college-me' hated country music, and I would often tease Kristin and ask where her terrible taste in music came from (as if my love for techno remixes of pop music was any better). But she eventually won me over, and our rides to Baltimore were frequented with this song on repeat, blaring through the speakers, while we sang at the top of our lungs and laughed like the free, relaxed young women we were, without a care in the world except whether we could get to the bar in time to catch the drink specials.

We were relatively inseparable in those days, spending so much time together you would think we were roommates and not friends attending separate universities fifteen miles apart. Kristin was the friend who would pick you up from the airport at some horribly annoying time when everyone else rolled their eyes and told you to take a cab; the friend who would show up when you were having a bad day and drag you to Chili's for your favorite boneless buffalo wings; who would jump in the car and go on road trip adventures with you; the friend who would strike up a conversation with some random sweet girl in the bathroom and make friends; who would on impulse purchase a hamster and giggle uncontrollably while watching it roll around in its little hamster ball, spoiling it and showing it as much love as if it were one of her beloved cats; who would tell you that you looked beautiful even after you gained fifteen pounds and hated yourself standing next to her perfect, petite frame; the friend who would shock you and defy all stereotypes by changing her own tire on the shoulder of 476 in the evening, completely unfazed by cars whizzing by, because her dad taught her, whereas your dad taught you how to call AAA; the friend who managed to party with the best of them while still staying on top of her studies and planning for her future.

    A future that was tragically cut short, because she, like me, was also the friend who trusted that people were ultimately good and gentle, and kind. The baby's whimpers brought me back to reality, and I realized how horribly unfair it was that these memories were distant to me, while Kristin would forever be twenty-one in our minds.

A Dream

I'm alone in a fairground at night. The scene is in shades of blue and black. It feels like the kind of a night that transitioned from a scorcher of a day. I don't know if I have ever been here before. It's eerie but also peaceful.

All is hushed, apart from an occasional cricket chirp. There are bare light bulbs strung overhead, furtively waving *thank yous* to a mild breeze that allows them to dance. The lights attach to poles on one end and corners of exhibit halls at the other. They allow a scene to play before me.

There is no backstory because dreams are well-practiced at keeping secrets. This is a tale with no beginning.

A breeze kicks up spirals of dust that encircle my feet as if it wants to tell me something. Out of the distant darkness, a young woman approaches slowly. It's Kristin. She is recognizable first by the smile that trademarked her life. It's good to see her happy after all she endured at the end.

Neither of us is surprised to see the other. Kristin is here, and that is enough. Nothing is said. I haven't seen her for so long, all I want is to take this vision in. This is my dream come true.

Wait ... my dream?

Kristin knew what this was.

She nods with her eyes. "You understand now, Dad ..."

I do. But a dream is worth something. A moment together. A feeling long awaited. A lost child retrieved.

Dreams impose their heartbreaking power of fading when they are discovered. This one loses its color and dimension. I slow it down a bit, but it's slipping from me.

Kristin knows, and before she turns her look says, "Dad, it's going to be all right."

She glides off in the direction she came. A look back, and she is still smiling. It's so sad and yet comforting.

I want to know she exists in some way.

It'll be okay. It's just different.

The Trial Date that Was Not

A plea is not coming, so the trial for the man who murdered our daughter will begin Monday, December 5. But there is a little wrinkle: I will not be allowed in the courtroom during the trial. That is, unless I am called as a witness.

This is correct. My wife and son will be there without me.

How does that feel?

The defense had this tactic in mind months ago. I became a witness because Kristin and I exchanged several emails during the last hours before she was murdered. Either the defense or the prosecution could call me to the stand to testify. That makes me a potential witness. Witnesses cannot sit in the courtroom during a trial. So, I will spend trial days in a hotel room somewhere near the courthouse, awaiting a call to testify. A call that might never come. I expect this was to keep me out of sight of the jury. I will be one less parent for them to study and maybe feel sorry for.

Still a novice to the wheels of justice, I'm receiving a practical education. There is no fairness, and only one side will win.

Murder is the unlawful killing of another person without justification. It's considered the most serious crime a person can commit. The prosecution intends to put Nick away forever with no possibility of returning to the general public. This would be first-degree murder. Life in prison is the outcome of a first-degree murder conviction in Pennsylvania.

First-degree murder is the goal. It would be a resounding victory if we could get that. In some states, "life in prison" is not actually "life"; it's twenty-five years. But in the Commonwealth of Pennsylvania, life means the remainder of a person's life. No matter how much remorse the prisoner shows or how he behaves, he never lives in the outside world again. It is life. Life in prison sounds fair.

Second-degree murder does not apply here. It is murder committed as a principal or accomplice during the commission of a felony, such as a bank robbery, rape, or burglary. As an example, someone robs a bank or a convenience store and kills someone in the course of the robbery. Presumably, the perpetrator did not go into the bank or store to commit murder, but murder happened.

Third-degree murder is all other kinds of murder and is punishable as a felony carrying a prison sentence of multiple decades. The penalties are on a sliding scale. At most, Nick would receive thirty years in prison. But the catch is this thirty is not a full thirty. He would be eligible for parole hearings at fifteen years. If a parole board wanted, he could be released at that time. That would be in the year 2020. We feel it's still an extended sentence when someone is giving up fifteen years of their freedom.

We are warned the court-appointed defense team will employ every legal trick either to free Nick or at least to lessen his punishment. A successful self-defense outcome in court would free him altogether, and he could be set free that day.

What about voluntary manslaughter? This is a real concern, too. A person who kills an individual without lawful justification commits voluntary manslaughter if at the time of the killing he is acting under a sudden and intense passion resulting from serious provocation by the individual killed. I do not know what will happen in that courtroom, but if things go sideways, Nick could be out in what seems like no time. There are cases similar to this when someone received three to seven years in prison.

But wait. Two weeks before the trial is to begin, Charlotte calls. "It's not in a posture to go to trial."

This means there will be a continuance, a postponement to a later date due to a motion made by the defense. Had this gone down as a plea and not a trial, they would actually keep the December 5 date for his plea and sentencing.

Charlotte says the killer "is balking at the present plea negotiations. The lead defense attorney indicates there is a fifty-fifty chance this could go to a plea, but right now, he cannot say it is a plea. If the killer accepted a plea for third-degree murder, he would receive fifteen to thirty years … "

The truth is, Nick had at least one big "prior" in his past, and that could make him serve almost all of the thirty years. He and a friend, when they were twenty years old, used a pellet gun to rob a bank in Delaware. An elderly female teller put money into Nick's gym bag, but their dark blue Camaro was stopped soon after by Delaware State Police. They each received prison sentences and served five years. It is presumed this prior felony will now keep him in prison longer.

If this does go to trial, the soonest would be mid-January or early February. Nobody knows.

Charlotte tells us the defense team requested a toxicology report to get blood levels of both Kristin and her murderer. This buys them time. Later, I learned the report was never followed up. It only slowed things down.

Charlotte continues on the case by interviewing witnesses.

"Keeping the momentum going. Still going on like we're going to trial," she tells me.

She explains how the lead defense attorney is doing all he can to make the defendant "look pathetic as a person" to the judge when they have meetings. Charlotte counters by portraying how the Mitchell family is dealing with the holidays coming in November and December.

On the call, Charlotte warns there is always a risk that even if this went to a plea, everyone could be assembled in a courtroom, ready for the plea, and at the last minute, everything could change and the defendant might withdraw his plea. If that happened, this would go to trial. Sometimes, pleas backfire.

Charlotte insists Michele should plan to be in the courtroom on December 5 in case this trial still takes place.

"I need a parent there," she demands.

Charlotte also suggests Michele should bring a friend with her for moral support. If needed, the county will supply someone. She reminds me I will not be permitted to attend the trial.

Charlotte made a point to the judge that if this goes to a plea, to keep holding that December 5 date open "So the Mitchells can have some kind of a holiday. To give this some kind of closure."

December will see no joy or closure for us. Nor will any of the Christmas season. Everything is in limbo.

RECOLLECTION

Charlie's Initiation

In a conference room within a power company in Pennsylvania, buffet trays warmed an assortment of Italian dishes. For this voluntary noon meeting, the scent alone would draw a crowd.

By eleven-thirty a.m., my daughter's video was ready. On the screen, the name of my presentation was "When Dating Hurts."

A man in his early fifties entered and placed his pad of paper and pen on a seat near the last row. Then he walked over to survey the line up on the buffet. I just had to chat with him.

"Let me guess. You came for the food, right?" I took a chance on what his reaction would be.

"No, I came to hear you speak." That felt good.

After Charlie introduced himself, he said, "Four years back, I knew nothing about domestic violence except the stereotypical stuff. You know, guys from the worst parts of town who come home, get drunk, and take things out on their wives. That's what I used to think. But I remember when I learned the truth."

After a moment's hesitation, he continued.

"Yeah, it was a Monday. I had to do an energy audit for a domestic violence agency in town. At Laurel House."

Charlie needed to meet with the agency's director and her assistant. Before the meeting, he stood outside of a conference room waiting for them. They came out with a third woman who introduced herself to him. He remembered her. Maria was very friendly, very nice, and had a big beautiful smile. She might have been twenty-five.

After Charlie met with the director and her assistant, he surveyed the building and collected information for his audit. He made an appointment to return in two days and present his proposal and some solutions.

"So, I returned to Laurel House Wednesday," Charlie said, rubbing his eyes, "and I handed out binders. I was starting to speak when the assistant put up her hand and stopped me."

She asked him if he remembered the young woman he met Monday at the conference room door. Maria. Of course, he did. As it turns out, she was having trouble at home with her boyfriend who was horribly abusive to her.

Laurel House had just received word about her minutes prior to this meeting with Charlie. She had been hanged by her boyfriend the day before, outside of her apartment.

Charlie said to me, "I shut down." He knew so little about domestic violence before this. But Maria put a face on it.

"I thought, here was this precious little lady who was gone in the worst way. Just like that. She's gone. I mean, I just met her. I was stunned. I still get choked up. Like I am right now ... "

Charlie's story made domestic violence real for him. I could see Maria in his story. These are real people. Real, innocent people who become caught in harm's way and cannot escape from it. These are people we pass on the street every day.

They need our help.

A Holiday Bonus

A couple of days before Christmas, I have an impromptu end-of-year meeting with a senior manager at work. He feels the need to reflect on my 2005.

"I have some advice. As you enter 2006, do yourself a big favor and leave 2005 in 2005. It'll be better for you, and it'll be better for everyone else who works here." In other words, don't bother people with that little ripple of bad luck I have in my life.

Well, that was kind of unsympathetic of him. My inner rage complicates my response. But here I go.

"You know, even if I tried to do that, I mean, leave 2005 in 2005, it isn't quite so easy. My family is facing a murder trial. So, I don't get to control what's coming, or when … "

I shift from defense to offense. I'm not a happy guy and say, "But I want you to do something for me."

He tries to stop me. "Look, you don't need to say anything about this. I'm just trying to help you … "

I will have none of it. Not with this guy. This is the same man who tried to compare our daughters months ago: his engaged daughter and my dead daughter. This man clearly doesn't have the filter that stops most people from inserting themselves where they don't belong. No matter what comes from what I'm about to say, I'm putting it out there.

"Allow me to speak? Okay? You spoke to me, so let me speak."

I draw in a breath.

"Okay, think about your daughter for just a moment. Imagine she's twenty-one. Just finished college. She's excited to have landed a nice job. Picture her face. Do you see it? She's dating some guy and, to all appearances, things seem to be fine.

"There comes a night, and you get a call. It's a detective. Your daughter was murdered. There she is. See it. Stabbed fifty-five times … all over the place. See it in your mind. Hold that thought for, oh, how about fifteen seconds?"

He interrupts. "Hey, look ... "

"Can you be quiet for fifteen seconds?" I could just about jump at him.

I stare at my watch, waiting for fifteen seconds to pass.

It feels like fifteen minutes. The watch on my right arm finally hits fifteen seconds.

Wham! My right-hand slams down hard on the desk in front of me.

"Okay, wipe that out of your mind, and get over it ... !"

I storm out, pulling his door nice and hard behind me.

Christmas 2005

We think about the way it used to be. How can we not compare this with previous holiday seasons?

Michele, David, and I attend midnight services at Saint Paul's Catholic Church in Ellicott City, Maryland. The same church where Kristin had both her First Holy Communion and her funeral service.

I bring along a leather-bound journal Kristin gave me. It has never been written in. We arrive half an hour early, and I will use this opportunity profitably. This is the first time I write the first of my "Dear Kristin" entries. Each will capture feelings about life without Kristin, and I will speak directly to Kristin in a conversation. I truly expect she will be able to read what I write. For all I know, this is the only way I can communicate with her.

Earlier today, Michele and I put Kristin's ornaments on our tree. We knew it would be too painful, so we waited until today. For Kristin, we also have a present: a stuffed bear doll that wears a red vest. The bear's face reminded me of Gatsby, Kristin's dear Siamese who joined her in her final resting place four months ago. This bear will soon take its rightful place on a rocking chair with other dolls in her bedroom.

Christmas Day. A constant rain aptly colors our mood. Before a Christmas visit with some dear friends an hour away, Michele, David, and I stop by Kristin's grave.

It's marked by a two-foot tall wooden cross Poppy fashioned together in his workshop. Kristin's name is in raised gold letters along the horizontal piece. On either side of her name are two red hearts. Attached at the top is a little angel in white.

This cross marked Kristin's grave the first year.

It's a downpour as we three speak with Kristin at this gravesite. We finish with prayers.

Christmas Day, in this place? This is so wrong. It should never be like this for any family.

We return to our car and circle around for a last look. A claustrophobic gray sky has a seam trying to open and let light peek through. Is this to give us hope? How foolishly sentimental we can be, always attaching a storyline to everything that happens.

We are pathetic.

But an unmistakable rainbow appears, and it stretches horizon to horizon. It seems improbable since there had been no hint of sun. I roll down all the windows and capture it to prove miracles can appear in our lives. Miracles? Yes, I said it, miracles.

Couldn't get it all in one shot, but it happened.

Had we arrived here any earlier or later, we would have missed it entirely.

New Year's Day 2006

There is no *Happy* New Year's Day this first day of 2006.

Palpable dread comes closer to describing it. Not only with an impending trial but a continuance the judge has approved. No new trial date is set. It's a marathon without a finish line.

I often resort to calling Charlotte Stark and hope for new insights. I learn the continuance is to allow time for more evidence to be run through a DNA lab. Each DNA test costs the Commonwealth hundreds of dollars, so prosecutors and defense lawyers cannot submit every blood stain for a test. They have to be judicious.

This DNA testing, requested by the defense, is intended to accomplish something at the trial, but nobody I speak with can imagine what.

One extremely helpful piece of information from Charlotte makes so much sense. We're glad she told us. The defense team, although court-appointed and not costing Nick a penny, needs to fight to win, of course, but also needs to make it appear they are using every lawyer-move possible. Getting a continuance is one of these moves. The truth is, if the defense were to lose this case, and if Nick could convince the authorities he was not represented well, he might get himself retried.

This is something called the Post-Conviction Relief Act. It's a direct appeal when the accused loses a case and wants to challenge some aspect of it. Maybe he feels his attorney was not exploiting all available strategies and tactics to win his case. With Charlotte's explanation, the defense's actions make more sense.

The judge issues a continuance. Although this particular postponement has been granted, the defense did not use the time to do further DNA testing. It was a tactic with no further action.

For the first time, I understand why the defense files these kinds of motions. If they aggressively pursue this case, which they appear to be doing, and if the result is a conviction, the outcome would have a better chance of remaining a secure outcome.

If the defense attorney does not put up a good fight, we could be back in a courtroom with another trial in a couple of years.

Charlotte shares her strategy. "If this goes to trial ... " She stops and composes herself. "Look, this is a horrible tragedy. This was a girl on her way up. She had a college degree. She had a great job waiting for her. She had friends. She had a beautiful apartment. He wasn't going anywhere. He's not going anywhere. He's on his way down. His dating her was a reach."

To Charlotte, our daughter is not a case number. Thinking about the way she would portray Kristin in a courtroom, she follows up and says, "The fact of the matter is, with her, I have so much to work with ... "

Charlotte is on this case almost every day. She tells me, "You're getting the full-court press here. The horror and the tragedy are not lost on us. You've got to realize that. And when these homicide cases are assigned, this is a top priority. There's that part of me that wants to put this guy away, you know, murder one. He's gone for life, and that's it, he's done. But, on the other hand, what if he gets voluntary manslaughter? Then it's all for naught. And you know how juries are ... " Her voice trails off.

This could go to a plea. This could go to a trial. This could be a murder conviction, and he gets life. Or maybe he gets fifteen to thirty years. Or it could be manslaughter, and he gets four to seven years. And maybe time off for good behavior.

So far, 2006 is feeling as dismal as 2005.

Working

In my other reality, my job, I am busy dealing with the kind of days any creative director goes through. I not only see ideas in development, but I have to push through what is going on at home. It's not always smooth. No matter the circumstances in my personal life, I must take good, and sometimes not-so-good, advertising campaign strategies and make them stronger. There's no letup in fighting for the kind of high-level work our creative department is expected to create.

Nobody gives me much slack just because our family had a little mishap. I knew who my friends were before my daughter's disaster, and they remain friends. They have my back. I need them. They know when to ask about our family or the trial, and I don't mind explaining it to those who care.

The owner of the agency wants the distractions in my life to go away. He wants me to get back to the business of making work happen. I am one of the highest compensated employees in this company, and this company relies on me to behave like it. They don't want my mind wandering off to the unfixable parts of my life. They want me to be present.

I feel I am bringing it. Maybe I don't see myself 100-percent clearly, but work is done well, and it goes out on time. My department has nothing but pros, and I feel as if they have stepped up while I am in this life turmoil.

When I have a few moments, I call Charlotte from my office with a frequency that feels reasonable. She knows why I call. I am hoping she will reveal progress. Often, I hear her thinking out loud, "What a lovely daughter you had," or "What a horrible loss this is." In our conversations, she talks about her own daughters. There is one she finds quite like Kristin. In fact, her daughter also attended Saint Joseph's University.

And momentum with the case has stalled, and there's nothing any of us can do about it.

The Devil's Horn

It's not uncommon for Michele and me to ask the unanswerable question: "what is Kristin doing right now?" Of course, she is not alive. But then, where is she? In Heaven? On some other spiritual plane?

Some parents who have lost children call on mediums or seers to establish connections with the *Great Beyond*. Our neighbors tell us about a medium named George Anderson, called the "Stradivarius of Mediums." Anderson lives in Long Island, New York, and he supposedly contacts the deceased.

Whether or not anyone believes what Anderson does, his services are an unbelievable $1,700 per hour. When he does a session, Anderson is precise about how your loved one died and what they are doing currently. Some feel he is able to communicate with the dead, and the dead talk through him.

Our consciences and religious upbringings tell us not to go near any of this. We hear, "It is not your loved one communicating through that medium. It is Satan speaking!"

Well, that could pose a problem.

At work, I learn about a local medium. She lives a few miles from our home. "She's so insightful and has helped so many people by contacting *the Other Side*," is what I hear.

We don't want this medium to study Kristin's story via a Google search, so we have our neighbors set up an appointment. These are the same neighbors who lent us books by George Anderson.

The night arrives for the medium. It is seven p.m. on a face-numbing January evening. Michele and I arrive a few minutes early and feel jumpy. We hope the talk about contacting Satan is nonsense.

We ring the doorbell, but nobody seems to be home. Where is this medium? Do we have the wrong night? We notice the way the house is laid out, to our left there is a window directly into the kitchen. Through the window, on a table, I see a book. Oh, it's only *The Devil's Horn*.

Oh, my God. Who are these people?

Michele sees it and wants to abandon this entire session. I hold her off so we can talk about it, but headlights wash over us. The medium is pulling into her driveway.

As she lets us into her home, she introduces herself and her husband. This super-sized man says nothing as I offer a hello with my hand extended. He could be Lurch from *The Addams Family*, which would be flawless casting for tonight's outing.

The medium, Michele, and I sit in the living room which is reasonably chic but uncomfortably dark. Maybe this lighting is part of the act. She tells us how it works. Nothing complicated. Like George Anderson, she will attempt to contact our loved one while asking us simple questions. We should answer only with a yes or no, and that's it. Apparently, contacting the dead is relatively straightforward.

I hold up a tiny silver recorder I pulled from my pocket and ask if I could record our session. George Anderson's books suggest recording is better than taking notes. In fact, some people bring several recorders because communicating with *The Beyond* can cause electrical interferences that play havoc with some recorders and make the results unintelligible.

The recorder is enough to throw things off. I guess I blew it. My request to record unhinges this medium. She is not happy and prefers to do this reading with only Michele. I am told I need to remain in the dark living room.

This turn of events reminds me of something I also read. Recording a session could signal I'm a cop—which I'm not. Bogus psychics sometimes get busted when they take someone's money without the ability to do what they claim they can do. It amounts to stealing someone's money. She thinks I'm a cop putting evidence together on her.

While I sit in the darkness, Lurch passes by several times and never acknowledges me. Maybe he can't see me. The medium is in a room with Michele, attempting to use her special powers.

Her reading goes nowhere. She babbles all over the place.

"I see a young boy with dark hair. He's wearing knickers. Does this seem like someone you know?"

Michele says, "Well, no ... "

The medium then begins to recognize someone else.

"I see a child. He's on a tricycle ... "

She's on a fishing trip and not catching anything. It doesn't get better.

"This doesn't normally happen to me. I'm a little *off* tonight," she says.

She is probably thinking about the "cop" and his recorder in the living room. The reading stops in less than ten minutes. She does not charge for this aborted session. She acts relieved to see Michele, me, and my recorder leaving her dark residence.

When we arrive home, I look up that book we spotted, *The Devil's Horn*. I am prepared for this to be about devils, devil worshippers, witchcraft, evil spirits, spells, Lucifer, and all kinds of soul possessions.

Not even close.

The Devil's Horn is the 175-year history of the saxophone, an instrument once banned by a pope. The sax was once considered the most seductive and feared instrument in existence. A symbol of decadence in some countries, it was forbidden by the Nazis and Communists.

The saxophone was considered cursed, which stemmed from the life of its mad inventor, Adolphe Sax, a Belgian inventor and musician who died in 1894 at seventy-nine in abject poverty.

Like many things in our lives, tonight will become a story for a book to be written one day.

New Trial Date

The reassurances we received about this going to a plea are not taking form when and a new trial date is set.

The trial for the murderer of our daughter will begin the week of June 5, almost exactly one year after Kristin's death on June 3. It will also be the day after David graduates from high school. Naturally, our emotions are reaching levels that owned us leading up to our first trial date back in December.

Lest we forget, I will not be allowed in court for the trial except if I am summoned to answer a few questions about that final evening when Kristin and I exchanged emails. It's insult to injury.

Looking ahead, anything can happen with a jury. A defense lawyer could win over a jury with words like, "Ladies and gentlemen, why ruin two lives when one is already ruined?"

What if the outcome of the trial were a voluntary manslaughter conviction? Compared to what this killer did to Kristin, imagine him serving four to seven years for manslaughter. And maybe being paroled in three years. An outrage.

But there is another outcome. The longest of long shots: convincing a jury this was an extraordinary case of self-defense.

I hate to imagine such a scene as this:

Nick is on the witness stand and says, "It was very late. I was tired. We argued about whether I could stay at the apartment that night. The argument escalated with pushing. Some shoving. A slap, I think. Then, it got rougher. A push. A punch. We were in the kitchen, and I pushed her again. Some things got knocked on the floor, like kitchen knives. She got up and screamed, then swiped at me with a knife. I mean, I had to defend myself, right? The rest I cannot remember very well. I guess my mind blocked it out. All I know is, I was scared and felt threatened. The rest is a blur."

Maybe the jury is fed this:

The defense team portrays Nick as a well-meaning man who treated his girlfriend like a princess. This man, twenty-eight, with his whole life ahead of him, spent money he didn't have trying to make her happy. He lent his car to her sometimes.

His lawyer might say, "This is not murder. Sure, someone unfortunately died, but this is a crime of passion. It is love gone wrong. He meant no harm but was left no choice. He was only defending himself ... "

And I also imagine somehow that the jury buys it as self-defense...

The jury is thinking, "You poor thing ... all six-foot tall, muscular you ... attacked by this five-foot-three girl. How did you get out alive? We're willing to overlook most details. Your life's what's important. You are the one at risk ... "

I have to stop imagining this scenario.

If the resolution of this case were self-defense, this murderer would walk out of that courtroom and resume his life as a free man. What a disaster that would be! Why would the most important decision we will ever face include fairness? Life is not fair.

Is any outcome too bizarre?

I ask myself this question, what if this were me? It comes with a very easy answer. Having taken someone's life, the most precious gift a person could possess, I would likely get in my car and drive 100 miles an hour into a brick wall. I would not deserve to live.

And to be painfully precise, while in that car, I would ask for God's forgiveness for doing the unforgivable. I would shout out, nice and loud, the "Our Father." Approaching that brick wall, I would try to time it out perfectly with, "... And deliver us from evil ... Amen." *BOOM.*

Nonexistence. Eternity. I would not deserve to live. But I'm not the one on trial.

If the defendant decides he wants to offer a plea, he has to understand what he is pleading guilty to, and what his prison sentence term would be. It is not his attorney's decision. It is this killer's decision. Third-degree murder carries a thirty-year term with the possibility of parole at fifteen.

If Nick decides to plead this case, his court-appointed attorney will take the request to the judge. If accepted, it will go to the prosecution team to accept it or not.

The prosecution team would confer with the Mitchell family. Together, the prosecution team and our family would discuss the merits of the plea. This is *our child*, but this is *not our decision*. It belongs solely to the Commonwealth of Pennsylvania.

Although the defendant-murderer, Nick, gave an interview and admitted to his murderous participation the morning he killed Kristin, he still would have power over some aspects of his fate.

He knows he will receive prison time unless this goes down as self-defense, which is a far cry from what the evidence indicates.

We are prepared to be soundly disappointed with just about any outcome.

The Headstone Fiasco

I think back to Saturday, June 4, 2005, the day after Kristin was killed. We needed to decide on a funeral home and a cemetery. We requested four plots in a row in case we needed them. You never know.

As discussed earlier, Michele, David, and I arrived on a day when nothing could relieve us from the news that had beaten us down the night before. Roberta, the salesperson, was pleasant enough but had only three weeks of experience at Leighton Park Cemetery. Identifying availabilities on plot maps for this 350-acre cemetery presented her with plenty of challenges.

Nearly eight months after Kristin's burial, the little white cross has been the only grave marker. It's about time we decide on a gravestone. I leave a voicemail with Roberta about discussing Kristin's stone.

Roberta calls back and informs me there can be no headstone. Leighton Park Cemetery cannot allow a headstone on Kristin's grave because it would back up against another family's headstone, back-to-back. Instead, they will allow a footstone if we desire to go that way.

We have seen footstones at this cemetery. These are sad afterthoughts. Our daughter is not getting a sad afterthought. And worse yet, at Leighton, every footstone we have seen eventually sinks into the ground and tips over.

A footstone? This cannot be happening. We cannot catch a break. I ask Roberta for someone I can speak with who's higher up in the organization. I am fully prepared to unleash on these people. Kristin might not be living, but she will always be our daughter. We feel this is happening to our daughter.

She tells me, "Mr. Mitchell, I can give you his name, but I'm sure it will be a footstone only."

John Donaldson meets with Michele and me in a cramped conference room. He begins by saying, "I'm very sorry about your loss, but as Roberta explained to you back in June when you picked out these plots, there was no possibility of a headstone."

What are you talking about? That never happened.

I say to John Donaldson, "You're telling me you think we knew about this back in June? And you think that eight months later, we are trying to change what we were told?"

That loud pounding inside of my head is my heart beating.

"That is correct, Mr. Mitchell," Donaldson says.

"And you think we made this up," I ask in disbelief.

Donaldson indignantly returns with, "What I'm saying is I believe what Roberta told me."

Angry to say the least, I become very descriptive. "Let me tell you what I think you're saying, Mr. Donaldson. You think we arrived here eight months ago, in June—the day after my daughter was massacred. And even though we were experiencing the worst nightmare any parent could ever endure, you think we still had the presence of mind to hear what Roberta said and figured that one day we'd come back and try to pull a fast one on you? To see if we could shove a headstone in anyway? Like we knew we would be burying our daughter and be stuck with a quiet little footstone? That's what you're saying, isn't it?"

Donaldson raises his eyebrows and almost smirks. It's his way of saying, "Yes."

Soberly he says, "Mr. and Mrs. Mitchell, maybe we can find another four plots that will accommodate a headstone for you."

Am I hearing this man correctly?

I ask, "You mean, *move* our daughter?"

Donaldson seems proud to have found a workable solution. "We would disinter her vault and then bury her someplace else in the cemetery. Leighton Park Cemetery would assume both the cost of the disinterment and the reburial."

I shake my head "no" at Michele. She agrees.

But Donaldson warns, "Understand now, if in the process of doing this, the concrete vault breaks—since concrete can break apart—you would have to assume the cost of a new concrete vault."

Somehow, he found a way to make me angrier.

My response is clear.

"Oh, really? That's interesting. I have a couple of thoughts for you. One: your guys had better not break that vault because I would imagine if it broke, my daughter in her casket would come tumbling out of there onto the ground. That's not going to be good. Two: you and your cemetery got us into this situation, and we're not paying to fix this. And here's why. Roberta, your salesperson, who represented this cemetery as much then as today, could barely read a plot map in June. It was her third week, and I'd bet my life she didn't know she sold us four plots that could not take a headstone."

Donaldson leans forward on the conference room table. "Mr. Mitchell, I'm sure this was explained to you clearly by her. Back in June."

I will not be run over by this guy.

"No, she didn't. But let me ask *you* something. It's obvious you couldn't possibly be the person who runs this organization. Who's above you? There has to be someone ... "

Donaldson tells me about Robert Montgomery, who is associated with the Office of Cemetery Oversight Advisory Council on Cemetery Operations. He is the one person we need to convince to arrive at a different outcome. Montgomery supervises cemeteries from the Northeast to the Southeast. It is not supposed to be easy getting in touch with him. But I locate him and we set up a meeting.

Days later, we meet in the same conference room where we saw Donaldson. We are prepared for war. When the subject is Kristin, Michele and I do not need to be urged into action.

Robert Montgomery looks the part as he walks into the room. Tall and dignified, he wears a perfectly tailored gray suit. He asks for our explanation about what happened. Michele and I give our highly emotional account more calmly than we anticipated we would.

Our overview of Kristin's tragedy helps Mr. Montgomery picture the fragile state we were in while walking that painfully hot cemetery with Roberta in June. Michele, David, and I would never have accepted four plots knowing we would be not be allowed to add a headstone.

Montgomery concurs. "I'm sorry for what happened. What can we do?"

Is he actually going to help us?

I say, "Okay, if you make the final call, we only want to get back to where we thought we were. Leave Kristin where she is and put in a headstone like we thought we were doing."

Montgomery is right there with us. "That's fine. We can do that. Here's what I'd suggest if you'd like. I will show you types of granite we carry. Take your time. You don't need to settle on anything until you're totally ready. This is important. Whatever you select, the cemetery will pick up half of the cost. How does that sound to you?"

Michele and I are delighted.

Montgomery continues. "I don't know if you've ever considered this, but some people add pictures of their loved ones." He hands us a sample. "Usually, these cameos are oval. And since they're ceramic, they hold up remarkably well in sun and weather. We would create this for you. No cost."

I'm still not sure why everything turned around, but we say, "Great. Thank you."

Montgomery suggests next steps. "Okay, I'd like you to work with Bonnie on this. I don't know if you've met her, but she's been with us forever and will make you very happy. She will keep you informed as things progress."

Well, that felt better.

Bonnie was a bright spot in a storm of disappointments. Her knowledge, insights, and artistry guided us until the day the headstone arrived on the back of a truck.

Maybe it was because she helped us achieve our wishes, but Bonnie was treated as an outsider by both Donaldson and Roberta. They shunned her. Bonnie was our star, but a very lonely star.

Being a mom, she must have felt some kind of kinship with our sad story. On one of our calls, she opened up about how some salespeople at this cemetery took advantage of grieving family members, upselling them when they were not able to think clearly.

Never so pleased to see a gravestone.

The day our headstone arrived, Bonnie called and said we would be very happy with the results.

The final product, with a cameo showing Kristin on graduation day, was precisely what we wanted. Across the top edge was emblazoned "To You, O Lord, I Lift My Soul."

There was Kristin's name, her birthdate, and June 3, 2005. Below her dates, it reads "Love Forever, Beautiful Angel." Bonnie said this call would probably be our last. She had been fired that morning. She needed to tell us the stone was completed then she left.

Weeks later, Bonnie called again. She landed a similar job at another area cemetery with nearly twice the salary.

On Kristin's cameo, in the flowers you will see David, Michele, and me.

Flowers for Kristin

Kristin strongly disliked artificial flowers. She was not afraid to let everyone know. No matter how pretty or how well they lit up a room, to Kristin, fake was fake.

There were no exceptions.

Kristin understood why people bought and displayed the artificials. Of course, people want flowers to look nice and healthy for long periods. But to Kristin, God bless her, no excuse did it for her. Real or nothing.

This constantly presents Michele and me with a dilemma at Kristin's grave. Real flowers typically wilt, dry up, and look sad in a few days. Even though the headstone has an eastern exposure and misses hot afternoon sunlight, flowers don't fare well there.

At Christmas, and on special occasions, Michele and I pick up fresh roses and sometimes sunflowers. Kristin's grandparents usually have arrangements placed directly at the grave by a florist. There is always a white ribbon with gold handwriting saying something like, "God Bless Kristin. Love, Gaga and Poppy."

In life, Kristin had little patience with fake flowers.

Most of the year, flowers at Kristin's grave are artificial. Michele never misses the need to apologize. "Kristin, you don't like fake flowers, but we wanted to bring you something that will last."

We have other artifacts on display in front of the headstone. A little angel statue that looks like Kristin at about five years old. This angel holds a kitten. There is a different angel who kneels with his head bowed. A beautiful red stone with a multi-colored horse rising out at its top is a replacement for one just like it that was stolen from her grave.

Who steals from a grave?

There is a light-brown stone someone left years ago. It is a Jewish custom to place stones or pebbles on a headstone to indicate you have visited the grave and to indicate respect for the deceased.

For a long while, there was also a "Special K" bar left by my cousin's daughter. Angela drove three hours from Richmond to deliver it when she was going through a rough patch in her life. She was calling upon Kristin to get her through. She gave Kristin the Special K nickname years before she passed. When the bar became weathered, we replaced it with a fresh one.

Finally, there is a gray-and-white cross with "Hope" prominently displayed in raised letters. It also says, "May the God of hope fill you with all joy and peace." This is from my cousin, Mike, and his lovely wife, Suzanne. They had lost their high-school-aged son six months before Kristin died. I remember thinking at the time, "How will they ever get through such a devastating tragedy?"

I have a firm understanding now.

RECOLLECTION

Yvonne's Story

People often approach me after my presentations on dating violence. This is after they gather up their courage. They bare their souls and tell me personal stories. They feel like I am one of them, and they can open up to me. They are correct.

Some stories took my breath away, like this next one.

In Plymouth Meeting, Pennsylvania, my presentation ended, and I was preparing to leave. Two women thanked me and said how sorry they were about Kristin. I always appreciated the sentiment.

The woman to my right, Yvonne, asked, "Can I tell you my story?"

Her friend, Linda, added, "Her story is amazing."

Yvonne was married to a serial abuser. Her husband was physically abusive, emotionally abusive, and economically abusive. The trifecta of domestic violence. Why she would marry someone like this was not the important part. She did. They had six children. Why did they have six children when they could not afford them? These relationships aren't based upon perfect decision-making.

An acquaintance of theirs blew the whistle on Yvonne's family for not having the financial wherewithal to care properly for their kids. Child Protection Services (CPS) served papers and, soon after, removed one of her children citing the poverty conditions in their home.

The truth is, forty-seven percent of families who have children removed have trouble affording basic necessities. Yvonne and her husband were barely scraping by.

Yvonne worked long hours waitressing at a diner nearby. Her husband dropped her off daily at six-thirty a.m. and later picked her up at five p.m. In the meantime, he did little but drink.

Her story got worse. Not only was her husband not working and abusive, but one-by-one, her children were being removed by CPS.

Five, four, three, two.

In time, Yvonne was down to her last child.

At the diner, a coworker suggested, "Honey, when your last child's taken away, you'd better disappear."

That was easy to say but not quite so easy to execute being trapped in her home. Her angry abuser-husband was in control of everything she said or did.

Sure enough, CPS gave Yvonne the date and time when they would come for her final child. She hit rock bottom. She had had enough.

Coworkers pressured Yvonne to make a clean break. She needed time to execute her escape. She knew this man would kill her if he caught her. Vanishing was her last resort, and that became her plan.

The next day, Yvonne put on an extra layer of clothing under her waitress uniform. At the diner, it was folded and stashed in the backroom. Bringing extra clothing became her daily routine. She also brought photos and mementos of her children for safekeeping. In two weeks, she planned to break away from her miserable life.

The day arrived. Her husband dropped her off at the usual six-thirty a.m. He yelled out, "See you at five," like always. Then he muttered something unintelligible under his foul breath and roared off.

Yvonne worked most of that day, but her friends knew this was it. Around three p.m., a weather-beaten red Ford F-150 pickup swung behind the diner and parked near a dumpster. Her chariot had arrived.

Yvonne lifted her belongings over the tailgate and dropped them. She waved to coworkers and disappeared.

Police were contacted by Yvonne's husband later that evening. Nobody at the diner could say where she was. They said they assumed she had gone home early.

It was as if she had vanished.

All Yvonne knew about the man driving the pickup was he owned a horse farm in Northwestern Pennsylvania. The possibility of tending to horses was the most refreshing life change she could imagine. In no time, she felt something she had missed for a dozen years: a feeling of safety.

As Yvonne told me her story, she added this detail: "I waited about a month before calling my dad. He's the only one I could trust with where I was. He wouldn't tell anyone. Not even my mother knew."

Her father did not let her whereabouts slip. Returning home would have been a death sentence.

Yvonne leapt to a different part of her story. She left out when or how she became divorced, and whatever happened with her children. She offered no details on those. But when she learned her ex was dating someone, Yvonne contacted this woman and warned her about him. The woman did not heed her and married him. She was later serially abused.

Yvonne took another giant leap to another part of her story. Her ex was doing time in prison. She didn't say how he got there but said he was constantly getting in fights with other prisoners.

Yvonne's friend, Linda, cut in.

"Bill, now she's going to tell you the best part ... "

Yvonne continued.

"A few prisoners were out to get him. So, one day, on the second floor of the cell block, two inmates grabbed onto him and dangled him over the railing. They dropped him headfirst to the concrete floor below."

Yvonne finished her story.

"He was in lots of pain and suffering for about a month before he died." Yvonne had some trouble telling me this part because she was giggling. "It's what he deserved. Don't you agree, Bill?"

Maybe it was karma that stopped me from expressing any reaction. I try not to wish harm on people. It's something I've been working on.

I just wish the suffering would end.

The Possible Plea

The trial is four months away.

This means the beginning of June is shaping up to be quite a challenge. The first anniversary of Kristin's murder is Saturday, June 3. David's high school graduation is Sunday, June 4. And now, the start of the trial is Monday, June 5.

This is the formula for a panic attack.

Michele knows all about panic attacks. I've experienced only one, but the memory of it is enough to cause a second one.

A panic attack is absolute horror. I remember sitting in a parked car when it happened. I lost track of everything, including the ability to see or hear anything. I felt as if I were falling inside of myself into an endless dark pit. Spinning around, I went deeper and deeper. I neither heard nor saw anything outside of myself. I have no idea how long it lasted but found myself gasping to breathe; my heart was racing. But knowing I was breathing was the first sign I might be returning to normal.

The reality that our family, and our daughter's case, will be on display in a courtroom for a murder case is agonizing.

Then one afternoon at work, I receive an unanticipated call from Charlotte Stark. Nick is seriously considering a plea, although his court-appointed attorney is dead-set against it. His lawyer believes Nick will get a better result going into court and having a trial. It's clear Nick is concerned about being found guilty of first-degree murder and receiving a life sentence. But if Nick pleads to third-degree murder, it's likely he will receive a sentence of fifteen to thirty years in prison.

The District Attorney

Bruce L. Castor, Jr. is the district attorney in charge of our prosecution team. Castor wants Kristin's case to go to trial, even though a plea is discussed. Castor feels his prosecutors can nail Nick with murder one and put him away for life.

Life in prison is the right outcome. We know that, but during the eight months since the killing, no evidence shared with us indicates Nick acted in a premeditated manner. An argument in Kristin's apartment escalated into a horrendous catastrophe, but is there evidence of forethought? Can the prosecutors prove a premeditated intent to kill? Michele and I are not so sure.

If Nick's plea is not accepted by the prosecution, specifically by Bruce L. Castor, Jr., himself, we will go to trial. In a trial, if the jury does not find premeditated murder, our best outcome would be third-degree murder.

But wait.

Already on the table is the possibility of Nick's plea. That means he would accept the third-degree murder outcome—*without any trial*. He would go to prison without putting up a fight. Michele and I need to convince Bruce Castor to accept this murderer's plea if it's offered. Charlotte Stark has schooled us on how brilliant, and tough, Castor is. He is legendary. Current circumstances call for Michele and me to speak with him in his office in Norristown, Pennsylvania and talk him out of taking this case to a jury trial. This will be one big mountain to climb.

A sage piece of advice comes from Charlotte.

"If this is what you want, state your position clearly and strongly. Demonstrate a firm resolve with your position to accept this plea. You'd better look like you mean it."

The last thing Bruce L. Castor, Jr. wants is for people like us to push him into accepting the plea and in a few months or years say we wish he had taken this to trial.

If we want the plea, we need to ask for it and stick with it forever.

Plea or Trial?

The district attorney's dark wood conference room mirrors the sets of the television show *Law & Order*. Michele and I settle uncomfortably into our seats, awaiting the entrance of the formidable Bruce L. Castor, Jr., District Attorney.

We are plenty nervous.

Directly across the table sits Risa Vetri Ferman, who is not terribly tall but is considered a giant here in the prosecution's offices. One day soon, she will become the next district attorney. She is brilliant, tough, and has the heart of a lion.

Sitting next to Ms. Ferman is Charlotte Stark, who told us this meeting would be "no piece of cake." Seated around the table are other prosecution attorneys and Sam Gallen, our lead detective.

Bruce L. Castor, Jr. enters, and things get real.

Castor is six-three, strikingly good-looking with perfect dark hair, firm chin, and Hollywood-bright teeth. He is central casting for the part. An imposing figure in a perfectly starched white shirt, French cuffs, and crisp suit pants. He owns the room.

After shaking my wife's hand and mine, Castor begins.

"It's our opinion that your daughter's case deserves to go to trial. For what this animal did to her, the Commonwealth of Pennsylvania wants to put him away for as long as possible. Maybe life. As Kristin's parents, I would expect you would want to do the same. We want to nail him to the fullest extent of the law for what he did." Castor lowers his voice, "But I've been told by Charlotte that you would consider accepting this man's plea. So, talk with me about that."

Good thing we came prepared.

I open a folder and spread eight-by-tens of our daughter on the table directly in front of Castor.

"This is Kristin riding horses, which she loved from the first time she rode a rocking horse that was a birthday present. At home, one hundred equestrian competition ribbons remain hanging on her bedroom walls."

I pull out the next photo.

"Here is Kristin with David. He is four years younger. Here she is napping with her favorite cat, Gatsby. This is her college graduation, the last day I ever saw her alive. Such a sweet and precious person."

Castor interrupts.

"Allow me to ask you something ... Aren't you trying to talk me out of taking this to court? These pictures and what you're saying are having the opposite effect. I want to go into a courtroom and get this guy. I want us to go in there together and fight for Kristin."

We were warned our approach could set Castor off.

Looking around the table, I ask, "Does anyone here have anything, any evidence that would convince a jury this guy acted with malice aforethought, or whatever you call it—or whatever it needs to be, to put him away forever?"

Silence. Nothing.

We're disappointed there is no reply. I feel surprisingly calm so I shift gears.

"Your prosecution team has a ninety-eight-percent success rate in cases won. That's correct, yes?"

Castor agrees. "It is ... yes."

I continue. "If you accept this guy's plea, don't you get another win? I mean, your ninety-eight percent win rate will only go higher, right?"

Castor says, "That would be correct."

I appreciate Castor is allowing us to speak our minds. So I ask the confounding question.

"Without even playing the game, so to speak, your team will get a win if you accept the plea ... yes? It's all the same?"

"Yes."

"*Then why play the game?!* We've not heard anything from anyone seated here that makes us think you can get this guy for premeditated murder."

Is Bruce L. Castor, Jr. about to give us what we want? Will he accept the plea? So I continue.

"So, you win just by accepting his plea. That's good. He goes away for up to thirty years. That's pretty good, not great. And Kristin can rest in peace. So, what are we missing here?"

Castor is thinking. Everyone seems to be thinking. Nobody is talking, so I add this, "Okay, one more thing ... "

I try not to lose our momentum.

"Mr. Castor, let's say we do go ahead with what you had wanted. We go to court and proceed with this trial. What if the jury looks at that guy and thinks, 'Gee, such a cute guy. His girlfriend is gone, why ruin his life too? Even though his killing her will never be right, this feels more like a crime of passion—or maybe temporary insanity on his part ... '"

I finish with this ...

"So, what if this goes the wrong way? Think of famous cases—not that long ago—when DNA pointed to only one guy in the entire world. That one-in-a-billion-percent of accuracy from DNA *didn't get him convicted*. I mean, what if that jury gives our killer a voluntary manslaughter verdict? How many years will he get then? Four to seven? Maybe he does less time if he makes 'prisoner of the year.' Who's going to feel okay about that? I can tell you, we won't."

Bruce L. Castor, Jr. decides to go with Michele and me on this plea. He accepts what Nick is offering. There will be no trial.

Third degree murder.

We are walking on air for a few minutes.

But we don't get too happy; we still have a deceased daughter. Momentary euphoria crashes back to earth.

When we arrive home late in the day, Michele and I send an email back to Bruce L. Castor, Jr. We do not want him to forget what we said or, even worse, we do not want him to change his mind.

Plea and Sentencing

It is April 20, 2006. Today, Michele, David, and I are seated in the Montgomery County Courthouse in Norristown, Pennsylvania for Nick's plea and sentencing. We want to see this "daughter-killer" led away to prison for a very long time. It's the fair thing to do.

Let this be a giant step toward closure at our house.

Today's procedure was almost delayed. We received word Nick's family is traveling, and he requested the postponement of the sentencing so they would be able to attend. I almost forgot about them, since only one of his brothers has attended any legal proceedings thus far.

In an email written to a friend I wrote:

> We received word that the defense asked the judge to delay the guilty plea and sentencing hearing until Nick's family members return from a trip to Europe. This is so they can be with him when he is sentenced.
>
> Forget about fair.
> Forget about the surviving family members (us).
> I cannot believe the defense attorney requested such a postponement. Or that the judge even considered it.
>
> Like we're supposed to await the return of this family to be there for his sendoff? A family that has missed his two previous court appearances.
>
> I don't believe his family is in Europe any more than I believe they're on Jupiter. This entire thing could fall though.

As it turns out, the judge did not grant a delay.

Samantha, Kristin's college friend, joins us as she did at the formal arraignment seven months ago—and the preliminary hearing a month prior to that. I feel she has changed before our eyes over the ten months since Kristin's graduation. She looks about as somber as we do. Each of us is breaking new emotional ground these days. Just when we thought we reached our limit, we have needed to stretch even more.

This courtroom is enclosed by dark wood-paneled walls. The ceiling goes up a couple of stories as one might expect in a courthouse building constructed in 1854. The judge will be seated at a raised desk one level above all participants at the back-left corner. There are jurisdiction seals and flags located behind where he will sit. A half-level down, to the judge's left, is the witness stand.

Our family is seated on the right side of the gallery. We picked the row directly behind the prosecution's table and Charlotte Stark. It affords an unobstructed view.

To the left of Charlotte is the defendant's table. I see Nick's lead defense attorney leafing through papers, making notes, and readying himself. Frankly, he scares the hell out of me. I fear he will pull something out of a legal bag of tricks and take this day off course.

He walks over and confers with Charlotte; they seem to be agreeing on whatever they are talking about. To my untrained eyes, this feels good. Things must be moving in the right direction.

Apparently, the judge does not appear until all parties are in the courtroom and prepared to make this procedure happen. There is no sign of Nick, either. My family waits. And waits. And waits. We feel there is no hurry as long as this happens today.

Then I watch Nick's defense attorney quietly leave the courtroom through a side door along the left wall. Minutes later, he reappears and crosses the courtroom to speak with Charlotte Stark.

She abruptly stands up and says, "What?"

Both attorneys leave through the same side door the defense attorney entered from.

I check my watch. We are forty-five minutes past our scheduled start. From what we have heard, this proceeding should already have concluded by now. This delay cannot be to our benefit.

To distract myself, I gaze around this large room and imagine echoes from a thousand cases heard in this place. A very long history of pain and suffering brought by people misbehaving. Countless numbers of men and women illegally taking advantage of someone else. White-collar crimes. Blue-collar crimes. Any-collar crimes. Attempted murders and successful murders have funneled in and out. Some defendants walked free. Some went to prison.

What brings me back to the present is wondering where Nick is going today. Which state prison? Does it really matter as long as he goes away? Not at all.

From that side door, Charlotte reenters the courtroom looking at wit's end. She hurries toward our family, not looking cheery.

Charlotte gives it to us straight.

"It's going to trial. He wants to drop the plea. This happens sometimes. Our guy's talking about backing out of his plea."

My family goes where we have been often of late. A place of stunned shock. It's already been a journey into uncharted emotional territories, but we were not prepared for this. We thought today would transition us into some relief for fifteen to thirty years.

Now, we are going to trial? This is astounding.

Michele is in tears. David is staring straight ahead with his mind processing what this means. I hear my breath and feel my heart pushing the inside of my shirt.

Charlotte says calmly, "Look, this is pretty normal. All of a sudden, it hits him. He goes from not wanting to face potential life in prison to feeling like he's giving up his freedom if he pleads today. So, he freaks out. It happens."

Charlotte is the essence of patience. Such a contrast to the pyrotechnics display blasting throughout my nervous system. She glances back at the defense table and suggests, "Okay, we need to wait this out. We're not done here."

She heads back to the prosecution table.

I resort to the one antidote I have relied upon this past ten months: prayer. Days like today are more consequential than I can handle alone. I believe there are unseen forces at work, and the One listening to my prayers has a large say in how everything proceeds. Today, we need help.

I pray for the outcome that benefits the greatest number of people. Of course, I hope the result today is for this man, a man who murdered a person so precious, to be taken where he cannot affect innocent lives for a very long time. But there is always more at work than meets the eye. I just pray for a positive result.

In the courtroom, the only sound is an occasional cough or a creak issued from a wooden chair or bench. Forever cannot be measured on a timepiece, but today, forever ends in just short of fifteen minutes.

Charlotte returns with guarded optimism.

"Okay, our guy's coming out, and he's back to the plea. Let's hope this goes smoothly. Fingers crossed."

A side door opens, and two guards lead our daughter's killer, Nick, into the courtroom. He is secured at the hands and feet and wears his navy-blue prison jumpsuit. He doesn't look our way this time, which is fine with me. We don't need more drama.

The judge enters and is seated. According to my watch, it is two-forty. We were advised the initial part of this procedure involves a seemingly endless chain of questions asked of the killer. This is so he realizes he is giving up his right to a trial along with his freedom today.

The judge leans toward the defendant's table and says, "You understand the reason you have been called to the stand is for the purpose, specifically, of questioning you with respect to your understanding of the Court's determination, primarily with respect to your guilty plea, and whether or not it is knowingly, intelligently, and voluntarily entered. Do you understand that, sir?"

Nick, showing no emotion, says, "Yes."

The judge comments, "Thank you."

The defense attorney reads no less than sixty-six consecutive questions. Each one is to be entirely sure, in every imaginable way possible, that Nick understands how he is being charged. He has to clearly answer yes to each question. Some questions sound like the previous ones slightly reworded. This is intentional. The court does not need this to go wrong if Nick were to later say he did not understand what he was agreeing upon. This litany is dizzying but necessary.

Papers are handed to the judge, and unintelligible words are spoken by the two attorneys. The judge asks Nick if he feels he was represented fairly and properly by his defense attorney. He asks Nick if he totally understands the trade-offs between this plea versus taking this to trial.

He does.

Charlotte Stark discusses the differences between first-, second-, and third-degree murder. When she gets to third-degree murder, she makes it clear this is how Nick is being charged. She asks if he understands.

He does.

Our Words to the Court

Before sentencing is handed down, our family is given an opportunity to speak before the court. Each of us has prepared statements. We did not share with each other what we will say beforehand.

MICHELE
Papers in hand, Michele leaves my side and enters the witness stand. She gently clears her throat and begins.

"This tragedy truly was the end of the innocence. As I remember Kristin's life, from the delicate tiny baby I held in my arms through the last weekend I spent with Kristin after her graduation from Saint Joe's, I will always remember her beauty, her intelligence, her quiet depth, and her love of her family and pets.

"As a parent, you protect your children as long as you can. But eventually, they become adults, and you must let them make their own decisions and form their own judgments about people.

"Kristin was very trusting and still, I believe, naïve about the dangers of the world. She never believed anyone would hurt her. In fact, she often tried to fix those who needed help.

"Nick, you ended the innocence, and you ultimately took away my daughter and her brother's only sibling. You took away her future. The opportunity to be successful at the wonderful job she was going to begin at General Mills. Her chance to groom and ride a horse again. Her opportunity to raise her own Siamese kitten, and her chance to cook Pasta for the Angels, and so much more. You brutally murdered her, and you left her to die.

"When I pray each night, I ask God to please not let me forget her beautiful face, gorgeous smile, silky hair, or laugh. Her perfume, her tiny feet, small wrists, and hundreds of special qualities and moments we shared.

"I only have Kristin's loving notes and cards. Childhood dolls, stuffed animals, other childhood playful items. Her clothes. A few pieces of jewelry that she would wear each day. And two saved messages on my cell phone where I can close my eyes and pretend she's still here.

"A special locket that I wear each day contains Kristin's picture and a strand of her hair that was taken before her casket was closed. I've learned to dread the question, 'How many children do you have?' I feel guilty saying one, yet I can't bear to explain why I had two, but now I only have one.

"I finally found an answer, which I use. I have two children. One is here on earth, and one is in Heaven. Kristin, I believe, is with God in an eternal place of peace and rest, and that Heaven for her is everything she could have ever wanted on earth to make her feel loved, secure, and safe. I need to believe in this to help me get through the day.

"Kristin's personal relationship with God is reflected in her Dear God note. This was written on a small piece of paper and found among her belongings that we were going through. It said:

> *Dear God, please protect me and keep me safe.*
> *Love me and let me love you all the days of my life*
> *and when I am with you for eternity.*
> *Please guide me always and love me forever.*
> *Love, Kristin.*

"Kristin is now safe. She has God's love for eternity, and she will be waiting for me.

"Nick, your final right to judgment rests with God. No court can decide that fate. I hope you're truly remorseful for what you did and will accept your punishment and deal with your guilt each day. May God be with you. Thank you."

DAVID

Next, our son enters the witness stand, collects himself, turns, and speaks directly to the man who murdered his sister.

"A piece is missing. A number I still can't bring myself to delete from my cell phone. Some various holiday cards and Post-It notes with her handwriting on them, and an empty room in my house that is colder than all the others, because the door is closed, and no one lives in it anymore. These are the things that I'm left with.

"I don't hate you, Nick. I realize that if we switched roles, you would probably hate me.

"I hate what you did, and I hate any circumstances that allowed for that to happen.

"The reason I don't hate you is because I believe, somehow, you loved Kristin, and you needed her, and your actions prove to me how desperate you were to have her.

"Nobody has her now, but God. And if you don't believe in God, then ask yourself what force there could possibly be in the world that drives me to say I'm trying to forgive you for what you did to my sister, and I hope when you walk the streets again, alongside people like me, that you're a changed person who can manage to use your heart and strength to do some good.

"I hope in your own mind, you have taken responsibility for the destruction you have caused. I hope you realize that no matter where you are during the remainder of your life, you have the capacity to help people and change lives for the good. I'm offering you that chance.

"The God I believe in always offers it to you, and one day society will once again offer you that chance.

"For God's sake, or Kristin's sake, and for my sake, take it."

With that, David solemnly walks back to where our family is seated.

ME

I enter the witness stand. My thoughts are conflicted with what I really want to say to this man, but it will do no good. He could be back on the street one day. So, I have to keep this positive.

I look directly at Nick.

"Today, as I stand here, I still have not absorbed the full impact of Kristin's death. I hope I never will. I don't think I could live with it. Simply stated, death is just too permanent.

"A lot of good would have to come out of something this terrible. We had that thought the evening we learned about Kristin's murder. Maybe the attention caused by our tragedy will become a loud and clear warning to people in relationships to be more careful and prevent themselves and others from becoming victims of violent acts.

"Our tragedy has already urged people to help prevent friends and loved ones from becoming victims. Our tragedy has caused some people to return to God and prayer and for their families to find peaceful and safe answers in their lives.

"Our tragedy has caused people to look at violence against women in new and meaningful ways. This is an epidemic. It is entirely out of control. As soon as we can, our family is going to give a good portion of time and talents to this important cause.

"Nick, you saw the photos taken at Kristin's graduation. She never looked more beautiful to me than on that day. But weeks later, those happy pictures became imagery for covers of funeral programs, or Mass cards, or thank-you cards.

"Nick, at Saint Joseph University, on a warm Saturday, the fourteenth of May last year, I met you for the first time. Ironically, the same day I met you was also the last day I ever saw Kristin alive.

"Fewer than three weeks later, she was dead. She was gone forever. I told Michele and David that I felt sorry for you. They could not believe it. But I did. I still feel sorry for you, just as I feel intense sorrow for everyone who ever knew and loved Kristin. We are all feeling the deep effects of shock and loss in our lives and hearts. And today, we find it more difficult than ever for most of us. We are all victims.

"What took place in that apartment was completely horrific. Not only is it a parent's worst nightmare, but it's a nightmare from which there is no awakening. The effects of this act will stay with us for the rest of our lives.

"Today, standing here, I still feel sorry for you. I mean that sincerely. And one day, I expect I will find forgiveness. It might take a little while longer, but I will get there.

"You and I will be united forever by this tragedy, and there's nothing we can do about that. Horrible circumstances like this murder and all the pain and suffering that come with it remind me we were not born to stay forever on this imperfect planet.

"Kristin would hope that maybe her life was taken away from her so others might never suffer and die as she did. But that can only happen if we learn from this tragedy. Kristin would want us to pray. She would want us to forgive, forget, and move on with our lives, to deal with what's important in our lives.

"So, this can be an opportunity, only if we allow it.

"In an email, Kristin wrote these loving words a year ago:

Dear Mom & Dad & David,

It's amazing how much you value people when you can't see them all the time. I miss being at home so much—and I didn't get a chance to tell you all that— nearly as much as I wish I had.

I can't wait until fall break, so I can sleep at home and wake up to the three people that love me so much.

When you were all walking out of my room and downstairs to leave, I wished you weren't. I even shed some tears when I saw you walking to the car outside. I enjoy being here—but not as much as I love being at home with all of you, so I can't wait to see you again!!! Well, I'm going to run, but I'll call you guys soon.

I love you all so much!!!
Love always,
Kristin

"Kristin was special. She was fun. And so full of life. One of her favorite sayings, which she added next to her picture in her high school yearbook was ... 'Live and savor every moment. This is not a dress rehearsal!' She knew she would only get one chance at life. Here is a short poem sent to us by Kristin. It's called, "An Angel to Watch Over You."

Some people come into our lives–and quickly go ...
Some people become friends and stay a while,
leaving beautiful footprints on our hearts ...

"For those who never had the privilege of knowing and loving Kristin, I also feel sorry for you. You missed out on someone great. Thank you."

While I was speaking, I occasionally glanced over at the man who left a deep scar across my family's future. Nick wore no expression. I would like to know what he was thinking. I am certain it was not about what I was saying.

We are ready for him to go away, and for us to go home. Our family needs to turn the page and get away from anything that has to do with the disturbing end of Kristin's life. We have relived the events of June 3 in our minds, and we don't need to do that anymore. We want to remember what it was like to feel good about Kristin, to recall her smile and laugh, and the only way to get to those memories is to leave this area.

Kristin's Murderer Speaks

The judge offers the man who slaughtered our daughter an opportunity to speak before the court. Maybe he will make sense out of the senseless.

This will be the only time we hear his voice before he is led away in handcuffs and chains. He will board a van and begin a long sentence in Rockview Prison, a state penitentiary near Penn State University. They call it "the State Pen near Penn State." It is situated in Happy Valley.

Facing the court on the witness stand, Nick speaks.

"I'm so sorry. I loved her. I've always loved her. I am always going to love her. I think about her every day. It's killing me. For the rest of my life, she's all I am ever going to think about. Truly, I'm sorry, Samantha, David, her parents, everyone. I can't change it. I would. I don't know what to say. There's nothing I can say. My words aren't significant enough, but that's all I ever think about. Every single day. Every minute. Every second. Every hour. I loved her."

I sense this is coming from his heart. This man will be locked away no less than fifteen years, likely longer. A cinder block hell. What a miserable future he made for himself.

The judge has extemporaneous words for the court.

"I find great hope and encouragement in the resources that have been demonstrated to all of us by a remarkable family, the Mitchell family.

"Their compassion, their strength, their caring for each other. The great love they have for their sister and their daughter is encouraging. It gives us all hope. Hopefully, it will sustain them and her friends and her extended family in the future. And the memories of their beloved daughter will help to ease the pain of their lives.

"From what I have heard and learned from this case, not just here in this courtroom today, but from what I have read and discussed with counsel for the parties, she was indeed a remarkable young woman, whom anyone could set as an example for their lives who were fortunate enough to call her daughter, sister, or friend."

The judge shifts his focus over to Nick.

"So, that having been said, are you ready to receive the sentence of this court, sir?

"Yes," Nick answers blankly.

"Do you have anything else you wish to say?"

"No."

The judge reads to the court, "The defendant is sentenced to undergo imprisonment for not less than fifteen years nor more than thirty years in such state correctional institution as shall be designated by the Deputy Commissioner for Programs, Department of Corrections. Additionally, the defendant is sentenced to pay the costs of prosecution."

We are depleted at this point but thankful this chapter of our lives—and this killer—will be shipped away for a while. This was quite a day. Nick is finally heading to a place where he cannot hurt anyone.

Outside of the courtroom, several reporters ask the obvious. Mr. Mitchell, how is your family? Do you feel justice was served? How do you feel about the man who killed your daughter? Did he seem remorseful to you?

With Charlotte Stark standing directly behind and to my left, I must sound like the nicest father to have ever had his daughter stabbed to death.

Summing up where we are, I say, "I just hope some good can come from all of this. He sounded like he meant it ... "

I do not show emotion. I feel I should speak about what just happened. When I look as if I will answer every question, Charlotte shuts it down. "Okay, thank you, the Mitchells need to go."

She physically turns me around so we are face-to-face. She asks pointedly, "How do you really feel about what Nick said in there today?"

"Well, I actually feel sorry for him. And ... "

"Listen to me," she cuts me off. *"Never feel sorry for him!* He wasn't crying his eyes out for you and your family. Or Kristin. That was *all for him*. Don't fall for that bullshit. Another manipulation to make everyone go boohoo for his screwed-up life. Just remember what he did to Kristin. *That's who he is.* Never, ever feel sorry for him."

In my fragile state, I am not expecting to be verbally slammed by Charlotte. I feel embarrassed and immediately realize she is correct.

Snap out of it. I fell for that manipulator just like everyone he has ever exploited. He killed our child. *That's who he really is.* A killer.

In time, I will learn how con men prey on sweet, innocent young women like our daughter and other people's children. And when these accomplished predators do not get what they want, they lash out, and someone pays for it. They punish people. They punish everyone.

If it gets bad enough, and they do not get what they want, someone gets punched, disfigured, strangulated, shot, stabbed, or burned to death. One day, I will meet survivors of this kind of unhealthy behavior. I will realize Charlotte speaks the truth gleaned from experience. She has seen this hundreds of times.

It's time for me to wake up.

On I-95 South

We put Norristown, Pennsylvania, in our rearview mirror and drive home. Near the Delaware line on I-95 South, an AM radio station broadcasts a short segment on today's sentencing. It is barely understandable with the interference.

"Norristown ... guilty ... the killer of twenty-one-year-old Kristin Mitchell ... a 2005 Saint Joseph's graduate ... murdered ... sentenced today ..."

At home, my insatiable appetite for details and closure finds an article on a Philadelphia website.

> A Montgomery County man has been sentenced to 15-30 years behind bars after pleading guilty to brutally stabbing his girlfriend to death in her Conshohocken apartment last year. The father of the victim, Bill Mitchell, told the court that the last time he saw his daughter was the day she graduated from Saint Joe's, last May.
>
> Bill Mitchell believes that one day he'll be able to forgive the 29-year-old man who killed his daughter: "People who have faith need to build on that. So, when something rocks their world like this, they've got something. And I think that it's increased our faith over time."
>
> Her killer broke down on the stand, tearfully telling the court that he still loved Kristin. The family believes she was about to break up with him and he couldn't handle it.

This particular article appeared the day after the sentencing:

> The captain of the Montgomery County, Pa. domestic violence prosecution team recalls Kristin Mitchell's murder as one of the worst she has seen.

"She was a beautiful 21-year-old recent college graduate," Charlotte Stark, an assistant district attorney, said Tuesday.

"It's heart-wrenching. She was awaiting a new job that looked very promising. She had great friends, and she had her whole life in front of her, and this guy cut it short tragically. Nothing will ever bring her back."

Mitchell's boyfriend, 29, pleaded guilty to third-degree murder in Mitchell's death and admitted to stabbing her 55 times, including 11 times in the back, after she attempted to break up with him.

He was sentenced to 30 years in prison and will be eligible for parole in 15 years, she said.

"Over the course of the months, I worked very closely with the family," Stark said. "They were in agreement that the plea deal would be acceptable."

Friends and family of Mitchell have started a charity in part to drive home the point that domestic violence can happen to anyone.

"There are other domestic violence organizations, but most of them don't put a face on the issue," said Bill Mitchell, Kristin's father.

"She was so special, because she did everything right. She went to college. She graduated. She had a great job lined up. She was a good person, and she wouldn't hurt anybody."

With this behind us, the stress we have carried for ten months begins to leave. There is no need to be calling Charlotte or wondering what the next step will be. We just received the next fifteen years off from trying to guess how this will turn out. The outcome is something we can live with for a very long time.

Emails from Charlotte

Three days after the plea and sentencing, I receive a short note from Charlotte telling she couldn't imagine how hard it must have been for Michele, David, and me when it looked as if we were going to be headed to trial. She acknowledged it was just what we had dreaded. She also called attention to Nick's change of mind.

She wrote, "It was a long ordeal, but your lovely family made it with dignity and grace. The whole thing is still with me—and will be for a long, long time. Most likely forever. Take care, Charlotte."

The following day, another note was sent from her.

"The flowers just arrived and they are beautiful! Thanks so much. Of course, we can stay in touch. I hope you are catching your breath and getting ready for David's graduation. He is quite an impressive young man. More later, Charlotte."

We were warned how defense attorneys demonize victims, especially deceased victims who cannot defend themselves. How they go to extraordinary lengths to manipulate juries in an attempt to lessen prison sentences for their clients. For the first time, there is no need to think about this.

With the plea and sentencing accomplished, there will be no crime scene photos on a screen in a courtroom to scar family members and friends. No vicious newspaper feasting on the massacre of our child—a despicable crime potentially turned into tabloid exploitation or sensationalism, and sales. We escaped that.

And to think, I would not have been allowed in that courtroom. I would have sat in a hotel room down the street.

What will life be like in our new normal? The numbness that protected us from the outset continues, but how long can that last?

RECOLLECTION

Fatal Steps at Great Mills High School

The electronic sign on Point Lookout Road in front of Maryland's Leonardtown High School reads as if someone made a mistake.

It says, "We Are Great Mills." But Great Mills High School is a rival high school miles away. But it's no mistake. It is solidarity.

Months earlier, on March 20, 2018, at eight a.m., a shooting took place at Great Mills High School. A seventeen-year-old male student was lying dead in a hallway from a self-inflicted gunshot to his head. He had used his father's semi-automatic handgun. Minutes earlier, a sixteen-year-old female student, had also been shot in the head. She was able to cling to life but passed two days later. Along with them, a fourteen-year-old male was wounded in the leg from the shot that passed through the girl and hit him. Fortunately, this young man survived.

I was driving to this school system that morning to give dating violence presentations at Leonardtown and Great Mills. With the shootings, all speeches were called off.

On June 7, ten weeks after the shootings, I was about to give a speech at Great Mills. I met that morning with the mother of the young woman who was shot. I considered it an honor she let me speak with her.

Parents of murdered daughters form bonds quickly. I knew what she was feeling from my family's journey through "a parent's worst nightmare." This mother was brave and she faced her pain head on.

God bless her. It's the best way.

I asked her if she would take me to the location of the shooting, the place where her daughter was gunned down. She accepted my request and wanted to start at the door where her daughter entered school that morning.

As we walked the hallways, I imagined her daughter's last day held all of the promise of any talented high school honor student. The sixteen-year-old was saying hi to friends and getting ready for her classes.

Some students said hello to this mother, as did teachers.

We walked a while when, in the middle of a hallway, she stopped and said, "Right here. This is where it happened."

This was a hallway where students passed through daily without any sense of tragedy hanging over them. While we walked, this mother was carrying her baby son in a pouch in front of her. He was one of nine children. Or did she count them as eight now?

At the location of the shooting, I recited a quiet prayer for her daughter and all other victims of dating violence, including Kristin.

Her daughter stopped being interested in this boy in January, two months before the shooting. She never considered him a boyfriend. They barely knew one another. Much like Kristin's situation, the relationship meant more to him.

Besides the damage he had already inflicted, the police believed this seventeen-year-old was going to kill the student who took this girl to the prom. Fortunately, his search for this other boy failed. As the school's resource officer was bearing down on the shooter, the young man shot himself. The mother walked me to the hallway where it happened.

Days after these shootings happened, at the University of Maryland Prince George's Hospital Center, the girl's mother said her daughter was brain dead. She and her husband made the decision to remove all life support.

She spoke to the press.

"She will not make it. There's nothing. No life left in her. Our lives changed completely and totally forever. My daughter was hurt by a boy who shot her in the head and took everything from our lives."

I was told the Great Mills High School community remained intensely emotional about the tragedy. When the unthinkable happens, there is no telling if it will ever settle down.

So, I hoped what I said was helpful. I wanted to give these high school students a few tools to help them recognize, understand and deal with dating violence. It's a lot to ask from a forty-minute speech.

After my speeches, I often hear words from students like, "I felt it was odd when I was dating, but I never knew what it really was." Or "I didn't know it was abuse. I didn't see how it could end up as it did. I didn't know where to turn to, or who to go to."

My aim was to turn newly recognized symptoms into realizations that lead to healthier directions in people's lives. I wanted to head off tragedies like the one trying to heal at this school.

We all can say, "We Are Great Mills."

A Picture Worth a Thousand Tears

Michele has left for work. I'm dressing in our bedroom, relieved to have courtroom days behind us. That's when I notice.

Standing outside of my closet, there is something odd about a framed picture on Michele's dresser. I would never have seen it, but the sunlight catches the glass and gives it away. The glass is unexpectedly spotted and smudged.

The photo in a narrow, brushed metal frame is actually a series of selfies taken by Kristin six hours before she was killed. These eight consecutive smiles indicate Kristin had no idea what evil was coming her way that evening. She was having fun spending time with friends from college. These photos, downloaded from her graduation-present camera, were sent to me by detectives. Every unseen photo of Kristin is a precious gift under our circumstances. It's like that.

A mother's love transcends death.

Today, however, the smeared glass undermines the power of Kristin's magnetism. So, I walk the frame over to the bathroom sink and reach for Windex and paper towels. This will only take a second to clean.

How did Michele let this get so grimy? It's unlike her.

But I discover what is actually here. Those somewhat circular, pinkish smudges appear to be lipstick. Michele must have held and kissed over every one of the faces. Eight Kristins, eight kisses. Multiple times. I almost blundered into cleaning it.

I am overcome. Have I ever seen anything in my life so genuinely mournful? Is there a more powerful yet unspoken expression of a mother's feelings about her lost daughter?

I replace the frame on the dresser. I almost ruined it.

It rests directly in front of Michele's jewelry box, and you would never notice the kisses unless I took a different viewpoint.

On this sunny morning, Kristin, Michele, and I notice them.

Padre Pio

It's a Tuesday afternoon at work. Our ad agency's top copywriter needs to write a brochure and attend a client meeting at the same moment.

"What a perfect opportunity for bilocation," I suggest.

He has no idea what that means. I tell him about a Franciscan Friar by the name of Padre Pio. Kristin heard about him in a religion class at Mount de Sales Academy, her high school outside of Baltimore.

Born in Italy in 1887, Pio's life sounded as outrageous as any Marvel Studios superhero with superpowers. Many believed Pio possessed the unique capacity to bilocate, to appear in two places simultaneously. Pio was witnessed in a chapel solemnly praying, while at the exact same time he was seen miles away giving last rites to a dying man. In another instance, he was seen kneeling in prayer in his monastery room and visiting a woman in her home—at the exact same hour.

It's reported he was also able to read the sins on people's souls. He encouraged hundreds of life-altering healings and miracles attributed to his praying for people, young and old. He made it clear he could not produce miracles but asked God to allow them.

The discussion at work reignites my interest in Padre Pio. With all that is happening in our lives, I ask him for guidance so I know what I need to do and the strength to get it done.

Pio lived most of his life among many people who are alive today. This makes Pio seem more accessible to me. I purchase *Padre Pio: The True Story* and can't put it down. His intimacy with God is an inspiration. I have room for improvement in that area.

One evening, before closing the book and turning off the nightstand light, I arrive on page 384: the story of Mrs. Vera Calandra, who lived in Pennsylvania. In 1966, this mother of four gave birth to a girl with little chance of surviving her first day. The baby was born with organs that had developed outside of her body. There were also congenital defects in her kidneys and urinary tract.

After her baby's birth, Mrs. Calandra's obstetrician suggested she not have her baby brought to her. He advised it would be better emotionally to let this child pass, never being seen.

No. Mrs. Calandra demanded they bring her child at once. She insisted her baby would not die, and these doctors needed to do everything to save her.

After multiple surgical interventions, her daughter, Vera Marie, was healthy enough to be taken home for the first time. It was explained to Mrs. Calandra, however, that ongoing complications would eventually bring an early death.

This child was returned to the hospital often for surgical procedures. At two years of age, Vera Marie was alive but faced another great threat. Poisons were emanating from her failing bladder. It needed to be removed. Bladder removal was a death sentence.

After removal, catheterization was necessary. In 1968, this meant tubes protruding from the child's side that emptied into test tubes. Little Vera Marie was declining; her destiny seemed incontestable.

Mrs. Calandra had already been praying exhaustively to God, Jesus, Mary, Joseph, all the saints, and anyone, living or dead, who might intervene. Health professionals had no further therapies or answers.

With her daughter's death approaching, this mother had run out of ideas. One evening, while her husband and children were in bed asleep, she sat alone in her living room reading a book about a poor friar who lived in San Giovanni Rotondo, near Italy's east coast. A Capuchin priest, Padre Pio, had numerous miracles attributed to him.

A miracle was precisely what her daughter needed.

Vera prayed desperately to Padre Pio. She was interrupted by an unmistakable fragrance of freshly cut roses drifting into the room. She checked throughout her small home, trying to pinpoint their location. The fragrance continued to release. This was no dream.

She was not aware the fragrance of roses was the sign of someone, living or deceased, who was very holy. In this case, the scent of roses was a charism of Padre Pio. She returned to her chair and prayed more.

This is when her story joins the supernatural.

Out of nowhere, Mrs. Calandra heard the unmistakable words of a man saying, "Bring your little girl here to me in Italy and do not delay, come immediately." She could only attribute this voice to the friar in the book, Padre Pio.

She heard it once more. "Bring your little girl here to me in Italy and do not delay, come immediately."

She prayed aloud, "God, if you help save my little Vera Marie, I promise I will do something big in this country in the name of Padre Pio."

She was being compelled to travel on an extended mission to the San Giovanni Rotondo monastery in Italy. In 1968, the complexity of arranging travel to such a remote location was daunting. It took Mrs. Calandra two weeks to plan for the journey to Padre Pio's home.

The closest lodging was situated at the base of a mountain. Miles of uphill roads led to the Our Lady of Grace Chapel, where Padre Pio's Masses commenced at five a.m. every morning.

On September 1, 1968, Mrs. Calandra's initial attempt was arduous and fruitless. By the time she and her ailing child arrived at the overflowing chapel, there was no way to gain entry. It was packed.

The following dawn, Mrs. Calandra and Vera Marie started considerably earlier only to be seated along the back wall of the chapel. After Pio's Mass, often three full hours in length, Vera and her frail daughter waited. She had been told Pio typically came through a narrow passageway, and she would certainly meet him.

Her first impression of him was nothing like the vibrant miracle worker pictured in her book. Ancient and withered, Pio was pushed slowly in a wheelchair by a young priest. People lined up to see and touch him. Close to Vera and Vera Marie, Pio raised his hand and signaled the young priest pushing the wheelchair to halt.

Was he going to produce a miracle?

He blessed the sick child's forehead, then signaled for the wheelchair to move on. He never glanced up at this mother from America who twice carried her dying baby up a mountain to his chapel.

Mrs. Vera Calandra was furious. She grabbed the first friar who spoke English and howled her intense displeasure about Padre Pio—the miracle man who summoned her to travel thousands of miles to see him and apparently did nothing.

Her only option was to return at dawn and hope for a better result. This next time, even though Mrs. Calandra could not speak Italian—nor could Pio speak English—she was prepared to make her anger known.

Just after Pio's Mass on the third day, the scene was exactly as before: a throng of admirers, the wheelchair, the venerable Padre Pio looking every minute of his eighty-one years, and Mrs. Calandra holding her dying daughter. She was fully prepared to unleash her intense frustration.

Padre Pio came near. Again, he held up a hand to stop the wheelchair. As he did the previous day, he blessed little Vera Marie's forehead. Mrs. Calandra's exasperation was culminating.

With his renowned past for summoning so many breathtaking miracles from God as the backdrop, Padre Pio shifted his glance away from the child and directly toward Mrs. Calandra. It was an all-knowing look. She realized at that precise moment he fully understood what was being asked of him.

In her mind, she heard him clearly. "I will do all I can."

While in the presence of the future saint, Vera kissed his hand and spoke to him through her heart. "Please God, make a miracle so that all the people will believe." She promised Almighty God that if her daughter were to live, the whole world would know the greatness of Padre Pio.

Mrs. Vera Calandra believed her daughter would live.

Do Not Delay

"Bring your little girl here to me in Italy and do not delay, come immediately."

Three weeks after those words were spoken to Mrs. Vera Calandra, they were fully understood. They applied to little Vera Marie and to Pio himself. He passed on September 23, 1968.

He knew when he first spoke to Mrs. Calandra in her home he would die soon. He knew her baby would die if she did not act.

The months following the visit to Padre Pio, baby Vera Marie's health appeared to improve. Her doctors were puzzled. A person without a bladder had no chance of survival, but this child was not only living, she was thriving. The surgeon who removed the dysfunctional bladder was shocked to discover she had grown a new, functioning bladder. This was technically impossible, since the human body cannot create new organs.

Mrs. Calandra, rewarded with a miracle for her daughter, set forth on her promise to "do something big in Padre Pio's name." The first iteration of the National Centre for Padre Pio was quietly launched in her living room as a card table with inexpensive brochures. She promised to do more when possible.

Mrs. Calandra spread the word about the life and miracles of Padre Pio. Followers from near and far contributed to further his name in the United States. Thirty years later, the National Centre for Padre Pio spans over 100 acres in Barto, Pennsylvania. Included are a church and a full-scale replica of Pio's chapel. A museum holds artifacts from his life. It is the ultimate homage to a friar who asked God to help people.

In this part of the book, I learn the first center started in Norristown, Pennsylvania, where the Calandra family once lived.

Norristown? Seriously?

This is precisely where we were in court last week at the plea and sentencing. We had never heard of Norristown, Pennsylvania before Kristin's tragedy. And now, Norristown continues to turn up.

RECOLLECTION

Award from Laurel House

Laurel House, the largest domestic violence agency in the Philadelphia area, informed us their annual *Breaking the Silence Award* would be given to the Kristin Mitchell Foundation. Representing our nonprofit, Michele and I received this honor at an event organized by a dedicated group of volunteers from the Laurel House Women's Committee. Our foundation was only a year old, but this acknowledgement underscored the fact that people were noticing what we were doing.

A program ad for the event said, "The father of a domestic violence victim is our powerful keynote speaker." It was nice of them to use the term "powerful." It set the bar high, considering I had given very few speeches.

The venue for this event, Philadelphia's dazzling Pennsylvania Academy of the Fine Arts Building, was the oldest art museum and art school in the United States. With high ceilings and long stairways leading to priceless collections, its interior was as famous as the art it exhibited.

The *Breaking the Silence Award* would be presented to our foundation first, followed by a fashion show by Saks Fifth Avenue and a catered lunch. The event would close with my speech.

I was trying to imagine how the agenda would feel to the audience of over 300. They would experience the delight of seeing the latest designer fashions, have a nice lunch, but then be plunged into a harrowing story about a family tragically losing their daughter.

Sitting at our table was Beth Sturman, the director of Laurel House. Charlotte Stark, who had prosecuted Kristin's case, sat to my left. What a pleasant surprise to have her with us *and* also Risa Vetri Ferman, the First Assistant District Attorney. Risa's oversight of our case, and her supportive words along the way, were soothing when our family needed them most. It was extraordinary to be in the presence of such heroic women once more. Added to that list of heroes is Michele. Facing days as we had was a challenge many said they would never have survived.

Also, joining us was Kevin Welsh. "Brother Kevin" always showed a bigger-than-life smile and an upbeat outlook on life. He belted out, "Brother Bill!" No matter how we felt, Kevin always lit up our world. Michele and I loved to be with him. We felt as if we had known him our entire lives.

We introduced Kevin to Samantha, Kristin's close college friend. With Kevin, Samantha had someone who wanted to know everything about her experiences with Kristin, his protector angel.

A few steps from our table sat the team of detectives who had worked our daughter's case. Sam Gallen caught my eye, and his handshake and hug were the equivalent of a bear's. Jim Carbo and Jim McGowan were also here. Their careful detective work made sure Kristin's murderer went to prison where he belonged. I wished I could have spent more time with these guys. Such courageous men.

When the fashion show concluded with generous applause, lunch was delivered to the tables. I had just received my meal when one of the women who organized the event leaned over and said, "Mr. Mitchell, will you be ready to speak in a few minutes?"

As with every presentation I have ever made, nervous energy caught up with me. I caught my breath behind the stage curtain. I asked Kristin to help make this speech powerful and motivational.

Matching my previous presentations, once I began, there was silence from a teary-eyed audience. It was out of respect for Kristin, I'm sure, but also for the intense content. I gave current information about dating violence, including the warning signs of an unhealthy relationship. I also included details of what happened to Kristin that fateful night and what we had been doing since her tragedy. When I finished, I appreciated the response. But mostly, I was relieved.

Looking Back One Year

With the turmoil of April's plea and sentencing fading, the calendar mercifully turns to warmer days in May.

I distinctly remember May 14, 2005, just a year ago, when I saw Kristin on her graduation day. On a pleasant tree-lined street, her loving smile was what I noticed first when we arrived.

She was a stunning, fully grown woman.

It took a moment to reassure myself it was Kristin. At one time, she was our little girl, then a high school student, but too soon, she was a college graduate with the start of a career.

Our little girl was now a woman.

Kristin was thrilled to see Michele, David, and me on what was our family's last day together. That Saturday, at Philadelphia's Saint Joseph's University, the Class of 2005 graduated under an immense white tent alongside Smith Chapel. The anticipation of new careers and success was on the face of every graduate along the bucolic sidewalks surrounding campus.

The ceremony was both an end and a beginning for 800 graduates and their families. Unlike every other family assembled, this day would hold greater significance for ours.

From the podium came prayers and invocations. We waited for the keynote speech by national newsman and author, Tim Russert. As expected, he kept the audience rapt with heartfelt stories about his father and topical insights from the world of politics.

This photo was taken by the man who would reduce us to a family of three only twenty days later.

After the speeches were given, grads were called to the stage for diplomas and photos with SJU President Timothy Lannon. Each name announced from the stage was returned with applause rising from classmates, friends, and family members.

Months earlier, during the fall 2004 semester, Kristin had won the position of sales associate with General Mills in nearby Dresher, Pennsylvania. This was the one job everyone in food marketing at SJU wanted. Kristin was launching like a rocket. Our years of wishing, hoping, and praying had paid off.

Although the temperature reached only the low eighties, it felt ten degrees hotter, especially on the parking lot fronting LaFarge dormitory, Kristin's residence her freshman year.

An SJU graduate with a job. Her mother couldn't be prouder.

Exiting the enormous white tent, Kristin appeared before us in her black graduation gown. There were hugs, kisses, and what felt like too many photos—but not enough weeks later. All around us, families showed the same feelings of jubilation, and probably relief. I glanced around wanting to remember it all. I thought it was our last opportunity to be here.

Kristin introduced Michele, David, and me to her close friend, Samantha. I first noticed her amazing curly hair. Samantha and Kristin hugged. I loved it when Kristin had this much affection for her friends, a trademark of hers since she was young.

Samantha, Kristin, and Felicity.

Next to be introduced was Felicity, Kristin's "sister" in high school. Felicity drove up from Baltimore. They double-dated to junior and senior proms and looked out for each other. Felicity's parents called Kristin their "blonde-haired daughter." No doubt the critical parts of Kristin's preparation for a college social life were practiced with Felicity during high school. They were wingwomen.

The final introduction was Kristin's boyfriend, Nick.

Twenty-eight, six feet, and gym-rat solid. I guess women would describe him as cute, almost handsome.

We exchanged a firm handshake, and a thought rolled through my mind: I'd never want to tangle with this guy.

Where did that come from?

I was not sure where that came from. Maybe his being closer to thirty than twenty? This was a man. My daughter was dating a *man*, not a student. Did that bother me? No, but there was something about him, but it was not the time to analyze thoughts like this.

We took plenty of pictures: Kristin and Michele. Kristin and David. Kristin and Nick. Kristin and Samantha. Kristin, Samantha, and Felicity.

Nick took shots of our family: Kristin, Michele, David, and me. Our final poses as a family of four were taken by the man who would soon put an end to it.

At one point, Samantha told me that, for someone's father, I was advanced for sending out text messages. I corrected her, since I did not know how to send texts. This was new technology in 2005.

"But, didn't you send texts to Kristin this morning?"

"I have no idea how that's done," I insisted.

Samantha heard my response. So did Nick.

Weeks later, I learned Kristin used "Dad" on her phone contact list to disguise a male friend of hers. Nick thought *he* should be the only male in her life. He was jealous of everything she did, and everyone she saw. It forced her to deal with him one way or the other.

Samantha and Nick brought gifts. Kristin opened them under a tree to avoid the harsh afternoon sun. One was a gorgeous pink Coach address and calendar book she used in subsequent weeks. The other gift? Unfortunately, it was a new set of kitchen knives from Nick for her new apartment.

As this graduation mini-celebration drew to a close, Nick appeared annoyed. Something was up with him. Michele and I quietly proposed an idea to Kristin about inviting him to join us at the approaching graduation dinner in Philly.

She said it was not necessary. She would catch up with him later. I was only being polite. I wanted this to be just the four of us anyway.

After leaving Saint Joseph's, we stopped at Kristin's apartment to pick up her Honda. We followed her to a Denny's on City Avenue where she parked. The four of us drove to McCormick & Schmick's on Broad Street in Philadelphia in my Ford Explorer.

I felt fully gratified walking to the restaurant with our college graduate daughter, my wife, and son. These were the exact days I longed for her entire life. Kristin had a diploma and the job.

Our dream was realized.

Inside McCormick & Schmick's, across the street from Philadelphia's City Hall, we walked past rich, dark wood paneling and original glass artwork to a four-person booth with high walls. This was the perfect setting to concentrate on Kristin's achievements.

The moment arrived to present Kristin with cards and graduation gifts. The most practical present was a compact digital camera. For the twenty days that followed, her Canon PowerShot SD200 captured many priceless moments hours before she was attacked by Nick.

Kristin was at her happiest that evening, but far too soon, our family returned to our car as the day drew short. Driving back to Denny's, the conversation centered on Kristin becoming more diligent in staying in touch with her elderly grandparents.

The last photo of Kristin and David together.

She confessed, "I know. I know. I'll do a better job contacting Gaga and Poppy. I can do it now. This year was crazy with papers and tests."

I looked forward to Kristin embracing the next phase of her life. She was ready.

After a day in total sun, evening cloud cover rolled in, and my windshield showed intermittent raindrops. Michele and Kristin would be driving three hours to our Maryland beach house to relax for a few days. The heat coupled with the emotional drain of saying goodbye to all of her college friends had to be taxing. What if my daughter or wife were to fall asleep behind the wheel?

It worried me plenty.

At the Denny's lot, I did the dad-thing and expressed my concerns to Kristin. She was confident she would be perfectly fine.

Maybe I worried too much.

We hugged and kissed Kristin as we stood in a light rain behind her tan Honda Accord. I remember thinking *this could be the last time I ever hold her like this. Or see her alive.* People get tired, cars slide and crash on nights like this one. And what if someone else's car ran into these women? So much of life is out of our control.

I told Kristin how pleased I felt. How much I loved her. And what this moment meant to me.

"I could not imagine being prouder of you."

"Thanks, Dad. That means so much to me."

How I looked forward to seeing her again soon. I burned this moment into my mind. I recalled other times I had thoughts like this. Like one afternoon with my grandmother when she was elderly. I knew time with her was running short. I promised myself to never let those vivid scenes slip away.

The last day I saw Kristin alive.

The next time I saw Kristin was in a funeral home.

The Murderer's Mindset

After Kristin's death, my yearlong search gained valuable insights into the last days of her life. One of her friends gave me her Yahoo email account password. I saw every email sent to her.

An example is the day following her graduation when she was with her mother at the beach. I saw an email Nick sent that day which recapped their past few weeks. He said the relationship had been stressful and hectic.

He was tired of the fighting. In this case, I figured "fighting" meant verbally arguing. He felt they needed to get back to the realities of life and things like working. He said they needed to trust one another, and he needed to change certain things about himself or he would lose her. He didn't delineate what it meant.

He said he was sorry for the pain he had caused her and the unnecessary drama, and he fully intended to show how much he loved her.

Today, knowing the warning signs of dating abuse, I could easily spot these red flags in his message:

- he referred to fighting
- they needed to trust one another
- he needed to change certain things about himself
- the pain he had caused her and the unnecessary drama

These admissions could pass as just any couple in a relationship, but this man killed Kristin nineteen days after he sent this email. As I have learned more about dating violence, the warnings jump off that email, too late to do any good.

But they can help others.

It's 2006 Not 2005

It's Saturday, June 3, 2006, the anniversary of Kristin's murder. Most anniversaries people look forward to celebrating, but this could not be further afield. It feels like a repeat of Kristin's funeral. I'm wearing the same suit, shirt, and tie, and it's the same church where both Kristin's First Holy Communion and Funeral Mass were held.

This five p.m. Mass, said in Kristin's name, includes Michele, David, Gaga and Poppy, and several of our closest friends. Michele looks especially solemn when we walk with David to a small side altar dedicated to Mary, the Mother of God. Michele had placed fresh flowers here a couple of days ago. They remain beautiful. We also created a card with Kristin's name on it that explains the reason these flowers are here.

After the service, we say goodbye to family and friends, then hurry twenty-four miles to the Cathedral of Mary Our Queen for David's high school graduation Mass service.

On Baltimore's North Charles Street, the massive cathedral can hold 2,000. Today's service is for the 2006 Class of Loyola Blakefield High School which will graduate tomorrow. Inside the cathedral, I wonder where the graduates are right now. I feel a need to find them.

I bet they're outside.

It leads me to the northern side of the cathedral. Even though every graduate is wearing identical white tuxes, black bowties, and black pants, I have no trouble picking out David. He looks sharp, and I have to take his photo.

It's not what David wants; his embarrassment is obvious, but his friends coax him into a smile or two for his father. *Snap, snap, snap.* Mission accomplished.

I realize today's feelings have risen from sad to cheerful.

Dear Kristin

In the "Dear Kristin" journal I started at Christmas Mass in 2005, I commit a few thoughts on the anniversary of Kristin's death. Here is what I wrote late in the evening of June 3, 2006:

Dear Kristin,

Today was the date you left this far-from-perfect world and passed into the next one. I hope it's every wonderful thing we heard it could be from the time we were little children.

Now only you know what happens after your life comes to an end. I wish you didn't need to learn quite so early in life. Or, so tragically. I love you, and I hope you are enjoying the eternal reward you deserve with God.

Love,
Dad
xxxooo

What makes this first unpleasant anniversary somewhat bearable is that David graduates high school tomorrow.

The lows, more lows, and hard-to-find highs of life are sometimes stitched side by side. Someone upstairs must have created a few highs as a way to keep us from becoming too dark or too realistic about how life can feel. Call it blessed relief.

These last few minutes tick away and end the worst 365 days of our lives. We look forward to the next 365.

It. Has. To. Get. Better.

David's Graduation

David's high school graduation is set against a cloudless blue sky.

It is exhilarating to be around people happy to be at this graduation. It is a contrast to the melancholia yesterday in the church service for Kristin, which was preceded by a visit to her grave.

Today's graduation speeches, prayers, and parading graduates closely remind me of Saint Joseph's University a year ago. Once more, I see the promise of possibilities on the face of every young graduate. It gives hope, which is something I need. I also need tangible reinforcement that things can work out, that there can be happier times. Of course, I know this, but there has been such a succession of unpleasant feelings, I don't take positive outcomes for granted. I expect to see things go wrong.

I am with Michele, David, and Gaga and Poppy Mitchell. I cherish every moment in their presence. It takes only one good day to start a streak, and what better day than this? I'm ready for new chapters and brighter skies. I want to see the good in people again.

It's difficult not to think back a year. On this exact day in 2005, we were shopping for cemetery plots and caskets. I should stop thinking about this sort of thing. Is it possible? Can I actually stop thinking about that day?

Congratulations, David. That's what's important today.

We're so proud of you. Just a little distracted.

Kristin Mitchell
WRITER & LIFE QUESTIONER

Kristin was a born writer. Her stories and poetry came from her heart. Poems featured in her high school's yearbooks were about the meaning of life, which was personally important.

How does it feel to be a relative of my soul?
to banter facetiously with that which I hold close?
to toy with my tender heart
and perplex my realizations?
for me to leave long-lost beliefs
and shred my intonations?

Religiously tight, we bond...
brashly leave behind all that is said to matter

Kristin Mitchell '01

In college, she wrote:

My fantasy garden would be a secret garden with stone walls much like the one in a book. I would have all kinds of flowers in it that created a medley of thought and life. It would be like a perfectly concocted soup. Vegetables, spices, oils, and creams would all dance together to create a rhythm in the garden that is irreplaceable and unending.

Stone benches would be like the leaves that are added to the soup to add flavor but are removed so that the flow and life of the garden can continue. Flowers that are pink and purple, yellow and white all intertwine and mingle, keeping quiet to themselves as if at a party where guests are soft-spoken before the drinks and food arrive.

The path of the garden would be like a ribbon, draped here and there, lying smoothly but equally hard and stone. The gray of the garden path complements the color and vivacity of the rich thrush. Bees hum and bugs crawl amidst the dirt and fallen leaves. The water that ripples over the edge of the fountains in the garden nourishes and replenishes the life of the garden and relaxes those who visit the garden with its easy, cool sounds.

Ears and mouth and throat are chilled and satisfied by the water that flows on and on and on. Eyes take in the garden and try to absorb its wealth. Rain starts to fall in the garden, and the sky turns dark. It deepens and thickens. Raindrops double in size and triple in amount. Water flows around the soil and on the path of the garden.

Kristin created a whole world in her writing. I wish she had shared more of it with us. It was typically found as a discovery somewhere. Not something she wrote and brought to us. She was a quiet writer. She probably didn't realize how gifted she was.

Kristin also took a sincere interest in Reiki healing, an alternative medicine that originated in Japan. It uses a universal life force that is transferred through the palms of the practitioner to the patient in order to encourage emotional or physical healing. Whatever its allure, Kristin was open to alternative approaches to life that went beyond what one sees and hears every day.

She was a gentle soul, and the way she left this world was as far from the way she embraced life as one could imagine.

RECOLLECTION

Memories of My Daughter, Hope for the Future

I begin to set the table for dinner. Four placemats, four sets of flatware, four napkins. No, wait. Remove one place setting, remove one set of flatware, remove one napkin. There are only three in this family now. Call for a dinner reservation for four. No, wait. Remember there are only three of us now. It's still incomprehensible that Kristin isn't here and hard to forget we used to be a family of four. Pull out the recipe for Kristin's favorite meal, "Pasta for the Angels", made for her when she was visiting during the college years. It was a joy to make and then observe Kristin's face as she savored this heavenly dish. Now it's made in remembrance of Kristin every June 3, the anniversary of her passing from this world. Gather the decorations for our Christmas tree. Kristin and David each have their own box with ornaments collected throughout the years. We open Kristin's box and shed tears as we hang her ornaments, now also including many variations of angels gifted and collected since her death. Open the unique jewelry box given to Kristin as part of her college graduation gift. Once holding only treasured earrings, bracelets and necklaces, it now includes a lock of her hair taken from her casket, Mass cards, and the small plastic bag from the morgue marked "evidence/property" that contains the two rings and bracelet Kristin was wearing when she was attacked and murdered. This is just a small insight into my family's new reality. Don't let it be yours.

Kristin was a strong woman and couldn't be easily manipulated. She experienced no violence in her home or among her friends. She believed that people were basically good and told the truth. She was nurturing, caring and found beauty in the world. She met the wrong guy and was wooed with gifts and dinners, while simultaneously being subjected to lies, emotional abuse, isolation, and ultimately power and control issues. The problem was that she did not recognize these "red flags". Why? She had no experience with these behaviors and no education to allow her to recognize the warning signs of an abusive relationship. She also didn't know how to safely end a relationship with someone.

As a former teacher, I urge everyone to raise awareness and educate our children about this issue. Elementary classes can focus on respect and appropriate behaviors, while middle school and high school students need the hard facts about dating abuse and dating violence. Work with your school and/or school system to be sure that primary prevention programs are initiated. Many local domestic violence agencies offer programs for schools. Most importantly, I urge parents to begin educating their children at home. There are many websites with resources which delineate the warning signs of dating abuse and dating violence, provide quizzes your child can take to assess if their relationship is healthy or unhealthy (and potentially violent), and offer help numbers to call for advice or chat sessions with counselors. These organizations are listed on the last page of this book. Don't wait until the college orientation day offers a short program addressing this topic. It may be too little and too late for many.

Kristin's story is devastating. People may tell you "this type of behavior doesn't happen in my community or among my friends", but the truth is that it does. Dating abuse is prevalent everywhere and affects people of all ages, backgrounds, identities and socio-economic groups. Don't let someone you know become a victim.

Kristin's legacy lives on. She would want you to learn from her tragedy and educate others to prevent this from happening to someone you care about or love.

Kristin and the jewelry box.
With remembrance and love.

Looking Back, Looking Ahead

I try to stay in the present, but specific dates from the past 365 days are burned into my mind.

June 9 is the anniversary of Kristin's funeral. In my mind I see the hearse pulling into our driveway, the remarkable eulogies, the heartbreaking burial, and the time with everyone at home afterward. We ran on boundless energy. We needed to be certain everything was as perfect as possible for Kristin—and somehow, we understood what to do.

We appreciated the way people rose to the occasion, jumped in, and helped. Many came great distances to bring comfort. Some who seemed like mere acquaintances soon became our most supportive friends. The cards, flowers, emails, calls, and hugs made us realize that some understood what we were living through, even though they had not gone through it themselves.

We hoped our friends, family, and coworkers could grasp what it was like to lose a child, especially in such a violent manner.

Most did, but not all.

Some did not understand the degree of our grief; they felt we needed to get over it. As if our recovery needed to fit their schedule. I am angered to think about this, and I know Michele and I agree on that. How dare they insinuate when we should gain acceptance and get over our tragedy. We will never be there.

How did we make it through those days? What kept us from halting? From saying, "Okay, we get it. It's over. That's enough. We're done."

That never occurred to Michele, David, or me.

Every date in June is another gut-punch of awful memories. Each one grips our emotions. None of it feels good except that it is a year later, and we survived it.

It does not feel as if a whole year has passed; it feels more like one continuous nightmare. Before we know it, we are finally, indeed, feeling free from that first year.

The Dominican Republic Escape

Michele, David, and his high school buddy, Eric, and I jet off for a week in the Dominican Republic. Resort vacations are nothing new, and we get what all-inclusive means from experience. I aim to get lost in a book under a cabana. Any positive distractions are welcome. The beach guarantees me therapeutic benefits.

The Iberostar Republica Dominicana hotel is the answer.

Wait, what is this?

Upon reaching the hotel, we depart the cool, air-conditioned bus from the airport, but an overpowering heat makes me all but incapable of breathing—and a little claustrophobic. This suffering is not playing nicely with my escape plan. I am no entitled prima donna, but I am human.

After a slo-mo check-in that reinforces the notion that the islands aren't built for speed, I hope to acclimate, but, wow, it is so hot down here.

This Iberostar hotel is international, which I like. It makes me feel less like a homebody, but being an American, with George W. Bush and Dick Cheney in the White House waging war in Iraq, some vacationers from Germany and other Euro countries sneer my way as if I endorse waterboarding.

They stare at me. I stare back. It is not feeling vacation-like.

The afternoon passes thanks to a few adult beverages and a nap on the beach. Later, after my initial all-inclusive feast and while the sun is still setting, we seek out the hotel nightclub situated a short stroll from our room. Michele and I enter to find ultra-bright lights zapping away that could cause electrical mayhem within our brains. The music is blasting until our eardrums cannot withstand one more deafening beat. Outside, we recover by taking a breezy walk around palm trees, and the sound of the surf is soothing on the way back to our room.

We stop by David's room to see how he and Eric are enjoying this tropical paradise. Eric is present but not David. David is still in the nightclub we just left, but we didn't see him.

Why is he alone somewhere on this Caribbean island?

We don't deserve nor do we want the perception of being overly protective parents, but *what could never happen* happened one year ago.

Michele stays in our room in case David stops by; meanwhile, I am in a rising panic looking all over this resort. He is not in the nightclub. Not in the lobby. Not around the pools. Not on the beach. Not in the bar.

This could be bad. He is nowhere.

Just as I am preparing for the worst outcome, I stop again at David's room where he is all cozy on his bed watching TV.

"Hey, Dad, what's up?"

He looks at me as if it was so nice of me to stop by. Soon, he sees I'm totally freaking out.

"What's up?! For God's sake, David!"

There is no such thing as overreacting anymore.

The next day, after my morning ritual of overindulging at the all-inclusive breakfast, I return to the peace and tranquility found on the beach under a cabana. I fasten my headphones, plug in, and resume Doris Kearns Goodwin's *Team of Rivals*, about Abe Lincoln's unorthodox cabinet choices and how he orchestrated men who despised each other. This could become helpful when I return to work.

I am a beach potato. I fall in and out of sleep seamlessly here. The only waking comes from the unexpected silence when a CD finishes. As long as my Energizers hold, I can forget about 2005 for a while.

Let us raise a glass to the beach staff. They supply my all-inclusive drinks. They are my heroes.

A Light at the End of the Tunnel?

Our Dominican Republic escape is a break from Kristin calling out from every framed photo throughout our home.

"Dada," she whispers from a photo when she was the cutest baby ever. She wore a little white-and-pink hooded sweater. So sweet. Just listening to her breathe was magical.

From another picture, she laughs along with her best high school friends just moments after their ring ceremony in junior year. They hold up their right hands and show off their trophies.

In the photo with her sparkling midnight-blue prom dress, she sounds like a young woman. Kristin carries herself wonderfully. She could put up a fuss about getting her gorgeous blonde hair just a little more perfect. So beautiful.

Throughout our home, carefully positioned keepsakes remind us of the best of what life can bring. Today, these same photos conspire to put us into a funk, and there is no moving or turning them away. We have to bear it. We cannot turn these pictures; it would be like turning our backs.

At this international resort, there is a cramped room lined with computer monitors where guests can buy internet time. A tropical morning sun pours through large windows and makes the screens absurdly difficult to see. I am here to connect for a glimpse at my email.

I am trying to make this quick, but the international keyboard presents challenges. Finally, I find my way to some good news from home.

What is this?

An email from Lauren and Stephanie, two of Kristin's closest friends from Saint Joseph's. Lauren was Kristin's roommate her last two years. Soon after, Kristin moved to the new apartment at the Riverwalk at Millennium Apartments. This email asks how we would feel about a 5K run/walk in Kristin's name, to be called

Kristin's Krusade. They suggest inaugurating this in a few months when Saint Joseph's University reopens in the fall.

I would do anything to keep Kristin alive and relevant, even in an artificial way. We have been made aware how crucial Kristin was to people outside of our family. She was essential in the lives of friends who suffered when she was ripped from their lives. I hold off mentioning *Kristin's Krusade* until it is an advantageous time to introduce it to Michele. But I love this idea.

Maybe it is unfair of us to be keeping Kristin all to ourselves, not when others also need to move through the stages of grief and find healing. *Kristin's Krusade* could be the pathway out of the misery everyone is feeling about losing her.

On the beach, late one afternoon, I present the *Kristin's Krusade* suggestion. At first, Michele does not want to share her daughter's life and especially her horrific death with the whole world. Reliving the facets of what happened June 3, 2005, for the remainder of our lives is an ordeal nobody would accept without careful consideration. Maybe we should let the whole idea of *Kristin's Krusade* settle for a bit. We are on vacation away from a bombardment of hard knocks that have owned our lives for an entire year. I should have waited on suggesting this run/walk.

Once home, one particular photo from our trip is displayed on our refrigerator. Taken on the beach by a resort photographer, I am looking quite tropical in sunglasses and a new tan. TeeTee, a friendly gray squirrel monkey, is seated on my shoulder. TeeTee and I are smiling broadly.

This picture gets a laugh every time. Kristin would love this photo of me with my monkey friend. Kristin was a bright spot in our lives, and she needs to become that once again.

It is up to us to get there.

Going Ahead with *Kristin's Krusade*

It's July 2006. After sufficient soul-searching and the weighing of many pros and a few cons, Michele and I endorse the *Kristin's Krusade* 5K Run/Walk concept. We tell Lauren and Stephanie, and they are wildly excited to take it on. This is taking our daughter's tragedy public, and we're not sure how this will be received. But we're doing it.

When Kristin's story is told, people want to know about her, and the more they learn, the more they relate to her. They see themselves in Kristin. They see their sister in her. They understand if this could happen to Kristin, it could happen to anyone. And that's the whole point. IT CAN HAPPEN TO ANYONE.

Lauren and Stephanie want the introductory *Kristin's Krusade* to begin in two months, on September 17, on Finnesey Field at Saint Joseph's University. We print a posterized version of Kristin's likeness on t-shirt fronts. The type font for *Kristin's Krusade* is Kristin's actual handwriting pieced together, letter by letter.

We believe *Kristin's Krusade* is what Kristin would want if she had a say in it. Her face represents the young woman with everything going for her; someone who could not envision the horrible outcome that awaited her in a dating relationship.

It will take a full-court press to pull everything together in the time we have, but this is important. It will happen.

Another Dream about Kristin

Dreams that include Kristin have been too few, considering her tragedy was fourteen months ago.

This short dream involves Michele and me enjoying a long weekend with Kristin. In the dream, we realize she is not alive in the human sense but alive in some three-dimensional way. As real as possible. Kristin perceives her existence is altered, but the main thing is, we are together.

Too soon, it is time for Kristin to slip away and return to Heaven or some other plane of existence. She quietly fades away. It is so uplifting to have seen her moving and interacting with us, even within my mind. It feels real, and it matters.

Who really knows what dreams are?

There is no breakthrough or revelation in this dream. But as the parents who lost a child the way we did, it is a blessing to be with Kristin.

Thinking about Kristin, caused by the dream, I fault myself for not admitting to her how strong I felt she was. She was one of the most determined people I had ever known. I kept it to myself. I didn't want to encourage her to be that way more than she was.

In direct contrast to the pleasant feelings of Kristin echoing in my mind, David will be attending college in two days. Imagining him away from home is depressing, even though this day had to come.

We will pack the Explorer and aim for Davidson College in North Carolina. I expect this moving day will find a rightful place among the hardest ones we will ever endure. Imagine how different it would have been if his big sister were still in his life to comfort and counsel.

I wish she were present for the moral support and coaching a college-aged sister could bring her brother. It would have been fun to see her playing the adult as she did in those days when David was entering elementary school. How interesting it would be to get her take on David as a college student.

No matter, I now encourage her — and God — to watch over and guide David through these days. To help him make good choices, give it all he has, and create his kind of success.

I remember when David and I walked the campus of the University of Virginia in Charlottesville three months before Kristin's tragedy. I mentioned what an advantage it was to have Kristin as his informed advisor on all things relating to college. He agreed she was perfect to turn to any time he needed coaching. Now it can happen only through prayer.

David Goes to Davidson

I didn't want to accept how much things would change in life. But there will be two of us living at this house soon. It was different when Kristin was alive. I figured we would be fielding calls and visits from her and David. I pictured our home as the base where we would collect, especially

David loved Davison from the moment he walked on campus.

once Kristin had graduated. Every parent has to face a quiet home one day, but ours is going to feel emptier than most.

Today, we need to deliver David to college.

The drive from Baltimore to Davidson, North Carolina, is challenging. Mostly highways and long hours of playing chicken with 18-wheelers barreling south. The best advice is to drive your car as aggressively as these big guys.

Upon arrival at Davidson, we recognize familiar sights: parents and students emptying SUVs and car top carriers. The last time we did this was at Saint Joseph's University with Kristin. We are proficient at moving a child into college.

We are in a place where new memories can be made.

David's meets his roommate, Alex, and immediately likes him. Alex has made friends with practically everyone on their floor already, and this is only move-in day.

David has orientation assemblies. Parents have their own separate meetings. Davidson College is easy to love. Organized assemblies and charming speakers come one after another. The Davidson staff understands what students and parents need to assure them this school is a right choice.

It feels good here.

The following day, David has one last briefing. The three of us decide it's time to wish him the best, then Michele and I will drive home. We walk David in the direction of his next orientation, give him a hug and kiss, and wish him well. He gives us a mini-wave, probably so other students do not see Mom and Dad are still here. Other parents also transition out of sight. We get one last eyeful of our only living child and watch him change from a high school to college student right before our eyes.

All grown up.

Our drive home includes another stampede of tractor trailers barreling north, but this time we're ready for them.

We heard, "There's nothing but trucks on this road!" Words that aptly describe Routes 77 and 81, those ornery asphalt twins who force drivers to play their A game or get out of the way.

We learn not to get boxed in.

Hours into the drive, ten miles north of Roanoke, Virginia, I give the wheel over to Michele so she can experience these thrills for herself. She is a superior driver and does not let the flatbed monsters get to her. Honestly, she deals with them better than I.

About twenty minutes into her turn as driver, a semi's massive retread comes flying at us. There is no avoiding this. It slams into and under our car; yes, there will be consequences. It is as if our car has been shot down, and we have little time to land this thing. Michele is equal to the emergency and keeps cool. There is an exit immediately ahead, and a gas station is in sight. Lucky us.

At the station, we pull in while the radiator hemorrhages its last. It's a goner. We can tell by the way it's emptying all of its antifreeze. A tow truck delivers our car to a dealership's service area drop-off. The driver takes us to a nearby Best Western.

The next day is lost waiting at the dealership. In the late afternoon, we mercifully arrive home.

The First Kristin's Krusade

The morning of Sunday, September 17, 2006, could not have dressed up more beautifully for our daughter's initial event.

We were invited to stay on the grounds of Saint Joseph's University in their modest four-bedroom Carriage House. This way, we did not have to face a pre-dawn race up I-95 from Baltimore to Philadelphia. The Carriage House rests adjacent to the residences of elderly Jesuit priests who have come from across the country in retirement.

Gaga and Poppy, Kristin's grandparents, join in this *Kristin's Krusade* celebration as does David, who flew up from Davidson. Wrens and robins chirp their anthems as we walk to the Loyola Center, a building that serves as a retirement and nursing home for Jesuits. We had been encouraged to take advantage of the breakfast set out for the priests.

We feel embraced by senior Jesuits curious to ask why lay people are in their midst this morning. When we explain the *Kristin's Krusade* 5K Run/Walk, they bless our efforts and say they will pray for us.

We have never seen priests as relaxed as these. Most wear plaid shirts and jeans. They appear to be enjoying this chapter in their faith journey.

We feel peace in this oasis of tranquility. These are men of God by our side on a day when all we can think about is our daughter, who we hope is with God. It's all coming together perfectly. Each of us feels heartened. What we are doing is exactly what we are meant to do.

The sign-up for the first Kristin's Krusade in Hagan Hall at Saint Joseph's University. So glad this is happening.

After a full breakfast, things will get rolling. Today marks a bright, new chapter. *Kristin's Krusade* is launching without any difficulty. Close to 300 are here, and we look like a real run/walkathon with our white t-shirts emblazoned with the words *Kristin's Krusade*.

We meet many of Kristin's friends and the members of SJU's faculty who taught her. We see family members from Virginia, Pennsylvania, New Jersey, and Maryland. There are friends from home who made the drive to show love and support for Kristin.

Just a few of the participants of the Kristin's Krusade 5K Run/Walk

We brought a video that summarizes Kristin's life. It holds people's attention after they sign in and receive their *Kristin's Krusade* 2006 t-shirt. The new video explains why this dating violence event holds special meaning for the viewers.

Laurel House and other domestic violence agencies share vital life-saving information about intimate partner violence.

Our first 5K Run/Walk is off and running.

Although my family has been bitten by domestic violence, we have minimal knowledge about why it happens and what can be done to prevent it.

We are aware of the stereotypes and myths, but want to know the truth. We will gain access to victims, survivors, and counselors who have studied or lived it, and promise to learn everything we can.

Counselors from local domestic violence agencies answer questions.

Kristin's Krusade has come together and drawn hundreds of people in little time. It's uplifting for Michele, David, and me. We owe everything to Lauren and Stephanie for creating this event and pushing it along. We are in their debt.

We are relieved this event went so smoothly, and there is a feeling our daughter belongs to hundreds of people now, not just our family. The event far-surpassed all expectations.

For years, people had told us they appreciated *Kristin's Krusade* and what Kristin's friends and family were doing. *Kristin's Krusade* was a fitting way to celebrate Kristin's life. Participants were thankful the epidemic of dating violence was put on display. *Kristin's Krusade* made them aware in ways that were applicable to their everyday lives. Our event helped them detect dating violence when it happened around them. *Kristin's Krusade* offered practical ways to deal with it and live more safely.

Kristin's Krusade 5K Run/Walks were held annually for eleven years.

Kristin's Personal Items

From: Stark, Charlotte
Sent: Friday, September 15, 2006 5:05 p.m.
To: Gallen, Samuel
Subject: Kristin Mitchell

Sam,
Risa has given the ok to return Kristin's personal items (camera, computer, etc.) to her parents.

Would you please contact Bill Mitchell to make the arrangements?

Thanks so much,
Charlotte

Approaching the fifteenth month after the murder, the lead detective, Sam Gallen, informs me it is possible to collect Kristin's personal belongings. This transfer will be in Norristown, Pennsylvania, the same city northwest of Philadelphia where we attended court proceedings.

For the first time since Kristin died, her personal computer, cell phone, digital camera, and who-knows-what can be returned. Anxious about the meeting and not knowing what I will receive, I ask a close friend to join me. Lou is an advertising agency buddy I've known over thirty years. He's thirteen years my senior.

We enter the Detectives Bureau located at One Montgomery Plaza. With Nick safely away in prison, and the pressure of a trial six months behind us, to me Sam Gallen is more like a friend than a police detective.

Watching Sam at work, I pick up on what a detective's job could be like. Some of it seems exciting. But it also seems like a lot of paperwork. One mistake and a bad guy could be returned to the streets to cause more harm.

He shares a few details about the cases they have handled and the awful things people have done to one another. It's hard being in my shoes some days, but I can't imagine being in Sam's.

I expect Sam's gentle handling of our family underscores his respect for what we have been enduring. We are the human-side of cases that progress through his department. It is important to Sam that our daughter is never thought of as a case number but a real person with a real life. I might be reading into this; maybe he's this way with all cases.

On this day, Lou and I also chat with a couple of detectives who worked our case in its initial hours.

Detective Jim McGowan was the first detective to speak with Kristin's killer at the ER when Nick's wounds were treated. "Self-inflicted" was the highly accomplished medical examiner's opinion at the conclusion of his evaluation. The murderer did that to himself to support his claim of self-defense.

The prosecutor, Charlotte Stark, said Jim McGowan is the best there is at conducting interviews. His is a job with so much riding on it. McGowan makes suspects comfortable and lets them talk their way into nice, long jail terms. Kristin's murderer talked plenty that fateful morning. The interview does not convey Nick as a sympathetic victim. The parts he fabricated, presumably to support his desire for a self-defense outcome, were simply unconvincing.

Jim McGowan is also the detective who calmly spoke with me on the evening of June 3 when the news was first delivered. Like most of the detectives I have met here, he is genuine.

The other Jim is Detective Jim Carbo. He followed Jim McGowan on the witness stand at the August 2005 preliminary hearing. The morning of the tragedy, Carbo had no choice but to crash through Kristin's bedroom door, only to find she had already passed.

Today, he expresses "I'm so sorry" twice. My life must seem more pitiful than I think. Maybe that's because he was the first to find the horrific murder scene.

But Detective Carbo faces his own challenges in life. His daughter was born with serious birth defects. Whether he believed in miracles before, he and his wife were told by a renowned neurosurgeon, "There is no reason for her to be alive." At three years old, she qualifies as a modern-day miracle.

Jim shows great empathy toward me. His daughter is alive. Mine is not. But Kristin lived twenty-one years with all of her faculties intact. She had a full life before violence took her down. At this moment, Jim feels for me, but I also feel for Jim.

Lou and I wait in a room surrounded by file cabinets when Sam carries in a sizable corrugated box containing twenty-five manila envelopes. Each is marked EVIDENCE in bold black type. Each has its contents listed on the outside.

Kristin's computer. Her cell phone. Her digital camera. Various phone and computer adapters. Cords and chargers. Some fashion jewelry. Maybe something here will bring insights. I will not rest until I reach home and comb through all of this. It's as if I am being handed clues.

Lou came as support, although he doesn't speak much. He understands this day doesn't require captioning. What is there to say, really? Lou knows what it's like to lose a child having lost his son, Michael, who was in his twenties when he passed. Today, stating the obvious wouldn't bring solace. Lou's presence is what I actually wanted.

Driving south on I-95, I tell Lou I was not permitted to see crime scene photos. The scar from that experience might have ruined me.

"Good," he says. "That's smart." He looks at me as if to say, "Did you have any doubt about putting yourself through that?"

Lou prefers to move our conversations to other aspects of our lives, like the good old days. Or life in general.

Whether those days were that good or not, they were happier than these.

Marked as Evidence

In my office at home, my one-track mind drives me to the evidence envelopes to study every photo, folder, or file on Kristin's computer. I look for anything that can open doors or answer the question, "Why?" I conduct this discovery without Michele at my side. I cannot imagine what I will find, and I'd rather tell her later than trip upon anything disturbing.

For sixteen months, Kristin's digital camera and cell phone have been holding priceless scenes from her final weeks. One of the shots on her cell phone is a selfie with her classmate and friend, Colleen, at graduation. This adds a reminder of the happiness she enjoyed that day.

Gifts like this are what I prayed for. The unseen moments from a life that should have blossomed over many decades.

Since the camera was her graduation present, photos were shot in the final twenty days before she was killed. Some within hours of the attack. Each photo that includes Nick is quickly deleted. When I see his face, I say out loud, *"How could you do this to my daughter?"* I know what he looks like, and I need no reminders. Maybe deleting him will symbolically remove him from our lives. When there is a photo with Kristin and Nick together, I save it after cropping him out.

Two days before she was killed, Kristin spent Wednesday, June 1, 2005, with Nick at Lum's Pond State Park in Bear, Delaware. It was an hour's drive southwest of her apartment. She emailed Michele and me photos of her fishing in a large freshwater pond stocked with hybrid striped bass.

Kristin holding a toad at Lum's Pond. Two days later, she would be murdered by the man who took this photo.

I locate a few photos of Kristin uncomfortably baiting a hook with a worm. For me, these shots underscore her disdain for hurting any kind of an animal.

Kristin Mitchell
TEEN & WOMAN

In high school, Kristin had immense talent for playing the flute. She played for the Maryland Youth Symphony Orchestra her high school junior and senior years, and she deserved the accolades she received. Kristin played with passion and flair.

The stage lit up when her prep school's flute players joined in concert with a local boys' prep school jazz band. There was such energy in every performance.

Kristin found her second voice with the flute. It would be impossible to decide if her playing was lovelier than she was, but it was all so immensely appealing. On stage or practicing in her room, the sounds were alluring. She was a pure spirit with an angelic face.

Equestrian riding was Kristin's foremost athletic interest after school and on weekends. This was her sport, and her skills came naturally. She was in harmony with the horses, and she bonded quickly with other riders. Unlike some riders, the long mornings and afternoons toiling in the dust and heat of the stables were not work for her. It was love. She cleaned stalls, hauled heavy feed bags, and lugged water buckets happily. Her hard work around these magnificent animals was a pleasure leading up to a beautiful, healthy horse to ride.

The event ribbons lining her bedroom ceiling colorfully proclaimed her proficiency from incalculable hours spent in practice. As a gifted rider, Kristin never backed away from being pushed by instructors.

Competitive riding events required negotiating and jumping obstacles which, from a parent's standpoint, were challenging to watch. Horses occasionally refused jumps which resulted in their riders dangerously slamming forward or making headfirst falls and dangerous landings.

Although the possibility of failed jumps terrified most riders, it drove Kristin to push her horses harder. Her strong will was on display. With boundless love for these powerful animals, she found her niche.

Kristin was a leader on teams in the National Capital Equestrian and Tri-State Equestrian leagues. With her sand-colored breeches, white shirt, black boots, show coat, and helmet, she looked every inch the first-class rider she became. She could not get enough time in the saddle.

After college graduation from Saint Joseph's University just prior to the summer of 2005, she was set on returning to riding. There was no quit in Kristin when it came to her horses.

Kristin's Last Day

I might have wondered once or twice how I would spend my last day alive. But I never thought about how my daughter would spend hers.

It's been eighteen months since Kristin's life was taken. Now, I have interviews, chains of text messages, and emails to fit like puzzle pieces for the creation of a timeline.

I also have some understanding of how unhealthy relationships work.

Extremely jealous, controlling, and manipulative abusers resent their partners spending time with other people, no matter who it is. Nick's intention was to control every aspect of Kristin's life. It is my view many out-of-control people cope by trying to over-control others.

Kristin enjoyed most of her last day, Thursday, June 2, 2005, with two Saint Joseph's University graduates. Austin and Sean had shared business classes with Kristin in her last two years. They received degrees the same day and walked at graduation directly behind Kristin. Months earlier, each had gained a desirable starting position at companies in Pennsylvania, Texas, or New York. June 2 was intended to be a get-together before heading off to careers in different directions.

When interviewed by detectives about June 2, Austin said, "When she was with us on Thursday, I could see there was something going on. She was happy to be out with us but got upset when she was on the phone with Nick. She made a couple of comments about him calling her. I got the impression that he was jealous and that he was checking up on her."

When asked by police how frequently Nick was checking up on Kristin that day, Austin replied, "It was constant. I got the impression he wasn't happy she was out with us. He told her."

Kristin would be attacked sixteen hours after sending this text to Nick at 11:54 a.m.: "Don't threaten me."

I have no information about why she said that.

Five minutes later, she texted again.

"I just don't like when you tell me to think about things when you are the one who has a different story every day."

There were no return texts from Nick. Maybe there were phone calls instead.

Kristin also sent emails that filled in the day's timeline.

At 1:57 p.m., Kristin sent an email to Michele and me. It was about settling into her apartment. She loved it and wanted us to visit soon. She attached photos of cheese soup she made from a recipe given to her by Michele that went "surprisingly well." She said, "I liked chopping the fresh vegetables and smelling the soup as it came together." Kristin felt motivated to cook in her new kitchen.

Kristin was excited to make cheese soup in her apartment.

She mentioned picking up her actual diploma at Saint Joseph's the next day; the "diploma" handed out at graduation was blank paper with a ribbon. She was about to send in final transcripts to General Mills for her sales position that would start in a month.

Kristin noted a post-graduation getaway with Michele in Punta Cana already booked for June 15. Michele had thought it wise to get travel insurance since Kristin's grandparents were advanced in years.

Kristin felt so encouraged about her new sales associate position with General Mills that would be starting in early July. She ended her email hoping to hear back from everyone soon. Signed: "Love, Kristin."

At two p.m. that same day, Saint Joseph's University graduates, Sean and Austin, picked Kristin up at her apartment and drove a short distance to TGI Fridays in Plymouth Meeting.

After a comfortable, conversational lunch, Austin and Kristin drove to his apartment building and pool. There must have been an unsettling call with Nick around that time.

At 5:13 p.m., Kristin texted Nick, "We are going to the pool. Calm down. It's not a big deal."

At 5:28 p.m., Kristin texted, "You are being ridiculous. Why can't I do something with my friends?"

At 5:42 p.m., Kristin put Austin on the phone with Nick in an attempt to explain there was nothing for him to worry about. Then, she sent a text indicating she and Austin were innocent friends going to the pool along with Austin's female roommate. The three stayed several hours at the pool.

Later, Kristin and Austin rejoined Sean at a restaurant in town where Sean worked part time.

At 8:40 p.m., Kristin was again tending to Nick's needy emotional state. She texted, "What's wrong? We are eating now. What are you doing?"

At 8:53 p.m., Nick texted Kristin in an angry mix of caps and lower case. His message was: if she loved him she should have paid more attention to him that day. He was feeling dissed by her—even though she had made it clear multiple times that this day was meant for her friends and not him.

Around 10:50 p.m., Kristin, Austin, and Sean were prepared to drive Kristin's Honda Accord to see the movie, *The Longest Mile*, at King of Prussia Mall. That changed when Nick needed Kristin to meet him at a Wachovia Bank ATM and get him money.

Soon after, the four met outside of Kristin's Riverwalk at Millennium apartment complex in Conshohocken. Kristin and Nick went into the building to her apartment while her two friends remained in Kristin's car. From inside the building, Kristin called Austin and Sean and said Nick was, "Taking his stuff from the apartment." She asked the guys to rent a movie at a local video store so they could watch it in her apartment.

Just before eleven p.m., at home near Baltimore, I read Kristin's email from early in the afternoon day. This was my first opportunity to see it. There was no hint of any deadly drama unfolding in Conshohocken, 125 miles away.

In my email back to her, I wrote my best fatherly advice. At 11:24 p.m., I hit send:

Hi, Kristin!
I really liked your email. Lots of good things that you wrote there for you to feel great about. I hope your apartment always remains as positive a force for you as it feels today.

I am also very happy about your positive approach to General Mills. Recently you said you were going to give it everything you've got. They will appreciate it—and so will you. You have already picked up so much momentum having won that job. Add to it and see how great you feel. That job will be the means to some well-earned happiness. As you succeed, you can honestly tell yourself YOU did it. This is your masterpiece. Do not let anything take your eye off what you're creating there with them.

Well, I'd better go to bed. It's 11:20 p.m. here. Which is late for me—although it might be early for you.

Goodnight!
Love,
Dad
xxoxx

Minutes later, I was surprised to see Kristin sent a reply.

Thu 6/2/2005, 11:33 p.m.

Dear Dad,
Thanks for the inspirational email. I really feel that General Mills will be a great way for me to start feeling good about myself for the right reasons. I am very excited about it and all that the company has already done for me to win me over to their side. I

feel wanted by a lot of people and appreciated for the right things.

As far as Nick, we got in a fight tonight because he was acting really jealous about the fact that I hung with my friends Sean and Austin all day.

They are people who care about me and are friends that I want to keep far into the future, and Nick didn't seem to understand that and kept calling and not trusting me all day. It was really annoying. He acts great when things are going well and we are doing things together, but when the tables turn and I want to spend time with my friends, he can't seem to handle it. I yelled at him tonight because he was acting mad that I had spent the whole day with my friends and was planning on seeing a movie with them tonight.

Sean and Austin are both moving away to start jobs in the next month to two months, and I might never see them again. It was a hard thing to do, but I had to tell him I needed space, and he left without making any further plans to talk or see each other. I am about to watch a movie at my new apartment with Sean and Austin, and they know the situation with Nick, so they are keeping me company. It is just really hard to deal with someone who seemed to be getting more and more controlling and not giving me space to be me. I know this is a really drastic change from my last email, but I guess I was trying to stay positive and recognize the good things in him. There are a lot. But this is on my mind right now. I hope to hear back from you with advice.

Goodnight
Love
Kristin

There were warning signs interwoven, but I knew fundamentally nothing about intimate partner violence or the red flags associated with it. If I had any understanding about these warning signs, I would have been frantically calling Kristin while speeding up I-95 North to ask real questions.

Here are several warning signs I missed in Kristin's email:

"...he was acting really jealous..."

"... [he] kept calling and not trusting me all day"

"...really annoying"

"I want to spend time with my friends he can't seem to handle it."

"...hard to deal with someone who seemed to be getting more and more controlling and not giving me space to be me."

She wrote this in her apartment while Sean and Austin were at a video store looking for a movie. Then Kristin called them to announce she kicked Nick out and had taken her keys back.

Sean and Austin arrived at Kristin's apartment around 11:45 p.m. They watched the shark movie *Open Water*.

Unlike most evenings, it was approaching midnight, and I remained wide awake. I read Kristin's email from 11:33 p.m., and responded. I blame myself for not calling Kristin instead of just emailing. A minute after midnight, on June 3, I sent:

Fri 6/3/2005, 12:01 a.m.

Hi, Kristin!

I saw your email, so I'll hold off on sleep to respond here.

If you really like Nick, and you do, you need to REASSURE him that he's important to you—but your friends are important, too. They're not MORE important than he, but they're a part of your life that you're NOT going to forego just for him.

The key is he needs to hear and understand that you having friends does not mean you care for him any less. Ultimately, we all need as many friends as we can get. That means friends at home, at work, at play. It's good to know people care for you. It makes life easier when you know you're wanted, right?

Kristin, the fact that he's a little jealous is a GOOD thing. At times it can be a royal pain, but it's a good thing. He likes you a lot. He wants to be with you. That beats the alternative.

At the center of it all, you need to level with him. He needs to know what friends mean to you. And he needs to know where he stands with you. Just be honest with Nick, and it should work out.

Love,
Dad
xxoxx

"Just be honest with Nick and it should work out"?
Did I actually write that?
I didn't know what I was talking about. If I had any training in this kind of behavior—and what the underlying story could have been—I would have called Kristin and asked what the fight was about. Maybe she would have opened up to me about it. Maybe I could have gained some insight and caught on.
The warning signs were present. I missed them.

While Kristin's two friends watched *Open Water*, Nick and Kristin sent each other several texts.
At 12:46 a.m., she texted, "Are you okay? I was just mad you were so controlling today." In the texts that followed, Nick is

yelling and acting out emotionally. This is underscored by his use of all caps and other forms of wild capitalization and lowercase.

At 1:03 a.m., Nick texted back that he didn't feel he received the kind of attention he deserved from her—even though she consistently explained she was trying to concentrate on enjoying her last few hours with her friends. He felt she had completely ignored him, and it was making him angry.

Kristin, Austin, and Sean watched the *Open Water* movie until 1:15 a.m.

At 1:27 a.m., Nick texted Kristin that he was sure she didn't want their relationship any longer, and that he wanted to speak with her about it all day. This shows he always had to keep the focus on himself. He knew she was with friends, and this day was intended to be about them.

Austin and Sean left fifteen minutes after *Open Water* ended. It was around 1:30 a.m.

In Austin's interview with police detectives later that day, he explained, "When I got home to my apartment between 2 and 2:15 a.m., I sent her an instant message from my computer to her computer. Kristin said Nick wasn't comfortable staying with his brother because of his brother's girlfriend, and that if worse came to worst Kristin would let him stay on the couch."

At 2:18 a.m., Nick texted to ask Kristin where she was.

Seconds later, Kristin texted back. "Home. You?"

Ten minutes later, Kristin sent the following email to me. She mirrored the positive vibes I sent her earlier in my email. She also expressed her frustration with Nick.

This was Kristin's final email:

Fri 6/3/2005, 2:28 a.m.

Dad

Thanks for the advice. I really appreciate you writing back this late. I am going to bed now myself. I ended up watching Open Water with Sean and Austin and although it was pretty disappointing, it was good to continue to spend time with friends who care about me tonight and not give in to a jealous-acting guy.

I love you and we should talk more. I got a voicemail from Gaga tonight that said they were thinking about me and had received my thank-you note for the graduation present and to call them. It was nice. I will give them a call tomorrow morning.

Love
Kristin

Kristin could have called it a night when she wrote, "I am going to bed myself." She could have turned off her cell phone's ringer. She would have lived, but she didn't.

Seconds after Kristin sent me that last email, still at 2:28 a.m., she sent Nick another text, "What's your plan?"

She wanted to find out where he was staying that night. With his brother? Someplace else?

"What's your plan?" was her last text. I assume they spoke by phone afterward because she decided he could return to her apartment.

That was a tragic mistake. Kristin called Austin, who had left an hour earlier, and said Nick was coming back to her apartment. She said Nick would stay on the couch, and she would sleep in her bedroom. They would pick up the argument/discussion the next morning.

That did not go as planned.

At about 2:30 a.m., Kristin put up an away message on her computer's instant message account, saying, "Thanks Sean and Austin."

Nick Returns to Kristin's Apartment

Law enforcement officials figured that just prior to 3 a.m., Nick returned to Kristin's apartment building. Earlier in the day, she had taken away his security card and apartment key, so she needed to let him into the building and the apartment.

When Kristin's college friend, Austin, was asked in his interview with police if he spoke with Kristin on her phone early that June 3 morning, he said, "Yes, she called from her cell phone at 3:04 a.m. She sounded a little distressed and said, 'Nick is here. He's in my bedroom, and I don't know how to get him out.'"

Austin continued, "I didn't really say anything, but I paused for a second. Then she yelled, really agitated, 'I'm talking to my friend Austin!'

"Then it sounded like the phone dropped and disconnected. I called back on my cell phone sometime after we were disconnected. It couldn't have been more than a half hour later. I got no answer. I called several times. I thought that if my cell phone number and name showed up on her caller ID on her cell phone, she wouldn't answer because she wouldn't want to interrupt talking to Nick. So, I called her apartment number from my cell phone. And I got no answer. Then I called her cell phone from my apartment phone. I got no answer."

Austin continues, "At about 5 a.m., I got a call on my apartment phone. When I answered, there was nobody there. Nobody answered. I hit *69, and it gave me Kristin's cell phone number."

Police knew it was Nick using Kristin's cell phone.

June 3, 2005 at 8 a.m.

At home, 125 miles from Kristin's apartment, the first thing I wanted to do that Friday June 3 morning was reply to Kristin's email sent at 2:28 a.m.

Thinking it through and wanting to offer advice, I wrote:

Fri, 03 Jun 2005   8:18 a.m.

Hi, Kristin,

I didn't know my parents called you. That's great they did. I might see them this evening and get a salad somewhere. I will also give them your graduation portrait that your mom gave me last weekend.

Try being patient with Nick. He cares—and this is his way of showing it. He's like the puppy that keeps jumping up on you. He craves attention—and, as I said last evening, it's a good thing.

What if he acted like he didn't care if he saw you or not? That would make you pretty unhappy at a time when so many transitions are happening in your life. Don't push him away.

Patience!
Love,
Dad
xxoxx

The problem with my email was the recipient died hours before I sent it. I would not learn Kristin was killed until late that Friday evening when I received the first call from a local police detective.

Nick's First Interview

What actually happened that night in Kristin's apartment?

The only version came from Nick in his police interview given that June 3 morning at 8:58 a.m., six hours after he entered Kristin's apartment. That's when Nick arrived in the ER reception area at Riddle Memorial Hospital in Media, Pennsylvania.

He reported to the ER desk nurse that he had been stabbed. When asked if he was aware of the condition of the other person in the fight, he indicated he didn't know whether his girlfriend, Kristin Mitchell, was still alive. The nurse alerted police who raced to Kristin's apartment. Police also hurried to Riddle Memorial Hospital to seize Nick.

Based solely upon Nick's explanation of what happened, the ER trauma bay staff incorrectly thought he was the victim of a stabbing. He led them to believe that. After he received initial medical attention, Nick's depiction of what happened in Kristin's apartment was taken in an interview that began at 11:50 a.m.

This interview was conducted by Detective Jim McGowan and a state trooper. Nick was the only one who knew what had taken place in Kristin's apartment. It can be assumed his aim was to make his participation in the fight appear to be self-defense. The following depiction of events was taken from his account. The words in quotes are directly from his telling of this event.

He arrived at Kristin's apartment before 3 a.m. An argument ensued in the kitchen. Kristin became angry and told him to *"Get out!"*

He told her, "I am on the lease and pay rent."

She said, "You don't anymore!" But he felt entitled to stay.

Nick said, "Kristin yelled, 'Get out now! Get out now!' at the top of her lungs." He refused to leave and went from the kitchen into the bedroom.

"Kristin, in the kitchen, started to call someone."

Phone records indicated a call was made from Kristin's cell phone to Austin at 3:04 a.m., as Austin indicated.

"Who are you calling?" Nick demanded of Kristin.

He said she didn't answer him.

Nick surmised it was a call to security to have him removed from the apartment. He was angered that she was not answering him.

Nick continued, saying that pushing and shoving ensued in the kitchen, and unfortunately, a set of knives sitting on the counter was knocked to the floor. Kristin also fell to the floor.

Kristin was screaming at the top of her lungs, "Just get out! Just get out!"

According to him, he was the first to be injured but thought it was accidental on her part. He said he tried to take a knife away from Kristin, and her neck was scratched in the process.

"I was not trying to hurt her."

This interview conducted by Detective McGowan needed to be halted three times while Nick's vital signs were taken by Riddle ER staff. McGowan had to step outside of the screen and wait to return to pick up where he left off. These interruptions work against keeping a suspect focused and under pressure, but McGowan had handled situations like this many times. He was not about to lose his place.

Nick continued with details of a vicious struggle. It was unimaginable. He said he was trying to stop the fight while characterizing Kristin as the aggressor.

Reading this interview, I knew Nick's story was untruthful because my daughter would never wield a knife around another person. Never. She was a gentle person, and this was pure fabrication.

He said Kristin picked up yet another knife and came into the bedroom. At this point, Nick said, "Things got crazy."

No matter how the story was distorted by this man, whether it was employing lies or truth, Kristin was the one who suffered an unbelievable number of wounds. That clear fact was not open to spin, speculation, or interpretation.

Nick said when she was unable to continue the fight, he was focused on taking care of himself. He called a couple of friends and his siblings to assist him.

He did nothing to help Kristin. That detail is, also, the truth.

He said, "I used my cell phone to call Carol, a friend. I called my buddy, Rob, and my sister, Millie. And my brother, Matt, who is a lawyer.

"I told my brother and sister what happened. They told me to turn myself in and tell what happened."

Hours into the interview, the detective asked, "At the time you stabbed and fought with Kristin, did you know what you were doing was wrong?"

"Absolutely," he said without question or emotion.

Detective McGowan inquired, "Are you sorry for what happened with Kristin?"

"Yeah, I am sorry I went back last night."

In every instance, it's clear Nick's only concern was for himself. It was as if he was the one who suffered the most from what happened that night.

The interview concluded at 1:37 p.m.

After interviews like the one conducted with Nick, Detective Jim McGowan looks for the reason a person commits a murder. Jim thinks it through carefully.

"Was it an addiction? Was it greed. Or intoxication? In this case, I could only find evil. He was manipulative and pure evil."

Carol's Interview

Later, still during the morning of June 3, Montgomery County detectives also interviewed Carol, a previous girlfriend of Nick's who drove him to the hospital. They had remained friends. He was twenty-eight; she was forty-three.

She told detectives Nick called from his cell phone while in Kristin's apartment at approximately 6:15 a.m. It was three hours after attacking Kristin. He said Kristin had cut his throat, and he was dying.

Carol rushed to her car and raced to the apartment complex where she hoped to find him still alive. Upon arrival, she observed Nick bleeding from his neck and his upper body. Although wanting to help, she had no desire to enter the apartment and potentially become involved in whatever had happened there.

Carol and Nick drove separate cars to her home in Media, Pennsylvania, to drop off one of the cars. Next, Carol drove both of them to nearby Riddle Memorial Hospital in her Volvo.

These details filled in gaps and answered questions about the sequence and timing of that tragic morning.

Nick's Second Interview

The next day, Saturday, June 4, 2005, Nick asked if he could give a second statement. At five p.m., at the Detectives Bureau located at One Montgomery Plaza in Norristown, Pennsylvania, Nick gave a supplemental statement concerning what happened in Kristin's apartment. The interview was conducted by Montgomery County detectives.

This time he came closer to telling what actually happened. He said he wanted to tell the truth concerning early Friday morning. He now admitted the wounds to the top of his neck were self-inflicted. After he was finished with what he did to Kristin, he went into the bathroom and got a razor blade. He cut his wrists first and then cut his neck which already had an open wound. He said he was trying to make it worse.

He said he was trying to kill himself.

Then Nick stopped and decided to get himself cleaned up. At that time, he changed clothes. He put on a pair of sand-colored khaki pants and was preparing to drive to a hospital.

The detective asked, "Is there anything else you would like to correct from your original statement?"

"That's it."

The interview concluded at 5:40 p.m.

At that same time, at our home, Michele, David and I were concluding a day spent interviewing funeral homes, picking out a casket, and securing cemetery plots.

Thanks for Nothing

We had wondered if anyone in an apartment adjoining Kristin's had heard noises the night Kristin was killed. Nick admitted she was screaming "at the top of her lungs," so someone must have heard something.

Someone did.

On Friday, June 3, a Montgomery County deputy chief interviewed a resident of Kristin's apartment complex. At 3:11 a.m., the man who lived directly above her apartment was awakened by the sound of a woman screaming from the apartment below.

He reported he heard a woman screaming, *"No! No! No!"*

Soon after, the screams stopped, and all he heard was the sound of a man's voice and some movement from the apartment below.

He said it became quiet in the apartment until about eight a.m., at which time he heard the apartment door beneath him open and close about a dozen times.

Had he done anything—anything at all—we know there is a strong possibility Kristin would have lived. Instead, this man in the apartment above hers went back to sleep.

When we learned this, Michele wanted to find him and scream at him. She didn't do it. We already had plenty to deal with.

It's hard. You want to blame someone, and the man in that apartment would be a candidate.

I have to ask myself if I were he, what would I have done? I never would have thought someone a floor below me was being killed. Nobody thinks that way. It's better this way. Leave him alone and move on to those things that can actually do some good.

The Last Text Sent to Kristin

On the evening of Friday, June 3, 2005, after I had spoken with Michele, David immediately sent a text to Kristin. A year and a half later, I see his text on her cell phone screen for the first time.

06/03, Friday 9:02 p.m.

DAVID to KRISTIN:
You have to talk to us right now!
Call me or I'm going to flip

God bless David for trying. He learned an hour after sending that text that his sister had been killed earlier that day.

And God bless Michele, too.
After I phoned and said I needed to meet with detectives on that first awful evening, Michele repeatedly called Kristin—pleading with her to please call back. Thinking about these failed attempts at reaching Kristin brings that fatal evening back in full force.

A Disaster Almost Averted

Kristin's murder might have been avoided. Nick almost bowed out gracefully a week earlier, and the upheavals of so many lives would never have happened.

It was Memorial Day weekend. Kristin intended to spend that time with Samantha at her parents' home on the Jersey shore. This was intended to be the break Kristin needed to get some objectivity about Nick—and life itself. The timing could not have been better. Kristin and Samantha drove to the shore home Friday evening and settled in.

An email Nick sent Saturday morning read as if he was acknowledging his relationship with Kristin was not going to continue. He said Kristin was "someone really special," and he admitted he tried to impress her by spending money on her he didn't have.

At the end of the email, he said he would not call or text her.

Kristin could have read that email and agreed it was time for this relationship to end. It wasn't comfortable anymore, and there were so many problems with it.

Knowing Kristin, she wouldn't want him to feel as forlorn as he depicted. She probably felt sorry for him. Nick's ongoing manipulation reached another milestone when the long weekend with Samantha was abruptly cut short. He won.

Nick drove to the Jersey shore and removed Kristin.

Having their weekend sabotaged enraged Samantha. The next evening, Samantha and Kristin spoke by phone. Samantha pleaded with Kristin for the umpteenth time to get some space from this man and see this dysfunctional relationship for what it was.

Their call ended abruptly with one of them hanging up.

Nick in Jail

The floor of a prisoner's cell at the Montgomery County Jail is small, approximately the footprint of a Honda Civic. This was where Nick spent his days after the murder. He could have used that time to review the myriad ways he deceived people, but one doubts that.

Example: Kristin was fond of his shiny white Jeep. Occasionally, he handed her the keys and let her take it for a few hours. The only catch? *It wasn't his car.* It belonged to Carol, the ex-girlfriend he was still seeing.

His nonstop texts and calls were made from a phone that was not his. Nor was his laptop. They belonged to his brother, Matt.

He made everyone think he grew up in foster homes from the time he was twelve. It was his go-to excuse for his often-erratic behavior. Not true. His home life was a typical nuclear family living in a five-bedroom home.

He told people about his mother's death when he was twelve. It worked for soliciting sympathy. It was not true.

Once, Nick showed Kristin a check. He said he pulled in $6,000 bimonthly. Another piece of fiction from someone acting more successful than he was.

On the brighter side for him, Nick thought his stay in jail would be short. He expected to be released on bail by July—meaning within weeks, and he was certain his case qualified as voluntary manslaughter because everything took place while in the heat of passion. He anticipated an eventual sentence of four to twelve years. Twelve being the maximum. And with good behavior, he would be out in six. Maybe five. He was optimistic.

You see, our daughter was just another female Nick met, charmed, duped, and then discarded. While Kristin lay dying, Nick was at work creating his self-defense story while readying himself to seek help at a hospital.

I wonder if he apologized to Kristin. Maybe saying he would try to do better next time.

Nick unfortunately entered Kristin's life. When the relationship no longer benefitted him, he took her life in the most-horrendous manner imaginable. His lack of remorse for his admitted senseless butchering of another human being doesn't match the sad man crying at his plea/sentencing hearing.

Charlotte Stark was correct: he was only crying for himself.

In jail now, awaiting prison time, he expected a light sentence. That way he could soon return to a life of promising to redeem himself and becoming a better person.

Dear Kristin

I enter my deepest feelings in the *Dear Kristin* journal.

October 7, 2006:

Dear Kristin,
I hope our prayers do some good for you. I hope you are able to pray for us now that you know the "secrets" we might know someday.

I say goodnight feeling a bit rattled by the knowledge I have gained these past few days. I had many questions answered, but with those, I have had my peace interrupted thoroughly. I would not change the events of this past week, but they have challenged me in new ways — they have made me feel close to you, which I love. But they have also helped to clarify what most likely happened to you in your apartment there at the end.

It's hard for me to "rejoice" at the life you had because I'd rather be sitting with you now and reviewing it — at the same time knowing you were adding new chapters to it. So, looking at pictures of your life only makes things so much sadder.

Thinking about June 2 and June 3 also brings sadness as the hours and minutes were counting down. No matter how many details are added to complete the picture, the ending is the same.

So, the place to go that makes me feel better is thinking of you with God. A place where you can be safe and away from Evil — the Evil which seems to run freely here on Earth. I'm glad you no longer need to suffer — as we will, and do, at this time.

Kristin, goodnight. I hope you see we are trying — and that we are never going to forget you and what you mean to us.

*I love you,
Dad
xxoxx*

I Know Too Much

At home, it has been a long time since we have felt good about anything. When we hear about other families celebrating their children's birthdays, our minds cannot help but to go directly to Kristin—someone who will never have another one.

Wedding invitations remind us of a day we will never experience with her. When I attend a funeral, I go alone because Michele cannot do it. Funeral homes bring back too many memories of Kristin's death and funeral.

Newborn babies remind us of Kristin, too, and how she embodied boundless promise. I feel happiness for the newborn's parents and yet horrible for my own family. I don't think about what we had, just what we lost.

By now, I have fixated on every aspect of Kristin's death, and I have gone to places no parent should ever explore. There is nothing more to say, study, or ask. I am in some state of emotional paralysis and can barely process clear thoughts or breathe normally. As horrendous as I imagined her attack on June 3, 2005, I grossly underestimated the destruction.

Kristin is gone, and she went in an unthinkable manner. From the beginning, I felt I needed to dig deep and learn what happened. Now it's different. I admit I know too much.

I cannot un-know any of it.

I have stopped searching. I have no choice. No motivation.

I was told what I have done is what many fathers do. As father and protector, I felt my job was to get to the truth. This was not a morbid fascination or curiosity driving me; it was a sense of responsibility to my child. I wanted to find out what this monster did to her. Now I know.

Along the way, I tried to find any redeeming qualities in the man who did this. I wanted to understand him. Maybe if I felt something worthwhile in him, it would lead to wanting to forgive him. But this man is no more than a predator, loping from prey to prey, and taking whatever he can steal.

This was no *crime of passion*. It was an execution. He used our daughter, and then he destroyed her.

A friend made an observation. "If there's any fairness in this world, I bet he'll meet his maker sooner than later. It's what he deserves, don't you agree?" I found a way to avoid offering him an answer. An eye for an eye would not achieve anything for our family. I didn't want to be associated with it.

I figure Nick has fifteen to thirty years to replay places where he went wrong in life. He has much to think about on that subject. Maybe he will fix it.

But it's on him. He is not my problem.

My wife and I are uplifted, however, to learn of the intense feelings Kristin's family, friends, and acquaintances have for her. These emotional connections run deeper than Michele and I were aware. We never knew until she was gone. A year after, her death continues to affect every person she ever knew.

A useful example is Art, a highly skilled auto mechanic who worked on Kristin's Honda. Art fixed a button from Kristin's memorial service to the middle of his bulletin board so he would spot it every morning when he arrived at his shop. He wanted to start every day remembering her.

Those times when Art called to tell me one of our cars was ready, he would ask how Kristin's case was progressing. He still cared about Kristin. She was more than just a customer in for an oil change or a tire rotation.

Kristin stood out in life and after.

Kristin Mitchell
PASTA FOR THE ANGELS

Pasta for the Angels was Kristin's favorite dish. Her mother made it for her on special occasions. Later, Kristin made it in college. Angel hair pasta, shrimp, tomatoes, olive oil, sour cream, fresh oregano, parsley, and Parmesan cheese. Simple, yet sublime, it's the way our family honors her every June 3. Kristin wrote this poem for her mother. Today it is displayed in our kitchen.

"Michele's Kitchen"

The most familiar place in my house
Where my mom cooks dinner every night,
packs our lunches in brown bags
She knows exactly where everything is
Made me snacks there and lunch when I was young
Cat hair in places that many would find untidy
She relishes each one and laughs if the cat jumps up on the table
when food is there
Grandma doesn't agree
She thinks cat hair on tabletops is dirty dirty
Michele, what a woman
Her kitchen is just like her
Each part of her has its place
Each utensil in her kitchen has its own place too
Sweets in the pantry to comfort you after a bad day
Turkey in the fridge to pack into a sandwich with mayo and
red red tomato, green lettuce
Pictures of her children and family taped to the fridge
Neatly folded towel hung in front of the stove
Fresh bread under the toaster
Washed dishes still wet sitting by the sink
Magazines with good ideas to try
Recipes to make stacked high and higher
Coupons clipped and used to save copper pennies
I love you, Mommy! I used to say when I was young
Now it's Thanks, Mom!
The same thoughts, the same good smells, the same classic meals
The same kitchen

Continuing Kristin's Krusade

From the devastation of June 3, 2005, we are awakened to the realities of this country's dating violence epidemic.

I sometimes hear dating violence is also referred to as sexual violence, sexual abuse, dating abuse, relationship violence, or intimate partner violence. Whatever it's called, it surreptitiously takes away our innocent young people emotionally, physically, and sometimes both.

I feel passionate about this cause, but without a level of mastery on this subject, I cannot speak with any wisdom in public. I will use my unbridled emotions stemming from Kristin's loss to find ways to help people hurt by dating violence.

That's what she wants from me, I believe.

I hope our family's efforts on behalf of dating violence will keep memories of Kristin in the present and not let her fade away into the twilight. I don't want her to become forgotten, like most who die young.

If intimate partner violence is as widespread as we are told by domestic violence counselors, we feel that contending with it is a superior option for channeling our energies. Keeping the *Kristin's Krusade* 5K Run/Walk alive is a first step.

The provost at Saint Joseph's University invites Michele and me to his office to discuss a continuation of *Kristin's Krusade*. We meet for ninety minutes and hear the university is encouraging a relationship with us for the next five years.

Any good news is welcome.

We are asked to meet with the head of SJU's Sociology department, Dr. Raquel Bergen, to see how she feels about this. Besides holding down her duties as a full-time professor, Dr. Bergen supervises R.E.P.P. (Rape Education Prevention Program). Students in R.E.P.P. are high energy female and male student volunteers who have undergone extensive training as rape crisis counselors. R.E.P.P. members counsel survivors of violence—and their friends and relatives, if possible. They are organized to help anyone who has experienced sexual assault, physical or emotional abuse, or have been impacted by a friend or loved one's experiences.

R.E.P.P. supports students, faculty, and the staff at the university. They are available twenty-four hours a day. All crisis calls are handled anonymously. Names of survivors are never revealed, even to other R.E.P.P. volunteers. All information is held confidential.

In our meeting with Raquel Bergen, Michele and I feel we have made a solid connection. Not only will *Kristin's Krusade* continue the following school year, but we want to work with Dr. Bergen to better understand domestic violence. We hope to find Kristin's legacy somewhere in all of this.

Charlotte, Six Months Later

After our meeting with Dr. Raquel Bergen, we join Charlotte Stark at The Pub of Penn Valley in Narberth. This bar and grill appears unremarkable from the road, but Charlotte frequents it because it's so "comfy." She deals with domestic violence offenders in Montgomery County; any amount of relaxation and enjoyment is heartily deserved.

Charlotte told us of a recent incident that took place in a department store. A woman in her fifties was verbally and physically attacking an older woman who was sitting in a wheelchair. The abuser was none other than the handicapped woman's daughter. This was in front of store employees and customers or, in this case, witnesses.

I am a rapt audience listening to Charlotte.

Another ongoing case involves a married couple. A month ago, the wife was preparing herself to leave for work. Her out-of-work husband was following her around their apartment berating her. While hiding a gun under a pillow, he shot her in the back as she stood in her bathroom. Wounded, she tried to push past him and get to her bedroom, but he dragged her back to the bathroom and fired again. This time the shot hit her in the pelvis and hip.

This horrific story got worse. Standing over her after she fell, he fired three more times, hitting her left earlobe, right hand, and the right side of her neck. For nine hours, she drifted in and out of consciousness on her bathroom floor. During that time, he also raped her. She did her best to make him think she was dead.

At 6 p.m., she awakened with pain throughout her body and realized she could not walk due to a paralyzed leg. With a cord, she attempted to shore up the bathroom door to keep him out. With a shotgun blast, the bathroom door blew open. He stood there with a gun in his hand and said he was going to kill himself.

After she pleaded with him over and over to call his mother, the police, or anyone for help, at nearly 10 p.m., he called the police.

He was charged with attempted first-degree murder and thirty other counts.

In cases like this, my personal opinion is unwavering: people should be prosecuted for what they intended, not what they accomplished. Had that woman been ninety years old, she probably would have died. Had she been a little ten-year-old child, she probably would have died. That man might have shot the only woman in Philadelphia who could have survived an entire day with six bullet wounds.

In my mind, that man was a murderer whose victim technically did not die. He should have been found guilty of first-degree murder. He should have gotten a life term.

Michele and I have a short list of heroes, and Charlotte Stark sits at the top. She is an intricate amalgam of intelligence, bravery, determination, and appropriately, "wiliness." That is Charlotte.

Since we have put some mileage between Kristin's case and what we are doing today, we consider Charlotte a friend. A friend who grinds away at her job six days a week and concerns herself with the life-and-death responsibilities she carries. She brings justice to the bad guys.

For all of this, the Commonwealth remunerates people like her with a shamefully low salary. That is insane considering what she does for the good of Pennsylvania. She could make three times that much in private practice.

Besides asking how Michele, David, and I are doing, it is refreshing to have Charlotte's time and attention and get to know her better. We are delighted when Charlotte tells us about a medium she sat with at a similar pub. Charlotte's fascination with things spiritual and mystical matches mine. Michele is highly skeptical. She sits back and listens to our conversation, wanting to believe but doubting its validity.

Five years later, in October 2011, I gave a keynote speech at Cabrini College's first Domestic Violence Symposium outside of Philadelphia. Charlotte Stark delivered a powerful introduction for me. She also included details about Kristin's case.

Charlotte's ten minutes were so moving, especially when she spoke about our family, that it was nearly impossible for me to speak when I reached the podium. Afterwards, Charlotte caught up with me, and we chatted about current cases she was handling, our families, and life in general.

During a discussion about this book, Charlotte talked about the countless sacrifices of time and energy given by detectives. She was in awe of the drive they gave to the cases she prosecuted. They saw the worst of what people do to one another. They faithfully chased down every lead—because one detail missed could turn a case in the wrong direction.

Charlotte concluded her insight about detectives.

"I felt when they had done their difficult jobs long enough, it was as if they began to lose that sparkle in their eyes."

Only Child

With two children reduced to one, David feels obligated to fulfill the hopes and dreams his parents might have had for both children. It's a weight he sometimes feels on his shoulders.

But David does not want to live in any manner other than a normal life at this point. He wants to have friends, try new things, and take life as it comes. He doesn't want to become an altered version of himself because of what happened with Kristin.

All we want for David is to be safe. And happy.

Michele and I tremble whenever we see him drive off in his car. People have accidents, especially teenage drivers. Neighbors have hit deer. Weather forecasts with rain and snow sound more ominous. So, yes, we go out of our way to warn him to the point of having arguments over it. We try to be reasonable.

When parents have been impacted by the "impossible," from that point on anything seems possible. Statistics go out the window. Perception is reality. We don't want to hear the numbers and percentages. There can never be enough seat belts. Windshields are never clean enough, nor wiper blades and tires new enough.

David at our initial Kristin's Krusade 5K Run/Walk in 2006.

So, it's a balancing act between letting him live a normal life and realizing that normal doesn't come with guarantees. Michele and I are merely trying to hold on tight.

David is a very smart young man and imagines his parents' hopes and dreams for both children have completely shifted to him. It's fortunate he told us this because it is simply not the case. He is one person. He is not Kristin *and* David. We are sympathetic to the burden he feels and ask him to let this go. He needs to be himself and live his own life.

Kristin meant so much to each of us, and inadvertent ripples like this should be expected.

Christmastime 2006

It's late afternoon on Christmas Eve.

Earlier today, Michele, David, and I placed red and white poinsettias at Kristin's grave. At the headstone's base, a pair of adorable little bear figurines are positioned just below Kristin's name. Two small ceramic Christmas trees, created a year before by Poppy Mitchell, were set into the ground on either side of a modest crèche—the familiar nativity scene of Jesus' birth with Mary, Joseph, and an angel.

Visiting one's daughter in a graveyard at Christmastime is about as dark as it gets emotionally. We ended this visit with prayers and then blessed Kristin's cameo.

Approaching midnight, we sit in the first row of St. Paul Church where the *Dear Kristin* journals began a short year ago. I brought this journal to pen another entry before the service begins. The events of the past few months will take longer to write than the time we have. I reflect on how Kristin's First Holy Communion was celebrated here, as well as her Funeral Mass. A beginning and an end all in one setting.

In a few minutes, a beautiful church service will encourage new hope and a rebirth for those who allow it into their lives. I appreciate the comfort I receive in this building. It is a feeling of being embraced by God and those spiritual connections I want in my life. I glance up at a life-size statue of Jesus on the wall behind the altar. I hope He keeps us in mind during these days that continue to test our family.

It has been eighteen months since Kristin's death. I know we have not felt the full measure of her loss as yet. It will hurt more, and it will hurt each of us in different ways.

There were so many facets of her life I wanted to talk about with her. Her new position in food marketing had connections with what I was doing in my career working for foodservice clients. This would have opened us up to new conversations. I also imagined watching decades-old family tapes with her. We could relive those nascent days and how cute she was as a baby and little girl.

Michele cannot deal with watching the old recordings as yet. The chasm between cherished moments and life today is too much of a contrast to endure. On a couple of occasions, I have watched parts of the tapes alone. I felt the need, even though I knew it would hurt.

There is one Christmas video where Kristin opens her presents and discovers a new Madame Alexander doll. She received these dolls annually from Gaga and Poppy Mitchell. When I recognized the precise doll on that video, I paused the tape and went to a display case in the living room. All of Kristin's Madame Alexander dolls have been frozen in time. I located the doll from the video and found myself crying like that first week when we learned about Kristin's murder.

I returned to the family room where the doll remained motionless on the screen. I immediately turned the television off and ejected the tape. It distressed me more than I had imagined.

I feel good about those times we had. There are thousands of pictures and miles of tape that can connect us with irretrievable memories. Maybe there will come a day when we can see what we *had* and not what we *lost*.

It's mid-morning on Christmas Day. The forecast calls for another rain, which adds a cold, wet blanket of gloom. It's a replay of last year.

Nobody associates Christmas with rain, except us.

Michele is at home preparing the dinner we will enjoy with friends and family members in a few hours. At the same time, I am driving to Kristin's grave again. Two days in a row. Samantha, Kristin's friend, asked me to take fresh flowers for Kristin. I will send her pictures later on. This is our second Christmas without Kristin, and it feels considerably worse than the first. "Time heals all wounds" is taking too long.

I didn't see it coming, but at a red light I launch into something I have probably needed to do for a long time. I lose it.

To be more accurate, I lose it with God. I am seething mad, and I want Him to hear about it in plain terms. It feels right to get it out.

Driving to my daughter's grave on Christmas morning? Really? This is our lives now? This gives me more than enough permission to say whatever I want, and I say it all. Loud.

Good and mad, I yell and scream as if I am giving it to anyone I have ever lost it with.

Yes, it is bad. No, it is good. It is just human.

When I'm done, I breathe. Then I apologize.

"I'm sorry, God. But you put us here, and we're doing the best we can. This is hard. You understand how hard this is. Help me. Help us."

Sometimes we just need to keep driving.

January 1, 2007

Happy New Year's? Not happy. Not happy at all.

At the beginning of the year, Michele and I reflect on what Kristin would be doing had this murder never happened. It's odd; this is the first time we are having this conversation.

She would be in the middle of her second year with General Mills, probably with a promotion. Although food marketing was her major at college, and even though she landed the job everyone at SJU's Food Marketing program wanted, we never believed she was meant for this career direction.

Michele felt Kristin would have been an empathetic psychologist. She deeply cared about her friends' lives. She was a giving soul, and her desire to help others was a core strength she never fully realized. Why did Kristin not pursue psychology? She did not want to face more years of schooling, so she settled for a solid direction that allowed her to graduate and pursue a career immediately. She wanted to get on with her life.

Is there anything to cheer about in 2007?

Yes, it's another year removed from the events of 2005. Time can lessen the severity of a nightmare, and hanging up a new calendar helps to dull the pain. We imagine so many possibilities ahead over the new months and seasons.

We do not expect to heal completely, and in some ways, we do not want to heal. Not if it means forgetting or letting go of Kristin. We want her as present in our daily lives as David is. We believe she's with us, right where we want her.

What lies ahead? I am without expectations. It is good I have my wife, my son, my parents, and a job I love. I realize I need to think about life more and my daughter's murder less.

RECOLLECTION

I was Kristin's best friend

My name is Felicity, and I was Kristin's best friend.

We technically met in passing when we took lessons with the same piano teacher in middle school, however, we became friends in the beginning of high school. I still have the movie ticket stub from our first official hang out, going to see "10 Things I Hate About You" in the theater.

Our friendship became so strong that Kristin asked her parents to transfer her to my high school, Mount de Sales Academy, for her junior year. Once we were in the same school, we were practically inseparable. Our bond was more than a superficial high school friendship. If we were not at school together, we were at her house or my house. Our families became second families to each other. We celebrated holidays and family birthdays as if we were truly sisters. My parents lovingly referred to Kristin as their "blonde daughter," as my family are all brunettes. When the Mitchells held Kristin's wake, I was part of the family's receiving line.

I have no doubt in my mind that if Kristin were still alive, we would be just as intertwined today as we were at fifteen years old. She was a beautiful girl, but she was so much more than her looks. She was kind; the type of person who wanted everyone to be included (which, it has to be said, is a pretty rare quality in high school girls).

She found joy in everyone and everything she encountered. She had a way of making the most mundane things more fun and bright, but she also had a deep well of empathy and was always available for her friends when we needed her. Over the past almost fifteen years since we lost Kristin, I have tried to recount to new people in my life exactly how special Kristin was; she had a duality of lightness and depth that I have not experienced in any other human. She was seemingly my first soulmate. She knew me better than anyone, and she always seemed to know how to balance me out.

Since I have lost Kristin, I think about her daily. That's every day for almost fifteen years. I think about the highs and lows in my own life that I would have loved to share with her.

She had a job lined up and she was on her way to a wonderful life. I think of all the memories that we will never make. Our travels. Our weddings. Our children. Her life being cut short had an incredible rippling effect, leaving so many people with a hole in their hearts.

The world needed Kristin and her light. I have tried to make her proud in my actions and how I live my life, but it never gets easier when I yearn to hear her voice giving me tough love or joyous support.

In the days following her untimely death, the Mitchells asked me if I would take on the responsibility of telling our friend group the terrible news, as they were consumed with so many logistics along with their intense grief. In addition to how difficult and traumatic it was to retell her story over and over to all of our friends, the second heartbreak was that in the following years, many of our friends avoided me because I reminded them too much of Kristin. I not only lost my best friend, but I lost the majority of my friends at the same time—friendships which have never fully recovered.

One of Kristin's best qualities was always seeing the best in people, especially when I was the more cynical and pragmatic one. Unfortunately, it was this seemingly positive quality that allowed Nick to come into her life. I met Nick only once, it was the night before her college graduation from St. Joseph's University.

I graduated college in North Carolina the weekend before, and I had not seen Kristin since Christmas break between our packed last semester schedule and the fact that we went to school eight hours apart. We chatted on instant messenger almost daily and talked on the phone, but it was not the same as the excitement of seeing her that Friday evening.

Kristin wanted me to meet her new boyfriend and she hadn't told me much about him. I took that as a sign it was not very serious. When I arrived at the restaurant with my boyfriend at the time, I practically leapt into her arms. There was so much to catch up on, and we could not believe we were finally graduating from college and *becoming adults*!

I politely made introductions between Nick, myself and my boyfriend, and we sat down at a table. Then Kristin and I quickly dissolved into our own bubble. We had often joked that whenever we were together, our boyfriends felt like the third or fourth wheels.

As we were catching up, talking a mile a minute, Nick began to get agitated. He was aggressively trying to interrupt our conversation, wanting me to know how much money he made. Or telling me that he was going to take Kristin on a fancy vacation somewhere. Finally, he went to get another drink and my boyfriend pointed out that Nick actually seemed jealous and that he should know better than to be upset that we were catching up. It was not as if I was threatening to him.

In hindsight, I realize that my bond with Kristin was threatening to him and that he had deep, emotional issues. Issues that led to him murdering my best friend because she wanted to break up with him.

First Speaking Engagement

I am surprised to receive a call from Carole Alexander, the director of House of Ruth Maryland, Baltimore's largest domestic violence agency. It is one of the most comprehensive domestic violence centers in the country. I have known about this organization since it was established in 1977 but have not thought about coming together with them on anything.

I learn that House of Ruth will hold an annual luncheon in three months and want me to speak. An audience of over 800 is expected. So, my first true public speech will be held in M&T Bank Stadium, the home of the Baltimore Ravens.

Coffee with Carole and Sande Riesett, House of Ruth's key marketing person, is when I share details of our family's last eighteen months. On my laptop, I run a video from our first *Kristin's Krusade.* They seem impressed.

Later that afternoon, Sande sends me an email. "You have the power to change lives. I can't remember the last time I've been so affected by someone else's story. I can't stop thinking about Kristin and the incredible strength with which you and your wife have dealt with her loss."

Our tragic story has strength. What our family has done since June 3, 2005 inspires people. Kristin's story is compelling. Some admire us for trying to overcome our tragedy and move ahead in our lives. Others want to hear what happened so they can prevent it from happening to someone they love.

This is more than a viable way to burn off some grief. It is not about our family's tragedy or only about Kristin any longer. It is about someone else's life now.

The level of interest in our story is unexpected. I had dreamed about sharing this horrible tragedy and seeing it work wonders. I wanted people to learn from Kristin's story. I am excited to see us transform lives. It will be an immense challenge, but the results will be worth the effort.

On the eve of the fundraiser luncheon, I was asked to drive to the stadium for a dry run of the speech. The stadium's large executive level is buzzing with workmen building a stage, setting up scaffolding, mounting video cameras, running cables, and arranging tables and chairs.

This is on a grander scale than I had thought. I catch up with Carole, who finds kind ways to ask, "Are you okay with this?"

I reassure her. "I'm fine. I will be okay with this. I'm good."

Actually, I can't wait for tomorrow.

The House of Ruth people aren't aware, but years ago, I was a terrified public speaker. Just petrified. As an advertising creative person, my job called upon me to present ideas to clients that would become print or TV campaigns. High pressure stuff.

On one occasion in the 1980s, I was about two sentences into a presentation when I totally shut down. I couldn't think or speak another word. Worse yet, someone had to present my work for me. Yes, pretty embarrassing.

It was so traumatic, I tried to concoct as many ways as I could to avoid presenting in front of groups. Fortunately, I left that ad agency a month after my meltdown. The new place didn't know about it.

Utter determination and uncountable hours of practice made me an average presenter. That wasn't good enough. I wanted to be as good as the best speakers I had ever seen. So, I read the books, watched the tapes, attended the seminars, and practiced as if my life depended on it. I wanted to beat this fear that had gripped me and made me feel inferior. I think I made it.

Speaking in front of a large audience at this House of Ruth fundraiser could not arrive soon enough.

The House of Ruth Event

At home, the morning of the speech, I practice a few times in our backyard using a Weber grill as my podium. My audience this morning is twelve Leyland cypress trees running along the edge of our lawn.

A few rehearsals and I am a mix of exhilaration and "What the heck was I thinking about when I accepted this?"

At Ravens Stadium, Michele and I ask how many attendees they are expecting today.

"Over 900, sir."

Michele and I are to be seated at table Number 1, directly in front of the stage. Seated at our table are Art Modell and his wife, Pat. Art owns the Baltimore Ravens NFL team, the platinum sponsors of this event. Their daughter-in-law, Olwen Modell, is lovely and gracious. She sits on my right. Carole Alexander is seated on Michele's left. Across from us will sit Maryland Governor Martin O'Malley's wife, Katie. The governor has not arrived as yet.

The final person at our table will be Tim Russert, the legendary host of NBC's *Meet the Press*. Tim is the keynote speaker today. We heard Russert speak at Kristin's graduation in May 2005.

Minutes before this function commences, feeling my typical nervousness with a speech coming soon, I find a men's room behind the stage. Washing my hands before leaving, Tim Russert walks in. It's just the two of us. I slow down drying my hands and wait for Tim to catch up.

He looks over and gives a quick hello. I tell him who I am.

Tim Russert says, "Oh, yes, the Mitchells. How is your family doing now?"

"We're okay. Taking it a day at a time. I heard you speak at my daughter's graduation at Saint Joseph's University in Philly. You were the keynote. May 14, 2005. Two years ago."

Tim sighs. "Oh, I'm so sorry for your loss."

We both uncomfortably blink back a tear. Here I am having a cry with Tim Russert. Never saw that coming.

Chin up, guys. We both need to be somewhere.

With a record 956 attendees, the lunch begins. Working to the detriment of speakers being heard will be a chaotic din of forks, knives, spoons and plates added to the dissonance of hundreds of water goblets colliding with wine glasses. It's such a distraction.

At the same moment I am listening to this racket, Michele whispers, "These people are so loud."

She's correct, but it is a luncheon.

Personally, I am super-sensitive to the noise, considering I will be speaking about my daughter in a few minutes. But I take it as a challenge.

"You won't hear any noise when I speak," I whisper back to Michele.

She glances with a look like, "What are you going to do?"

I will think of something.

On days like today, the price of tickets and the donations are ways of expressing compassion for people less fortunate in life.

Today, those "less fortunate" ones are us. Our family is this year's sad story. There was a sad story last year and there will be more sad stories in years to come.

The way I see it is this: if people select this domestic violence agency to support, sponsor, or to send donations, I'm all for it. And, you never know who in this group of hundreds of women and men might be in a troubled marriage or some other kind of abusive relationship.

Time to Speak

A reporter from Baltimore's WBAL-TV is our emcee. Jayne Miller handles the tough on-the-scene stories. It is what CBS' Dan Rather called the "fuzz and was" pieces, meaning police and death. Ms. Miller successfully outtalks the background dinner clamor.

She focuses on the recent tragedy caused by a gun-crazed student who killed thirty-two people at Virginia Tech. He wounded seventeen others. This man was a woman-stalker who had never been put away for his crimes. Now he is a serial killer, too.

Jayne Miller is a powerful voice for women's issues. Once she finishes, she notices the governor has not arrived. So, she introduces Governor O'Malley's wife, Katie, to the podium. Ms. O'Malley is a judge in Baltimore City's District Circuit Court and does a commendable job speaking off the cuff, although looking a little nervous.

Then Carole Alexander introduces me.

"I believe the segment that follows will challenge the assumptions that many of you still hold, and certainly those I held for many, many years.

"It begins with a video portraying the life of a beautiful young woman, Kristin Mitchell. It will be followed by the remarks of her father, Bill Mitchell, who is at the head table today with his lovely wife, Michele. They are both friends and supporters of the House of Ruth.

"Bill has given me a new perspective on the meaning of courage and the danger in our assumptions and beliefs."

Kristin's video runs with no noticeable competition from the audience. This is a good sign. They sit spellbound almost as if their dinnerware has disappeared. Although anxious about standing at the podium and speaking before 956 people, I begin when the video ends.

"Hi, I'm Bill Mitchell, and the young woman in that video is our daughter, Kristin Mitchell. Please come back with me almost two years ago. It's May 14, 2005, a hot and hazy Saturday afternoon. Kristin is graduating from college in Philadelphia. She is receiving a food marketing degree. The commencement speaker that day, ironically, is the host of *Meet the Press*, Tim Russert.

"After the ceremony, I took pictures of Kristin with her friends. More pictures of her hugging her mother and her brother. We're also taking pictures of Kristin and her boyfriend. We are meeting him for the very first time. She is proud of herself, and we are proud of her."

Gaga, Kristin, and Michele from 2007 House of Ruth video.

I speak about how she had won her sales associate position with General Mills and that she was ready to take off. Nobody knew she didn't have much time to enjoy that success.

I detail the first call from detectives and standing by the doors of a grocery store with the rain coming down wondering what was coming next.

I mention the video just shown, and I recall the high school proms and the college pictures, the birthday parties, and the vacations.

Kristin and David in the video we showed at the House of Ruth luncheon.

"Kristin had a good life. Probably a lot like most of your families enjoy today—filled with hope and promise. But the difference is, she is gone and she isn't coming back."

Then I bring it into the present.

"Ladies and gentlemen, before this happened to Kristin, I barely knew anything about domestic violence. Just two years ago I would have said domestic violence happens to other people. Not to people like us. Chances are this will never happen to you or your family. But I stand in front of you today, the father of a victim."

I tell the audience I envy those who are able sit back and listen to stories like ours but will never face this sort of thing in their lives.

"Our family is doing our best to try and make the most of this heartbreaking tragedy by talking about it and sharing what we have experienced." I commend the people who do the work of the House of Ruth. I liken them to angels living among us. Then I finish with the words. "My family and I thank you."

April 2007 House of Ruth speech at M&T Bank's Ravens Stadium.

People politely applaud. I am pleased it went well. This felt like a breakout day for taking the worst and finding how to turn it around. I want to do more of this.

Tim Russert Speaks

Tim Russert's speech mirrors the energy of his keynote speech at Kristin's graduation two years ago. He talks about today's politicians and how they played more nicely in the '60s. Tim offers anecdotes about Barry Goldwater and Lyndon Johnson.

He weaves in anecdotes about his father, "Big Russ," whom he admired for his guts and determination. A consistent Russert theme is family. He talks about his wife and son, and what it was like growing up and learning about life from family members.

Russert brings in points about domestic violence and mentions Michele and me by name. Looking directly at us, he says, "I thought about the strength, the character, and grace you're showing by being here today and talking about … " He halts and restarts. "And keeping Kristin's memory alive is so important to all of us. Thank you again."

The audience politely applauds.

Russert captivates the immense audience for forty-five minutes without referring to a single note. It's a level of expertise I admire. I also wonder how someone could do an NBC news program at dawn and be so compelling at noon. He brings such professionalism and polish. This man is at home at the podium with nearly a thousand listeners.

Russert finishes, and this event concludes.

While tables are cleared and the luncheon is winding down, hugs and handshakes are given and received.

Michele and I head home feeling Kristin would be proud of her mom and dad. I did what others said was impossible. I spoke about what happened to our child before a very large audience.

I am spent but see the power of Kristin's story. It makes me want to present this more often and influence more people.

A House of Ruth Luncheon Reaction

I saw this news article online the next morning.

WASHINGTON MAY 2, 2007
House of Ruth raises $200,000

Tim Russert, host of *"Meet the Press,"* may have been the headliner at Tuesday's annual fundraising luncheon for the House of Ruth, an organization that aids women and children who are victims of domestic violence, but the other guest speakers may have stolen his thunder.

More than 900 guests on M&T Bank Stadium's club level heard from District Judge Catherine Curran O'Malley, Gov. Martin O'Malley's wife and former member of the House of Ruth board.

O'Malley said, "It takes an entire community to enforce that piece of paper," intended to protect women from their abusers.

Another speaker was Bill Mitchell, father of Kristin Mitchell, a woman killed by a boyfriend in 2005 just three weeks after her graduation from St. Joseph's University in Philadelphia. Mitchell noted that his daughter's commencement address was given by Russert. Carole Alexander, executive director of the House of Ruth, said Russert was not told of the connection until he arrived at the event.

Russert tried to connect some of the national political content of his talk to the theme of domestic violence.

"We have to lower our voices," Russert said, in an age when the political discourse is all shouts and tirades.

House of Ruth Speech Aftershocks

Shock number one: Eight months after the House of Ruth speech, Michele and I are invited to regroup with the women who made that luncheon event possible. At the Artful Gourmet Bistro, a fashionable eatery in the Owings Mills area just outside Baltimore, we dine with leadership team: Carole Alexander, Sande Riesett, Olwen Modell, and Christy DiPietro. They tell us they continue to hear praise for the speech I gave last year. It is reassuring to know it was remembered positively.

After enjoying entrees named after famous Renaissance, Impressionist, and Cubist artists, Carole mentions a woman who attended the luncheon when I spoke.

She asks if we knew what happened to Jessica Mills. Ms. Mills, a House of Ruth employee, had severe domestic violence issues at home with her husband. He had received therapy and was using medications to lessen his anger issues, but with limited success.

Four months after my speech, Mr. Mills came home from work and shot Jessica to death. I had never anticipated a member of an audience where I spoke would be murdered in a domestic violence case. This is someone who probably stood near me that day. Someone who heard me speak. And now, she's dead.

Shock number two: Thirteen months after the same luncheon, I cannot believe the news. At fifty-eight, Tim Russert has died from a heart attack. Shortly after 1:30 p.m., he collapsed in the offices of NBC News Washington, D.C. bureau.

His last words were, "What's happening—?"

Bill and Hillary Clinton released a statement saying Russert "had a love of public service and a dedication to journalism that rightfully earned him the respect and admiration of not only his colleagues but also those of us who had the privilege to go toe-to-toe with him."

I sincerely believe he is with Kristin today.

RECOLLECTION

Be Careful What You Pray For

One June 2 evening marked the eve of another anniversary of Kristin passing. Late that night, I was praying about her in her bedroom.

I prayed for opportunities to help others. I never felt I needed to be descriptive when praying to either God or Kristin; they knew how to use me to the best of my abilities. Or not use me at all.

I prayed to be "an Instrument of God's Will." I heard those words in a song at church, and they stayed with me. No matter how corny that sounded, no matter what it might bring my way, I wanted to be put into action. My prayers could mean I would experience pain or suffering. But they could also bring a breakthrough where I helped a lot of people. Anything that was positive for others was welcomed by me.

In the past, when I had asked God and Kristin to put me to work in a meaningful way, in a day or so, something typically came my way. I didn't depend on it, but it always happened. It never failed.

I am nobody special. Just a man trying to bring some good into this world after seeing how much bad there is. It was not as if God and I had some special arrangement—at least as far as I knew.

The day following my bedside prayers, at 4:30 p.m. at work, a call came from a producer of ABC's *Good Morning America* asking if Michele and I would appear on a dating violence segment to be shot the following week in Washington. I hoped Michele would want to do this. Moments after ABC called me, I immediately remembered my previous evening's prayer. This had to be the response.

Along with taping for *Good Morning America*, I was asked to speak the next morning at the National Press Club. I would be one of several parents invited to give a brief speech before the press and national coalitions concerned with preventing dating violence.

The *Good Morning America* interview was conducted in a high-end hotel in Washington. We brought photos of Kristin on a thumb drive so ABC could use them in the video if they desired. Two other couples were also being interviewed.

Being taped for a national broadcast was anxiety-inducing, but ABC kept it uncomplicated. There were lights, cameras, a videographer, a producer, and an interviewer I recognized from previous ABC segments.

Michele and I sat side by side, and they began recording.

I was asked basic questions about what happened to Kristin in June 2005. It was not challenging to respond with the many facts I had given hundreds of times. My part was finished in a few minutes.

They repositioned the camera over to Michele. The interviewer opened with a few emotional, tug-on-the-heartstrings questions. Exactly what you would expect.

After asking about the kind of person Kristin was and how old she was when she was attacked, the interviewer drilled in. "Did you ever feel guilty about what happened to your daughter?"

Did I hear him correctly? Why would he ask that? Would Michele lash back at him for asking that?

Michele kept it cool, and handled his questions gently and politely, saying no, she never felt any guilt. She asked why she should feel guilt—we really didn't know the man who killed Kristin. We didn't know about his behavior. It happened in Philadelphia, 125 miles away.

Nobody would have blamed Michele had she stood and left that interview. This was not the final time the media attempted to "go for the sensational" with Michele. At all times, she kept herself together, remained cool, and answered. I doubt I would have been so reserved.

The next morning, as we prepared for the National Press Club speech, David, Michele, and I watched the *Good Morning America* dating violence segment in our hotel room.

It was introduced by Chris Cuomo, and the piece included stories of three young women, including Kristin. It emphasized that one in every three young adult women were seriously affected by intimate partner violence in this country. The story concluded with a photo I gave ABC with Michele sitting before Kristin's grave.

While we watched this segment, it was challenging to process all of the information. To be honest, seeing us on national TV, it was impossible to process at all.

Coincidences or Something Else?

Every curious coincidence is given consideration as a sign from Kristin. Is she communicating from *the Other Side*? Is she trying to tell our family she's okay? Are we fooling ourselves?

Maybe so.

I admit I have not accepted what happened to her. Maybe I'm candy-coating reality, but who wants to believe their daughter was killed? Or murdered?

How do we explain that visit to Kristin's grave on Christmas Day in 2005 when torrential rains added an even darker mood? And then, turning our car around to leave, the skies cleared and a Disneyesque rainbow arched horizon-to-horizon over the entire graveyard. Nobody expected that. And directly under the center of the rainbow? Kristin's grave. I have the photos.

There was the time Michele and I were kayaking at Tilghman Island, Maryland. Earlier in the day, she prayed for a kind of "sign" from Kristin—anything to tell us she was somewhere thinking about us. I didn't know Michele had asked for this.

The area has professional watermen putting to sea before dawn in search of rockfish and striped bass. So, when we put our kayaks into Dogwood Harbor to paddle into the Chesapeake Bay that afternoon, we anticipated fishing boats in the area.

As we launched our kayaks, one boat started its engines, left the pier, and crossed directly in front of us. We waited for it to clear before we paddled out very far. When the boat turned in front of us we clearly read the named painted in blue across the stern: Kristin Marie.

There are hundreds of boats running in and around that area. Each one has a name. The first name we saw that day matched Kristin Marie Mitchell's name. Was it a sign?

There was also the time we had a long drive north for my elderly aunt's wake in New Jersey. Aunt Marie was my mother's older sister and she had a long life, wonderful marriage—and a total of seven children. Aunt Marie's name greatly influenced us in landing on Kristin's middle name Marie.

During the drive to the Garden State, Michele prayed for a sign from Kristin. Again, I didn't know she had done this. A couple hours into our trip on Interstate 95, ahead in traffic we saw a tractor trailer with a logo design of a horse on the rear doors. As we drove closer, we saw the same design on the side. It was surprising how closely it resembled a precious little metal sculpture we had placed on Kristin's grave years before. We had never seen this on any truck before. Upon further inspection, we saw the two most prominent letters in the truck's logo were K and M. That's when Michele mentioned her prayer for a sign. It appeared Kristin had delivered once more.

I know my family attaches meanings to these events. We are the ones taking various evidence or pieces and weaving stories together. Anyone listening could be thinking, "Those poor souls. Everything they see they interpret as a sign from their daughter in Heaven."

What is real? What is a sign? What is what?

Over the years, we have witnessed hard-to-explain phenomena. Lights blowing out all over the house that first week; three of our family cars unable to start for a day each; Kristin's cell phone number magically going to the jeweler who made Michele's locket. Yes, those did happen. Only the meanings are open to interpretation.

Others might not believe me about this, but I do not accept every possible connection as a message from my deceased daughter. But some of our observations are impossible to dismiss.

They happened. We witnessed them. Then we asked ourselves and others, "What are the chances of that happening?"

So, here's a new one.

It's the middle of May 2007. Coming the first week of June, people from my creative team need to attend marketing research groups for a big, nationally known chicken-processing client. Focus groups will be conducted in Dallas and Philadelphia. My creative partner takes Dallas. I take Philly, which is two-plus hours from home. I can do this in a day.

I am expecting the Philadelphia groups will be somewhere in Center City, but Philadelphia is the sixth-most populated city in the U.S. So, these groups could be anywhere in the city or suburbs.

I learn the address for the research facility is 401 City Avenue in Bala Cynwyd. I have been in and around Bala Cynwyd several times. It is two miles north of Saint Joseph's University, where Kristin graduated.

I google it.

Look at that, the research groups will be close to that Denny's lot (see photo) where I hugged and kissed Kristin goodbye the evening of her graduation.

Denny's was at location 1.
The research is at location 2.

The day of the research, I drive up early so I can stop at the Denny's parking lot. I plan to search for the place where I last stood with Kristin. I want to stand there and take it all in.

When I arrive, I see my plans have been shattered. I mean literally shattered. It's a demolition in progress with barrier fences surrounding the whole area. Denny's has been flattened into unrecognizable debris. A sign tells it all: this site is becoming a TD Bank. I hear jackhammers and backhoes grappling to see which can be more deafening.

Construction machinery, dump trucks, and hydraulic equipment scuttle my father/daughter reunion. I am no newcomer to disappointments.

I notice a narrow opening in a fence where I might be able to crouch in. I just need to get to where Kristin and I last stood. With the lot completely torn up, I see it might be possible to pick up a few chunks of asphalt. There are yellow painted pieces probably from the lines that defined parking spots from the Denny's lot. This demolition is actually working in my favor.

I pick up two chunks. From behind me, an agitated construction worker wearing a yellow hard hat, requisite mirrored sunglasses, and safety vest asks, "Hey? What are you doing?"

I respond with an edge. "I'll tell you what I'm doing. I last stood with my daughter on this same spot two years ago. She was murdered three weeks later by her boyfriend. So, I'm taking these home."

He changes his approach. "Can I get you anything else?"

I look at the pieces of asphalt. "No, this should do it."

Two days after this, on June 3, 2007, marked the second anniversary of Kristin's murder.

Today, these pieces of asphalt are tucked away for safekeeping.

In that same block on City Avenue in Bala Cynwyd, so close to where I last hugged and kissed my beautiful daughter for the final time, I will make one more unfathomable connection in less than three months.

Take Back the Night

I am asked to speak at Saint Joseph's annual *Take Back the Night* event. They are allowing me twenty-five minutes as the keynote.

Take Back the Night vigils are powerful gatherings of students aimed at raising awareness about sexual and physical violence against women and encouraging victims to speak out.

This is held in Smith Chapel, where the university had held Kristin's memorial service three days after her funeral. It's the same chapel where a light kept shutting off and turning on during that the Candlelight Vigil.

I remember happier times not so long ago when Kristin, Michele, David, and I attended church services here. It is 100 percent different now. There are no smiles. No anticipation of what Kristin might do with her education and her life. That is all behind us.

It is time to use her story to save lives. I see my purpose is scaring audiences with the unvarnished truth about dating violence. Getting attention could lead to saving someone's life.

This is a news clipping I was shown prior to the speech.

Vigil Aims to Combat Sexual Violence

Bill Mitchell, father of Kristin Mitchell '05—who was a victim of violence— will be the keynote speaker. Mitchell will share his experience of losing a daughter to violence not long after her graduation from college.

The event invites members of the Saint Joseph's community to dialogue about physical and sexual violence. "While other Philadelphia schools host Take Back the Night events, the Saint Joseph's crowd is by far the largest," said Raquel Bergen, Ph.D., professor and chair of sociology…

> In a dramatic finale to the event, 70 candles in luminary bags will line the sidewalk leading from the chapel doors.

A five-minute video shows Kristin as a child, a cute teenager, and a college student. The audience sees how lovable a person she was—and so full of life. I'm sure they identify with this young woman who went to this institution. Someone who rode horses, loved cats, laughed with friends, but lived a short life.

What I don't anticipate is the effect the video is having on me. What a rush of emotion. I retreat into the darkness at the back of the chapel to get my mind off these memories and dry my eyes. Nobody sees me except Kristin.

Now, it's time to speak.

My voice resonates more powerfully than I expected. This feels unusual, and it helps me recover. The audience listens without moving, which is what happens when I speak about Kristin. They are captivated by what befell one of their sisters, and what our family is doing to make this devastating loss work to the advantage of others. People like themselves.

I have learned ways to urge people to rethink their dating relationships and not take life for granted. Kristin is probably watching over this, but nothing I do can change her future.

Padre Pio
VISITING THE NATIONAL CENTRE

Months ago, I was reading everything I could find about Padre Pio, the Capuchin friar who had hundreds of miracles attributed to him. I immersed myself in everything I could read about him. Life is about getting to the truth about why we're here and what we're supposed to be doing, so if driving three hours to this shrine brings us closer to the truth, we're going.

On this first trip, David and I drive three hours to The National Centre for Padre Pio in Barto, Pennsylvania. This is where they memorialize the poor Capuchin Friar who later became a saint.

Today, we will not be meeting Vera Marie Calandra, who, while still a baby, required miracles to survive inconceivable birth defects. But we will visit with her sister, Julia, who is a powerful emissary of the holiness within this place.

In the Centre's museum, Padre Pio's one-of-a kind personal effects, including his Franciscan vestments, are laid out. We stop and study exhibits while Julia gives us insight-filled descriptions of the miracles that gained Pio consideration for sainthood in the eyes of the Catholic Church.

One phenomenon happened in October 1995, in Salerno, Italy. A Mrs. Consiglia De Martino felt considerable pain in her chest and stomach. She also had been noticing a painful swelling in her neck, estimated to be ten centimeters in size. Scans revealed a liquid deposit resulting from a rupture of her lymphatic canals. Immediate surgery was advised.

Mrs. De Martino prayed for Padre Pio's intercession. He had died fifteen years prior, but she thought this meant he was closer to God.

A day later, prior to her approaching surgery, the fluid deposit in Mrs. De Martino's neck had reduced some, and she noticed less pain. The following day, health workers saw an almost complete disappearance of the swelling in her neck.

Scans showed no evidence of liquid deposits in her body at all. They released Mrs. De Martino with a clean bill of health.

Religious investigators of miraculous healings accepted the validity of Mrs. De Martino's cure. Two experts and a medical consultant unanimously announced the "extraordinary and scientifically inexplicable nature" of Consiglia De Martino's illness.

For someone to be considered a saint, it took at least two verified miracles where the saint-candidate intervened on the part of a living person. These had to occur after the saint-candidate was deceased. Canonization typically took decades, but in the case of Padre Pio, it took a "short" fourteen years for an investigation to commence.

Padre Pio's actual shawl.

Eight years later, Pio was declared a "servant of God," the first step in a meticulous process toward sainthood. Seven years later, he was declared "venerable."

Two years after that, he was declared "blessed." Three years later, in June 2002, Padre Pio was proclaimed a saint by Pope John Paul II in Saint Peter's Square. That amounted to thirty-four years, which was accelerated compared with most saints.

Padre Pio was also the first Catholic priest to receive the gift of the stigmata of Christ. To call this a gift might seem bizarre considering how painful these wounds were. Their locations corresponded with injuries Jesus Christ suffered during His crucifixion: hands, wrists, feet, side of the torso, and back. Padre Pio

David studying Padre Pio's actual glove within a frame.

had them, including scars on his shoulders where Christ bore the cross. Pio's stigmata didn't completely heal until days before he died in 1968, at eighty-one years old. From the stigmata, he endured ceaseless agony for nearly fifty years.

David and I see bandages Pio wore along with undershirts stained with faded blood. Afterward, in a private room, Julia encourages David and me to don a shawl Padre Pio once wore. With it wrapped about my neck, I ask for the strength needed to do God's work here on Earth, if that is my calling. I hope it is.

We also hold one of Pio's signature chestnut-colored gloves he wore to hide his stigmata from the public.

I would love to meet Vera Marie, the miracle child Padre Pio helped to save in 1968, but that moment will come in time.

The next day, I send an email to Julia Calandra.

Hi Julia,

Thank you so much for the time, energy, and attention you gave us yesterday. David and I are in search of answers, and our visit with you meant everything to us.

Although it was so fulfilling to see so many items once used by Saint Pio, plus articles given to your mom by Pope John Paul II, David and I agree the most moving part of our day was being there with you. You are the embodiment of all of the things your mother and Saint Pio wanted people to be. You are generous, and I would suppose you have given most of your waking hours over to helping people connect with Saint Pio and God.

I expect to see you again. Please give our best to Vera Marie; she was just wonderful when I spoke with her the other day. If I can do anything for you, Julia, please let me know.

God Bless your family,
Bill and David Mitchell

One year later, I returned to the National Centre, this time with Michele. We met Vera Marie Calandra, the woman saved in 1968 by the intercession of Padre Pio when she was a two-year-old. At forty-two, she looked like someone completely at peace.

Michele and I first noticed her honest smile. Knowing that she was still alive must have brought her feelings of the presence of God in her life. While the rest of us sometimes search to believe, she didn't need to look or question. She knew.

We unfolded the story of what had happened to Kristin, and Vera Marie appeared deeply saddened. Praying with her brought comfort considering who she was. She prayed for healing and for Kristin's immortal soul.

Vera Marie explained her lifesaving miracle did not end her physical afflictions in life. She continued to suffer with serious issues. Life had not been easy. But she was alive, and her perceptible positivity set her apart.

Vera Marie was saved by the prayers of Padre Pio and the Hand of God. It doesn't get more unearthly than that. This extraordinary woman was touched by God, and we were awestruck being with her.

We gave Vera Marie a graduation photo of Kristin. She carefully studied the face of a blossoming young woman who was murdered so horribly.

Padre Pio's confessional where Kristin's photo rests against the door.

Vera Marie indicated this picture would be placed by Padre Pio's confessional within the chapel.

Michele and I hugged Vera Marie, a woman saved from certain death by the intercession of a modern-day saint.

Before we left the Centre, we visited the exact re-creation of Padre Pio's Our Lady of Grace chapel. The tiled floors, domed ceiling, and architecture were a perfect reproduction of the original chapel where Pio said Mass in San Giovanni Rotondo, Italy.

The confessional used by Padre Pio in San Giovanni Rotondo rested along a wall in the chapel. There we saw Kristin's picture leaning against the door.

On the floor we saw photos of babies and children, pictures of old and young men and women, each with a handwritten appeal for Padre Pio's intervention asking to save or keep watch over someone's life or soul.

We lit a candle and said a prayer for Kristin. Then we placed a note by her photo.

God and Padre Pio,

Please watch over Kristin.

May she rest forever in peace.

7.16.08

A Donation from Verizon

Our nonprofit, the Kristin Mitchell Foundation, is contacted by Verizon Wireless corporate. We will receive a donation from their newest store in the Philadelphia area. Verizon's charitable focus is domestic violence, so our cause matches theirs perfectly.

Michele and I drive to Verizon's new store which could have been located practically anywhere in the greater Philadelphia area or its suburbs. Of course, it is located in Bala Cynwyd—a block from where Denny's stood (Position 1 in the photo); across the street from the research groups I attended three months ago (Position 2). You will recall, that was the day I collected the pieces of asphalt from the Denny's old parking lot.

Denny's was location 1.
The research was location 2.
Verizon is location 3.

It seems as if every instance when I need to be in Philadelphia, it's in Bala Cynwyd, within a block from where I last hugged and kissed Kristin.

In front of the store, Michele and I hold a four-foot-wide bank check written out for $3,000. Verizon representatives pose alongside us. Our tiny nonprofit is being awarded for making a difference, and this is encouraging us to do a lot more for the dating violence cause.

A Philadelphia website describes the contribution:

September 28th, 2007

BALA CYNWYD, PA – A cellular phone carrier is making a donation to an organization that fights domestic violence.

Verizon Wireless is also collecting old cell phones for victims of domestic abuse.

In celebration of its new retail store in Bala Cynwyd, Verizon Wireless is donating $3,000 to the Kristin Mitchell Foundation for Violence Against Women. Kristin was murdered by her boyfriend in 2005, three weeks after her graduation from St. Joseph's University.

Bill Mitchell is her father: "We can no longer help Kristin, but we can help other women."

A representative from Verizon Wireless: "It doesn't have to be a Verizon Wireless phone. It can be a phone from any cellular carrier. They bring them to the store and drop them into our 'Hopeline' bin, and then we'll have them recycled."

The Kristin Mitchell Foundation is holding its second annual 5K run and walk at St. Joe's University on Sunday.

The Second Kristin's Krusade

Two days after receiving the Verizon donation at 4050 City Avenue, we return to Saint Joseph's University at 5600 City Avenue. The two are a mile and a half apart. What are the chances they would be within walking distance?

This second *Kristin's Krusade* 5K Run/Walk is rewarded with the same clear skies as a year ago. Our first *Kristin's Krusade* t-shirts were white with black and purple inks. Rather basic. This year, everyone is talking about our latest shirts in a handsome sport gray. Our new logo is emblazoned across the fronts with the KK of the *Kristin's Krusade* logo. These double as both the initial letters of this event, and two human figures in motion. Each "K" was scanned from Kristin's priceless writing from her *Dear God* notes.

Domestic violence survivors use purple to represent peace, courage, survival, honor, and a dedication to ending violence. So, *Kristin's Krusade* uses purple as our predominant color.

We also unveil a new tagline that points out that young adult females have to take control of their RUN LIFE YOUR WAY® lives. We wrote *Run Life Your Way* not only to urge empowerment but to underscore this event includes a 5K run/walk.

We feel the enthusiasm build when signups total over 300. We might never become Susan G. Komen's *Race for the Cure* with hundreds of thousands, but we are growing.

At 7:30 a.m., on the northern end of Saint Joseph's Finnesey Field, our tents and tables are ready. Buildings are emblazoned with large banners showing Kristin's face and the *Kristin's Krusade* words in her own handwriting. Local stores have delivered caseloads of water, juice, and ice tea, along with an assortment of snacks. Saint Joseph's Food Marketing Association's connections make this possible. Besides refreshments, participants can pick up sunscreen, sunglasses, hats, buttons, and other practical items.

Volunteers from Laurel House, the domestic violence agency from nearby Norristown, hand out lifesaving information about intimate partner violence. They chat with all who stop by their table. The people of Laurel House confront the domestic violence epidemic daily, and it has to be draining to witness it face-to-face every day as they do. Our admiration for them matches their respect for what we are trying to do.

Our daughter's organization is putting on quite a run/walk. For those who race, *Kristin's Krusade* is awarding valuable prizes donated by the area's favorite running store, Philadelphia Runner. *Kristin's Krusade* also holds a raffle with a full array of prizes. The walk and the run are coordinated perfectly from the start of the race to the final prize awarded in the raffle. After we speak a few words to all who participated, we conclude this second event.

Our prayers were answered. This looks and feels like success. The interest we see boosts our family's mood sky-high. So good for us to see what Kristin's story can mean besides great personal loss, pain, and sorrow.

Only a couple of months before, Kristin's friends, Stephanie and Lauren, invested countless hours planning this.

Kristin's Krusade. Much more than a run/walk. A way to gain awareness about dating violence.

Their execution was flawless. They wanted *Kristin's Krusade* to become an annual event, and they are succeeding. All of Kristin's friends have learned what it is like to be so close to someone who is in harm's way and not perceive how dangerous it can become.

Nobody expects a friend to be killed by a boyfriend. That's why we're here. *Kristin's Krusade* aims to open everyone's eyes and change this.

Why Kristin's Krusade?

Before we close the books on our second *Kristin's Krusade*, we have to ask ourselves, "Why do we do it?" It's so much work.

Kristin's Krusade is more than one more run/walk in an already crowded calendar of 5Ks around Philadelphia in the fall. *Kristin's Krusade* is not just a race nor is it just a fundraiser.

Not the way you want to see your daughter's picture in the newspaper.

Kristin's Krusade exists for one reason: to bring awareness about this insidious epidemic known as domestic violence, dating violence, or simply DV. We want to shine a flood light on not just physical and sexual abuse but on psychological abuse as well. It is obvious this epidemic has low awareness and is not understood on campuses— or in the general public for that matter.

There is the myth that domestic violence only happens within stereotypically rough neighborhoods in the lowest income parts of cities. This is such a gross misconception. I thought this way, too. I was so wrong.

The truth: domestic violence exists *equally in all areas*, no matter how affluent the city or county. This was so far from what I had perceived that it took me time to accept it myself. Research conducted as far back as 1985 uncovered the truth. It's everywhere.

And *what is* domestic violence anyway?

I had to find a good definition, and this one is useful: domestic violence, also called domestic *abuse*, is violence by one person against another in a domestic setting. This could be in a marriage or any form of cohabitation. Domestic violence occurs when an abuser believes abuse is an entitlement, is acceptable, is justified, or will not likely be reported.

Domestic violence is more pervasive than we know.

Here is the truth: 1 in 3 women will be victims of serious physical violence in an intimate relationship in their lifetimes. This typically happens between the ages of 16 and 24, but can happen at any age. The research statistics also say *1 in 4 men* also suffer similar physical violence.

If this does not alarm us, what does?

From conversations with counselors, I learn very few men recognize themselves as abusers even when they are. They feel there is a good reason they do what they do. They feel it is not entirely their fault. They feel each instance is an aberration. And they don't take ownership of their actions.

Likewise, few women think of themselves as victims because they interpret their experiences as "family conflicts that got out of control." Some think they contribute to what happens to them—as if they deserve it.

They don't deserve it!

The overall awareness, perception, documentation, and understanding of domestic violence is low. This is why Stephanie and Lauren joined with us to create *Kristin's Krusade*. It's a way to help people gain basic awareness.

A one-day 5K run/walk in Philadelphia can barely touch this insidious issue, but those who take our cause to heart feel that saving even one life will make our efforts worthwhile.

The Foundation

Kristin's friends, Stephanie and Lauren, created Kristin's foundation with as much forethought and wisdom as they created the *Kristin's Krusade* 5K Run/Walks. Without their vision and generous efforts, Michele and I don't believe we would have undertaken this on our own. God bless them both.

By the end of 2007, "KMF" adds depth, maturity, and experience when Charlotte Stark joins the board. Charlotte, the prosecutor of Kristin's case, tells us Kristin reminds her of one of her own daughters.

Charlotte's dear friend, Beth Sturman, also joins the board. Beth is the executive director at Laurel House, the comprehensive domestic violence agency. It is a boost to our credibility to have Beth on our team.

Laurel House's commitment is "ending domestic violence in each life, home, and community." We pray Charlotte and Beth's knowledge of domestic violence rubs off on us. They will increase our ability to help people in tangible ways.

Jessica Mertz, who attended classes with Kristin during their freshman year at SJU, also joins. She intends to work in the domestic violence field and is taking classes to get this underway. We need young and energetic members like Jess. She's smart and motivated to help young women who become tangled up in unhealthy relationships. She champions this cause.

The Kristin Mitchell Foundation is a tiny but highly motivated foundation. Somewhere working behind the scenes, we feel Kristin cheering us on. We want her name to represent a positive force in people's lives for both empowerment and personal safety.

Turning our tragedy into a triumph for others will take some time. After spending so much of our lives reliving our loss for eighteen months, we now have a vehicle for looking ahead.

Charlotte, Beth, and Jess supply a vast amount of knowledge about DV, so our organization can speak to this. These women help us educate others about the warning signs of unhealthy relationships and what to do when a relationship is heading into danger.

Not long after Beth joins, an invaluable coworker of hers from Laurel House, Patty Goloff, has an interest in participating, too. Patty's phenomenal drive for getting things accomplished is a powerful asset. She becomes *Kristin's Krusade's* new treasurer and race director.

In succeeding years, the board adds Dr. Raquel Kennedy Bergen, the head of SJU's sociology department. Raquel has authored numerous scholarly publications, and she has written five books on violence against women. Her area of expertise is intimate partner sexual violence.

Dr. Rich George also joins the board. He was Kristin's favorite food marketing professor at SJU. Months after Kristin's death, Rich dedicated his teaching career to her. Rich brings the voice of reason when it is most needed in critical decision-making for the board.

Bob Teti, who taught Kristin first-year accounting, joins too and serves as our accountant. A peaceful man, Bob teaches master's level accounting at SJU. The last time he spoke with Kristin was several days before she graduated from SJU in 2005.

George Latella, another of Kristin's professors, brings us food marketing students who help the day of *Kristin's Krusade*. George's solid connections with generous outside companies generate truckloads of refreshments. His can-do attitude about everything is truly refreshing.

Of course, Kristin's brother, David, joins the board. He speaks out with force about dating violence with personal insights that captivate audiences. In meetings, his strategic thinking assists in crafting our mission statement. Michele and I are proud of David for his attention to an issue that changed the direction of our lives.

Our appreciation for those who serve this foundation, starting with Stephanie and Lauren, is endless. Besides the run/walks there are other fundraisers around the Saint Joseph's

University area. Each run/walk is a success, especially when viewed through the lens of awareness and education. The organization faces the dating violence epidemic head-on. We believe we help many, and we know we save a few.

From 2006 until the final *Kristin's Krusade* 5K Run/Walk in 2017, every event was held at Saint Joseph's University. It took an immense effort to make each one successful. We are forever grateful to SJU for their support and generosity. They helped this become a reality.

For each of the eleven years, the weather was crisp and clear, with only a cloud or two—but never a single drop of rain. We were fortunate.

SJU students and other participants came from near and far. We recognized many faces from previous years, and it was inspirational to be greeted by name. This familiarity brought us comfort, and it encouraged us to continue.

Besides the *Kristin's Krusade* 5K run/walk, we awarded the winner of the Kristin Mitchell '05 Memorial Scholarship to a deserving SJU undergrad. It needed to be someone who demonstrated active involvement in either service learning activities or displayed engagement in education and prevention activities in dating violence.

Awarding the scholarship was a highlight of every *Kristin's Krusade*. Standing beside our scholarship winners made us feel close to Kristin—a person who found it easy to help anyone in need. Her heart was huge, and our winners lived life the same way.

Remembering the Forgotten

When someone dies tragically, people reach out to comfort a victim's immediate family. The attention becomes a wonderful distraction from the realities of what actually happened.

Sympathy cards, books, phone calls, visits, and flowers are appreciated and remembered. Grief and heartache can take a lifetime to work through, but true empathy and assistance is offered. As a recipient of generous attention, I am sometimes torn between wanting to talk about the loss—or wanting to be left by myself to grieve. Mostly, I prefer the interaction.

Others who could use some attention typically get very little. People like Kristin's grandparents. They grieve mightily over the loss of their dear grandchild. The loss is as real to them as it is to us, Kristin's parents and her brother. And they face a dual predicament: they grieve for themselves while also attempting to soothe their own children—the parents of the deceased. Their feelings—their broken hearts—are sometimes overlooked.

The truth is, these are not the only ones suffering silently. The victim's friends, schoolmates, teachers, and acquaintances live with enormous holes in their lives. They are forced to deal with unanswered questions about life itself. They often suffer these tragedies without support or assistance.

You can understand how close friends of the deceased guilt themselves for not acting in time, or not intervening, or not recognizing the deadly peril, or not preventing it. They become the collateral damage of domestic violence.

Everyone is impacted in one way or another.

RECOLLECTION

Opposing Thoughts

I am David, Kristin's brother.

On the morning of June 4th, 2005, the day after I found out that my sister had been suddenly torn from our lives in an unthinkable manner, I experienced a moment of personal revelation that was critical in shaping my outlook on both my family's tragedy and on life itself. I decided to share it in this book in the hopes that it may help others coping with their own personal crises and tragedies, in whatever form they come.

My parents and I were in the funeral director's office attempting to iron out the details of the wake, funeral, and burial. The news was still fresh, our emotions were still raw and unpredictable, and our grasp on the reality of the situation was shaky at best. A ways into the meeting, the funeral director asked us, "Do you think you would you prefer a casket made of wood or of metal?" I don't mean this as a criticism of the funeral director – he was truly compassionate, professional, and did an excellent job for us – but subjectively, in that moment, the question felt utterly absurd and unanswerable to me. It was as though your house had just burned down, and the cleanup crew was asking if you preferred that they send a red truck or a blue truck to haul away the wreckage. I think the contrast of what seemed like such a trivial decision against the backdrop of a life-altering new reality struck a chord in me. Feeling that the collapse of my emotional house of cards was imminent, I walked out of the room, left the building, and landed on a concrete bench outside. The emotional release that followed was intense, and it was complete. I cried for my sister, I cried for my family, and I struggled through involuntary gasps for air in between outpourings of sorrow and pain.

I don't know if this went on for one minute, five minutes, or ten minutes, but a horrifying new thought gradually crept over me. I was not worried about Kristin – I believed she still existed, just in a different way now, and the pain she endured at the very end was over. But what about my parents and me? I began, for the first time, to come to the realization that this was a turning point in our lives. Things would never be the same. Was this the end of any semblance of a happy, fulfilling life? Was this the beginning of a dark new reality where life would be nothing but a sad, empty, deformed version of what it once was – a life that my parents would have to live for another 30 or 40 years? That I would have to live from the age of seventeen until the end of my miserable life?

Just about as soon as those thoughts filled my head with a future of misery and hopelessness, they were met with equal and opposing force by a new thought that formed: it was *my decision* whether or not this event would bring about such a future. The darkness, the hopelessness were not certainties – rather, they were only certain if I settled for the nearest, most obvious interpretation I could grasp of the event, namely, that this was "the beginning of the end". I decided in that moment not to settle for that. It was *up to me* to interpret what this event would mean for my life, going forward. Furthermore, it was *up to me* to decide if I would be controlled by it, or if I would find a way to become stronger as a result of it. Maybe I could even go a step further and find a way to harness its power, kind of like jujutsu, to become a better person and live a more intentional life than I otherwise would have. I don't know if those thoughts came to me from Kristin, from a higher power, or from a lucky firing of neurons at just the right time in my brain, but they have been critical in shaping the trajectory of my life since that day. It actually only occurred to me now, as I write this, that what seemed like an absurd, trivial decision that I couldn't comprehend in the funeral director's office, directly led to making perhaps the most important decision of my life only a few moments later.

We live in a world rife with judgment, canned narratives, and other noise. Maybe it's not so different than it's ever been in human history, but I tend to think that the deluge of entertainment media and the life-enveloping nature of social media have made it that much more difficult for us to think for ourselves and interpret the world independently. We're surrounded by simple narratives ("Bob got a new car!" – great, fun, smiley + celebration emojis…. "Patty broke up with her boyfriend" – sad, aww, crying emoji) that are too easy to adopt as lenses for assessing our own lives. It is all too easy to view life using the lens through which you think the rest of the world would see it: *something terrible happened to me, so now my life must be terrible*. Resist that interpretation.

I don't pretend to think that every person facing a tragedy or crisis can avoid pain and suffering. My family and I have suffered greatly. That being said, if you are one of these people, I urge you to believe that you have the authority to decide *what it means in your life*, even if simply to decide that *it will not destroy you*. That decision can have a powerful impact on the long-term severity of your suffering and the degree to which you can find happiness and fulfillment again one day.

It did so for me.

The Curtain Falls on Another Year

Two and a half years after Kristin's death, the aftershocks have settled down somewhat. "What happened" has been studied thousands of times, and it never makes sense.

It cannot make sense.

The "what-ifs" and "if-onlys" have been exhausted and vaporized into nothingness. There is only one outcome. The murder that happened.

Anger and revenge, those deceptive twins, are sure to promise more pain and trouble. I admit they sometimes pass through my mind. There will be anger but never revenge. We need to be looking forward.

The friends, family, and acquaintances who acted to help put out this fire in our lives will forever be in our debt. They did what we needed.

Our daughter's foundation was small but determined. *Kristin's Krusade* 5K Run/Walks took place yearly and brought awareness to thousands in time. Our knowledge and passion influenced others.

I hope our ability to stand strong and speak out against dating violence—by explaining what it is, how it happens, and how to avoid it—will always be our superpower. I hope that together we can transform the lives of innocent young adults among us. Not just women, but men as well.

Our tragedy, so unimaginable at its outset, could become a kind of resurrection for Kristin. This could be her phoenix rising from the ashes. With firm resolve, with enough time and effort, maybe a new legacy lies ahead for young Kristin Mitchell.

To move Kristin's story from unfortunate victim to the face of a cause is what we have in mind. Kristin did not fit neatly into stereotypes about domestic violence, and that is important. That is part of the power of her story. The stereotype was flawed.

Kristin's tragedy was completely unexpected. She was healthy, educated, clean-living, and from a nice family in a good neighborhood. She went to parochial elementary and high schools and a private university. She landed a sought-after job and was about to start an associate job with General Mills. Everything was all neat and tidy before the disaster happened.

Kristin was a trusting person who met the wrong guy. Like most of her contemporaries, she was never taught about the warning signs, or "red flags," of dating violence. She didn't know there were ways to break up with someone safely. So, she paid with her life.

This doesn't need to be the case for others.

A Dream Like No Other

Dreams have their own schedules. Whoever controls the showtimes isn't known, but it's not me. The following dream sequence, in content, style, and delivery was stunning.

I was in a crowded marketplace with people passing by in an ambiance of commotion. Within that busy flow, one person approached me. It was not my eyes but my subconscious that recognized her.

It was Kristin but not the Kristin Mitchell I knew at twenty-one. This was a much more grown-up Kristin Mitchell.

"Dad ..." was all she needed to say.

I was caught off guard. I hadn't seen her in over fourteen years. I instinctually gave a hug hoping it would make up for the thousands we missed.

As people busied about, we turned and walked. It really was Kristin. Close to how I remembered her. But more mature.

"Dad, everything you knew about June 3, 2005, was correct but with one big exception. I never died."

Somehow, despite a preponderance of life-stealing wounds, and a near-total depletion of her life energies, she had held on. Within a state of medical shock, and time decelerating to a crawl, she was permitted to ask God for one request.

"God offered me an alternative ending.

"He said, 'You have asked me to protect you, and I am doing that now. Come with Me at this time, or come with Me later. It is entirely your choice ...'"

In the early hours of that June 3 morning, Kristin's murderer asked a friend to drive him to a hospital to receive medical attention for multiple self-inflicted wounds. Upon his arrival, he apprised the ER staff about what happened to Kristin. Police bolted to the Riverwalk Apartments. Vital signs taken at the scene indicated she had, indeed, expired.

Well, not quite.

"They had a team of doctors on standby for cases like mine. People who were near death, but somehow clinging to life ..."

The interval separating Kristin's "death" in Pennsylvania and her funeral home viewing in Maryland was extended several days to allow for the creation of a replica—a figure of Kristin believable to family and friends. It worked. There was a viewing and a burial, but it was nowhere near the end for her.

The team that attended to Kristin accepted her as their own daughter. An exhaustive process commenced with the intention of returning her to the closest version of herself. Life-threatening wounds were repaired along with early stages of plastic surgery. She had a protracted road ahead of her.

For this "rebirth," Kristin was slowly being prepared to return to her friends, family, and a substitute version of her life. Focused physical and occupational therapies delivered a range of motion and strength doctors approximated to be a match for she enjoyed before the attack. She also needed to be psychologically ready to place herself in what would be a shock to both herself and her family. It took a decade and a half.

She was now nearly thirty-six.

Psychotherapists explained to her that some individuals have extraordinary in-born protective factors which enable them to cope with trauma that would destroy most people. Kristin was still that strong-willed girl, and more than anything, she wanted to live.

Her inner toughness saved her. We always knew it would pay off. She simply needed to wait until it was time. Now is the time for her return.

The person standing before me was Kristin. She looked and sounded like her. Older and, understandably, more reserved. We smiled while my thoughts turned to telling Michele and David. We would be united again. We would be four.

Then the dream ended as dreams do.

I remained in bed and replayed the fantasy. It was so real, I wondered if it was trying to tell me something. How amazing to be seeing Kristin alive again.

She really was with me. We will reunite in time.

Dating Violence Touches Everyone

A couple of years ago, I was asked to give a series of presentations about dating violence at various branch offices of a large utility company.

As part of my introduction, the company vice president would begin my intro with words like, "I thank God every day I've never had dating or domestic violence touch any members of my family, but seeing the statistics, there is a good chance it might have touched some of yours."

Knowing one in three women suffer serious violence in their lifetimes from an intimate partner, I imagined some of the audience members had already experienced it.

Before my final presentation, the room was packed with seventy strong men and women, the ones who operated heavy equipment and handled emergencies all hours of the day and night.

This time, the VP ended my introduction quite differently.

"At this point in my introduction, I used to say how thankful I was my family had never been touched by dating violence. Well, I cannot say that any longer. It's not true.

"At a recent family gathering at my parents' house, I told my sister how we were putting intense focus on dating violence here at work. I told her what I'd learned from these meetings. She reminded me of a guy she dated in high school, twenty years ago. I remembered him.

"She asked if I recalled the way he constantly gave her expensive gifts. I used to think he had money and just liked her a lot. No. These gifts were to make up for him physically abusing her. This guy was violently abusing my sister, and I didn't know about it until now. Twenty-plus years later."

Dating violence is everywhere.

So That's It?

We've all heard the tired old line, "Time heals all wounds." All wounds? Don't believe it.

Our family has learned how to wear our wounds over time. They are part of who we are. We will never accept what happened to Kristin, especially the obscenely brutal way it took place. It is sickening to know the child you cherished for almost twenty-two years was taken away like that.

We have learned to lessen some of our pain by forcing ourselves to look forward, not back. Although looking ahead, we miss the future ripped away from us that June 3 morning. Our family will keep her close in our hearts, minds, and lives.

Holidays afford us an awfully long time to reflect upon the past and our altered present. Holidays become annual emotional beatings. We would prefer to zoom past Thanksgiving, Christmas, and New Year's. Everyone else wants to slow these down, make merry, and give details about their children and grandchildren.

These are Kryptonite to us. We cannot help but make comparisons.

A useful way to allay our grief has been to keep busy. It temporarily gets our minds off our situation. We are also greatly lifted when we meet people who have been influenced by the work we have done in Kristin's name. This has happened often, and it's energizing. It proves our efforts are paying off in improving lives.

Thank you for reading this book.

I hope When Dating Hurts has opened your eyes to the truth about dating violence and what can happen when someone is not prepared. Awareness is a huge first step toward becoming safe and avoiding potential danger.

We were caught off guard. You don't have to be.

RECOLLECTION

Caitlyn's Story

I was the keynote speaker in November 2009 at Montgomery County Community College in Rockville, Maryland. Their "Choose Respect" conference drew an auditorium filled with high school students, college undergrads, and parents.

I always arrived at presentations an hour early to be certain the technology was set up and working. Thirty-five minutes prior to the start of my speech, someone walked up from behind me and asked, "Excuse me. Are you Bill Mitchell?"

I turned to find a woman who was probably in her late twenties. A cute, young girl of eight or nine was clinging to her arm.

"I was hoping it was you." She looked relieved. "I've wanted to meet you for a long time. I don't know if you remember me. I'm Caitlyn. You helped save my life."

All I could say was, "I did? I what? When did I do that?"

Caitlyn answered, "I called you. I told you what was happening to me with my husband. You said I needed to get out at the first chance. You talked about your daughter, Kristin."

Without any urging, Caitlyn told me her story. I don't know if there is such a thing as a "classic" domestic violence account, but her narrative would make Stephen King cringe.

She and her husband met when she was in college. She was twenty-three. He was tall, handsome, and quite strong. Caitlyn was a nursing student. He was divorced with four sweet daughters. He told Caitlyn he couldn't deal with his wife any longer because of her recurrent drug and mental health issues. He was able to keep the four girls.

For Caitlyn, this felt like a ready-made family.

In the beginning, she loved him and was prepared to spend her life with him. He seemed like a wonderful father but had a little bit of a temper. He would get mad and start yelling every now and then. Soon, he started to throw things when he was angry. His behavior escalated into controlling her and her friends. He forced Caitlyn to quit her job and end her nurse's training. He controlled not only who she spoke with but what she spoke about. It progressed into physical violence and constant verbal abuse.

What Caitlyn told me perfectly fit the template every abuser uses. The relationship felt like a fairy-tale romance at the start. Soon after, she became isolated from her friends and family members. She was threatened with violence, and finally, she received hard physical violence.

Over the three years of her marriage, Caitlyn gave up her dreams of a nursing career, and they had a son. She was frequently injured by her husband and needed to stay home to heal. He did not want her going into an ER for fear the staff would figure out what he did to her.

What she told me next, I will never forget.

In August of 2006, in the marriage's third year, he beat her unconscious with a rock they kept on a glass coffee table. That was after smashing the coffee table to pieces. He did this in front of all five children.

He thought she was dead, so he loaded her into the trunk of his Hummer SUV and drove to his mother's wooded property with the intention of burying her. He told all five children he was going to kill them too but changed his mind. But then he said he would only bury his baby son and wife so they could be together because she was his mother.

He dug a deep hole and put them both into it.

Then he shoveled on dirt.

"We were buried alive. He buried me and our two-year-old son."

As I listened to her, I visualized every gruesome torment, the deep misery, and a man's unearthly evil as it played out. I was listening to someone who should have been dead. I pictured Caitlyn and her baby boy lying in that cold grave.

She awakened when the cold dirt brought her back to consciousness. He pulled her out of the hole and began to attack her again. She begged him not to kill her, swearing she would never tell anyone what he did. He knew she could take care of her latest injuries at home as she always did before.

She begged to be left alive. No one would ever find out.

"My husband tried to kill me, and he thought he did. I was given another chance to live. God gave me another chance. For a week after he buried me, the children and I were held hostage at gunpoint in our home."

Obviously, she left him. But how?

One day, while her husband had fallen asleep, she snatched his cell phone, hid in a closet, and called me at work.

"Bill, you spoke about Kristin, and that it could be me one day. You said I could get help but I had to take the first step and leave. My husband awoke, and our phone conversation was cut short."

Caitlyn asserted that it took the strength of Kristin's story to push her to take action.

"Three days later, police came to our house looking for my husband who had outstanding traffic tickets. They arrested him. It gave me the opportunity to leave. I took my chance and left everything behind. I started over with my children and the support of my sister and mother."

Listening to Caitlyn's story in the auditorium where I was about to start my speech within minutes, with her voice breaking, she said, "I just thought about Kristin. I thought *that could be me.* I mean, one day, it could be my mom or sister telling the story about me being dead. After I called you, I gathered up enough strength. I got that extra reality check, that extra strength to know *I HAD to leave.*"

I checked my watch. It was less than ten minutes before the start of my speech. Besides my head throbbing, I felt as if I was running a fever.

"Caitlyn, please. Stop. I need to give a speech in a few minutes. Right now, I can barely breathe."

I promised we would speak when the speech was concluded.

I darted into a men's room and splashed cold water over my face, getting it on my suit, shirt, and tie. I groaned into the mirror, "What is happening? What is going on?"

I never anticipated someone like Caitlyn and her ordeal—so raw and distressing. How can this happen to someone so lovely and innocent? How did she survive? I wanted to help people with speeches and good acts in Kristin's name. But I was met with more than I could handle.

Something else bothered me. I was unable to remember Caitlyn's call. She was 100 percent certain it was me. How could I not remember that? With the insane trauma she experienced, there must have been PTSD and other complications.

After my speech, Caitlyn found me again. She was certain she called Bill Mitchell, the father of Kristin. She would not budge on that.

Caitlyn pointed to a woman in a business suit. Diana, a lawyer who specialized in family law, had guided Caitlyn to safety when her nightmare was still unfolding. I asked Diana about Caitlyn's recollections.

Diana insisted, "Mr. Mitchell, I can't say I recall hearing your name, specifically, but Caitlyn's got one of the finest memories I have ever known. She remembered every detail of her case. Every date, every punch, every broken bone, every awful moment. She never forgot one thing. So, if Caitlyn said it was Bill Mitchell, it probably was Bill Mitchell."

Eleven years after meeting her, Caitlyn and I have remained in touch. She told me she didn't want to give me details about her situation on our call because she was afraid I would search for her. If her husband found out she had contacted anyone about the abuse, it could have been fatal for her and her children.

She was certain I told her she needed to find a way to escape. To this day, she remains absolutely certain it was me.

After all she has been through, I truly believe her.

DATING VIOLENCE

Trying to Understand Dating Violence

Kristin wanted to break up with her boyfriend. I was told they had mini-breakups before, but this one appeared to be the end. She took back her keys and security card from him. It could have been a peaceful ending.

Only three weeks prior, she graduated from college with a food marketing degree and would soon be training as a sales associate with General Mills. She appeared to be set and ready. She apparently did not envision him in her plans any longer.

He didn't see it that way.

Kristin knew what was working in her life and what was not. One aspect not working well was the relationship with her boyfriend. It rarely ran smoothly. What was more bothersome than anything was his inclination to control every aspect of her daily life. His jealousy was annoying. Kristin's friends saw it and pleaded with her to "get some space" and understand him for the overbearing person he was. Her final emails to me, her father, indicated she was reaching the breaking point.

With this relationship suffocating her, at no time was it more on display than during her last full day alive, June 2, 2005. In the early hours of the following morning, June 3, while in her apartment—and with only her boyfriend present, an argument ensued when she tried to get him to leave. It escalated, became violent, and he murdered her.

How does an unhealthy relationship form in the first place? How can you detect it? And what do you do if it's happening?

There are warning signs, both physical and emotional, along with recognizable patterns that can signal to the person being abused that they are living within a potentially dangerous time, and they seriously need to consider safe alternatives.

Power and Control

I will share invaluable information I have gained from conversations with domestic violence counselors, prosecutors, parents of murdered daughters, and of course, victims and survivors.

These people know this nightmare. They have stared into its ugly face. For them and me it is an ongoing education.

One central explanation for dating abuse: it is all about power and control. Once you know that, everything falls into place.

I do not believe my daughter was in a physically violent relationship. Kristin was a peaceful person, and violence terrified her. But dating abuse does not need to be physical to exist. And the murder this book discusses started with one person's emotional grip and unstoppable manipulative personality. His power and control needed to win at all costs.

Dating violence (often interchangeably referred to as dating abuse, intimate partner violence, and relationship abuse) is one person successfully controlling another person. It is that simple. Although violence sometimes seems like the wrong term for it, *violence* is one person forcing their will (their power) over someone else.

Dating violence represents patterns of behaviors over a period used to exercise power and control over a partner (the abused). Offensive words, mannerisms, and actions are the means an abusive partner uses. Relationships differ, but what unhealthy and abusive relationships have in common are issues of power and control.

Dating violence is manifested in many ways and does not always appear obvious or alarming to the receiver. Here is a simple example of power and control.

You are sixteen. Or you could be twenty-four. Age does not matter. You are a woman shopping with your girlfriends or family. You are not with your boyfriend (or partner) who is typically very controlling. You told him earlier you would see him in a few hours. For most people, that would suffice.

But, while you are shopping, he texts: "Where are you?!"

You text back: "At the mall like I told you. At Macy's."

Not good enough for him. He wants you to prove it.

He texts back: "Get a photo of the Macy's sign and text it back right now."

Maybe that will make him happy, so you do it. Whether it quiets him down or not, you did what he commanded. In doing so, you showed you are under his power and control.

He barked, and you jumped.

That example can appear innocent. Nobody was hurt, but when it happens frequently, it is a pattern. Patterns add up to hard-core abuse. Patterns can indicate warning signs.

The man who killed my daughter used classic abusive behavior: power and control along with manipulation. He used rewards, punishments, and various mind games.

What are some examples?

He suggested Kristin should lose weight. He wanted to see if she would comply. So, she lost some weight. When she lost the weight, he acted bothered and then asked if she was seeing someone else. Control, manipulation, and mind games.

He bought Kristin meals morning, noon, and night. Later, he reminded her of all he had done for her. It was as if she owed him, and he wanted to be paid back somehow. He tried to buy her loyalty and gain power over her.

He asked Kristin's friends if they liked him. He urged them to tell Kristin they liked him because he knew that would help him. One of Kristin's friends said she had been around him less than an hour when he asked for this. She thought his request was weird.

Power and control.

That is what dating abuse is about.

Libby's Story

A few years back, I met Libby, a young woman in her early thirties. What made Libby's story so compelling?

She had previously been in an unhealthy relationship that had many of the classic dating violence warning signs I discuss in this book. One facet of her story jumped out at me. The abusive guy Libby dated—and broke up with—murdered his next girlfriend.

I asked her to write how it felt when she dated someone like this. I wanted to include this in my speeches given to high school students, college undergrads, and associates working for private companies.

This is Libby's true story:

"I think if I could say anything about abuse it would be that it starts off slow, and before you know it, you are in an abusive relationship. I grew up as the only girl around several brothers. I was tough, and I could definitely hold my own.

"I was the first to say when something was wrong and was always standing up for myself. I wouldn't take crap from anyone. Ever. It was almost a joke. I mean, my girlfriends would always say, if there was a fight, they would just stand behind me and let me take care of it.

"It was this way in every aspect except when it came to him. I didn't even realize it was happening until I was so far into it. He was a sweet talker. He showed me so much attention and made me feel like a princess.

"He showered me with extravagant gifts—multiple designer handbags, diamond earrings, and a ring. After our first date, he sent me two dozen roses at work. It was like I had found the most incredible man. It was good for a few months, but slowly, the mental abuse started.

"He would say things like, 'You look so ugly in the morning.' Or, 'People always wonder why I'm with you.' At first, the comments were so random and few and far between that I would just figure he had a bad day, or I misheard him, or he didn't mean it that way.

"Soon though, it was pretty constant.

He would say I was fat or that I wasn't pretty. It started to wear me down to the point where I fully believed him. Even now, more than ten years later, I still believe some of the things he would say to me, even though I know in my heart they aren't true.

"He constantly accused me of cheating on him. I would have my phone on me at all times so he could check in with me. I felt nervous if I was out without him because it was a guaranteed argument.

"He never did hit me, but he did pin me up against a wall once. That was as far as the *physical* abuse went. The *mental* abuse was brutal though. He got in my head and wore me down to nothing. When I eventually got out, I was a shell of who I was.

"My parents put me into therapy, but as I said, there are certain things I still haven't gotten back. I still see the 'flaws' that he used to point out. I don't think I will ever fully recover from what he did, but that doesn't mean I don't try my hardest every day.

"Mental and verbal abuse are just as bad as physical. I wish I knew at the time that I was being abused."

Libby and I chatted both by phone and in person several times. She said, one time, her boyfriend bought her an expensive gift which she totally loved. He knew she loved it, so every time they had any kind of disagreement, he threatened to take it away. He actually did take it back once. You see, that's how it works. There are rewards and punishments.

I was so happy to know the relationship ended and that she put plenty of space between them when she had the chance. She was finally safe.

Considering what happened to the next woman that man dated, whom he murdered, Libby was fortunate. Today, she is happily married and has children. She still fears the man she once dated, even though he is serving a lengthy prison sentence.

The Warning Signs

The Kristin Mitchell Foundation wrote, refined, and distributed warning signs cards. Some recipients kept the cards in their wallets or cell phone protectors. Some hid them in their shoes so their abusers would not find them. They kept them handy.

We described dating violence red flags using everyday terms. Reading through this chapter, it's possible you will recognize many and may have witnessed a few. What follows are the *classic warning signs* of potential danger in a relationship.

PREVENTION AGAINST DATING VIOLENCE STARTS WITH EDUCATION

Dating violence does not have to be physical. It can also be oppressive, coercive, or controlling behavior. It typically escalates physically, emotionally, and sexually, regardless of gender or sexual orientation.

No one deserves to be abused. Learn more about dating abuse from the following organizations on their websites:

thehotline.org
breakthecycle.org
rainn.org

EXAMPLES OF ABUSIVE BEHAVIORS

Coercive and controlling behavior may be emotional, physical, or sexual. It can sometimes be difficult to recognize the signs of abuse. Common examples:

Emotional/Psychological Abuse
- Constant put-downs
- Controlling or dominant behavior
- Checking your cell phone or email w/o your permission

- Extreme jealousy or possessiveness
- Explosive temper
- Big mood swings
- Constantly checking up on you via calls or texts
- Financial control
- Making you feel that nobody else would want you
- Making you feel you can't do anything right
- Isolating you from family and friends
- Telling you what to do
- Preventing you from doing what you want to do

Physical Abuse
- Hitting, punching, biting, kicking, strangulation (any form of physical harm)

Sexual Abuse
- Forced sexual activity without consent
- Threatening, manipulating, or coercing you into sex
- Taking/distributing private pictures without permission

IF YOU HAVE A FRIEND WHO IS BEING ABUSED

- Don't ignore it
- Point out specific behaviors that concern you
- Be a good listener/don't judge
- Talk in private and keep what is said confidential
- Let your friend know you care and will be there whenever they want to talk
- Guide your friend to resources and phone numbers

SAFETY IS EVERYTHING

When a relationship is over, the risk of physical violence is at its greatest.
- **NEVER** break up in private!
- Break up in a public place or by phone
- Let trusted friends/family know
- Have a post-breakup safety plan
- If you're in any danger, call 911

IF YOU, OR A FRIEND, ARE IN AN UNHEALTHY RELATIONSHIP, GET ADVICE OR HELP

The following assistance lines are always confidential, and they are always open:
- National Domestic Violence Hotline: 800-799-SAFE(7233)
- Break the Cycle: breakthecycle.org 424-265-7346
- Love is Respect: loveisrespect.org 866-331-9474
- RAINN: rain.org 800-656-HOPE(4673)

Reactions to the Warning Signs

Warning signs are not proof of dating violence or abuse in a relationship. But these watch-outs are cautionary "red flags" of potential trouble. That is an important distinction. After I have discussed warning signs in speeches or conversations, the reactions have been striking.

One female university freshman in Philadelphia said, "That sounds like what my roommate's going through. I'll speak to her."

A waitress in a Southern Maryland diner told me, "My daughter's boyfriend does that stuff all the time."

A high school sophomore remarked, "I didn't know it was abuse until I heard your speech. Glad I broke up with him a few months ago."

A university junior in Maryland said, "I thought he was just being a jerk, but I think it was a lot more than that."

A businesswoman said, "I didn't think it would keep getting worse. I thought he'd stop like he said he would. But he never did."

I often hear reactions like these after I share the warning signs. People in relationships feel something is not right but cannot figure out what is happening. They feel emotionally off-balance but cannot figure out why. When they hear the warning signs, they begin to understand what was actually happening to them.

For those in the dark, the warning signs often help people get to the truth. They have felt manipulated like human puppets. Those who have experienced uncomfortable "red-flag moments" should seek professional help immediately.

A good start is to call the National Domestic Violence Hotline: 800-799-SAFE(7233). It is free. It is anonymous. It is helpful. Make time and make the call.

If You Think It's Dating Violence...

Do something!!! Put down this book. Right now.

In an unhealthy relationship, power and control over a partner (the abused person) takes time and focused efforts on the part of the controller (the abuser).

Success is accomplished only through a continuous series of actions that include rewards and punishments, all with precisely one goal: establishing who the boss is.

The abusive behavior is often subtle in the way it is handed out, so the victim (the abused person) does not draw conclusions or catch on. It can be a little at a time. It is often said, if an abuser acted on the first date the way he acted on the thirtieth date, no woman would ever accept a second date.

Abusive behavior sneaks up on people.

After reading the warning signs in a previous chapter, you could feel alarmed. That can be good if you treat them like a wake-up alarm. An alarmed person might begin to take the initial steps in helping themselves (or someone they know), especially when it feels like an unhealthy relationship.

Being alarmed can lead to becoming motivated. Motivation can lead to searching out information and finding safe solutions.

Getting information and finding safe solutions are critical.

It follows that breaking the grasp of an accomplished controller takes time and careful planning. To be safe, an abused person (and her trusted friends and family) should consult domestic violence counselors. Domestic violence counselors are trained to help. Use them!

The warning signs, shown on previous pages, include directions about finding counseling from experienced professionals. There are domestic violence units all over this country. Help is standing by.

A victim's safety is all that matters to counselors. They keep everything anonymous. They will not send police unless you specifically request them to do so. They know domestic violence situations are dangerous, and they act accordingly. They are careful.

If it is your friend, and she is afraid to call the National Domestic Violence Hotline number, maybe offer to make a call with her. She can hang up any time she wants. Just get the dialogue started.

The National Domestic Violence Hotline is ready for your call: 800-799-SAFE(7233). They take inquiries and ask questions that lead to solid directions that help. Start the conversation.

These professionals are there to help. Use them!

The Template All Abusers Follow

Unhealthy relationships are not formed on the first date. They take certain types of behavior that are manifested over time.

What helped me understand how unhealthy relationships develop was to see how each step fits precisely into a template.

I will explain this template, or formula, which I have presented to thousands of audience members during speeches. Not once has anyone told me this template was either incomplete or incorrect, so I assume it is accurate and useful.

This template has only six steps. In this discussion, please allow me to assume "you" are the abused person, and "he" is the abuser.

STEP 1.
FAIRY-TALE ROMANCE

He seems perfect. He treats you like a princess. He always gets the door. He takes you to restaurants that are an upgrade over those anyone has ever taken you to before. You get "two dozen roses at work," as Libby spoke about in a prior chapter. He seems to be the most fantastic guy. He is the embodiment of Mr. Right. This makes you feel good.

Who doesn't want to be treated nicely? Of course, you want to stay in this relationship.

STEP 2.
ISOLATION

It is not noticeable at first, but he wants to do things with you. Alone. Away from your friends and your family. "Let's make it just us," you might hear. It makes sense to you. You want to get to know each other better, right? Time together seems like a good thing.

Sometimes his comments about your friends let you know he doesn't care for some of them. He might feel the same about some, or all, of your family. You want him to be happy, so you keep others away now and then. You love them, but you also want this relationship to work. You feel the need to make some compromises. He comes first. Your friends are a close second but a very distant second in his mind.

He sometimes acts strangely around your friends. Or he might be obnoxious or off-putting. Maybe he is uncomfortable. If your friends tell you they don't like him, he isn't bothered by it because he doesn't want them around you anyway.

If you have outside interests, like clubs or a sport you enjoy, it is possible he will try to urge you out of participating in them. Another example could be when he "accidentally" bought tickets to a show the evening of your father's fiftieth birthday. He says, "Oops, it's *that* night? I already bought us tickets for that night." Uh-oh. Guess you will have to pick between your dad and this guy. And you assume dad will understand.

STEP 3.
THREATS OF VIOLENCE

These are the near-misses that signal what you did or said bothers him, and you need to change it or stop. You get reprimands like, "You know what? That really makes me angry!" (Said with plenty of emphasis.)

Maybe he slams his hand down within inches of you to show you he means business. It's clear: if things don't change, it could get worse.

He might say, "When you did that, I wanted to slap you." You're relieved he didn't. In his car, maybe he jams on the brakes so you nearly hit your head on the dash. That was close. You'd better be careful.

At first, it scares you. But you figure if you're more careful about what you say or do around him, maybe things might get better. You hope you can return to the fairy tale that made your heart flutter back in the beginning. You want peace, love, and harmony. You want him to be happy. So, you intend to try harder to improve next time.

STEP 4.
ACTUAL VIOLENCE

You are heading into dangerous territory here. Something happens, and he doesn't like it. So, maybe something you own gets thrown or broken. Your dog or cat gets hit or kicked. Or you get pushed hard enough for it to hurt. Maybe you receive a slap or a punch on the arm. Something that makes a point or leaves a mark. It doesn't take much violence to make his point.

The message is: what you did or what's going on isn't making him happy, and someone is going to pay for it. This punishment is a reminder about who the boss is. It won't be you if you stay in this relationship. In time, violence typically escalates. As you accept or get over what happens to you, you are granting him permission to take it up a level and do more.

It is terrifying, but as you read this, violence could be happening to a friend, a family member, someone in your neighborhood, or someone at your workplace. It can be slapping, shoving, punching, kicking, or strangulation. It is any form of physical harm.

STEP 5.
THE CONVINCING APOLOGY

This part is crucial to maintaining unhealthy relationships. It is when the abuser takes current and former storylines and weaves them together into a credible explanation for why he did what he did.

As an example, after a violent incident, a male high school senior might say to his girlfriend, "Look, I worked hard to make that team. I worked all summer running hills, lifting weights, and busting my butt. So, after the coach cut me and picked the same losers who were on that losing team last year, I lost it. I'm sorry I slapped you. Give me another chance. Please?"

A male sales associate who works in a private company just hit his wife. Afterwards, maybe he says, "That was bad. I apologize, okay? You see the kind of pressure I'm under. I've put in nights and weekends to make my boss look good, and guess what? He turns around in a meeting and takes all the credit. He never mentioned me once. It wasn't about you. It was about him. I'm sorry, okay? I will do better."

A fifty-year-old gay male might say to his partner, "I snapped, okay? Something that you did reminded me of the way my mother used to come after me. She was always putting me down, making me her whipping boy. Just making me miserable. She hated my father but took all of her problems out on me. It was like a flashback. Let's try and move on. Okay?"

STEP 6.
REPEAT STEP 1. THE FAIRY-TALE ROMANCE

You start over. This second time around, maybe some pricy jewelry comes your way. Or you get a handbag you mentioned that was out of your price range. Any little thing to take your mind off what happened to you back in STEP 3 (threats of violence) and STEP 4 (actual violence).

He might say, "We're both better than this, right? Let's stay at that charming B&B near that antique row, the one you liked with the big fireplace and the whirlpool. Remember the spa and breakfast they put out?"

You slowly heal emotionally and physically. While doing so, you think of why this relationship can still work. He has so many good qualities about him. You see in him what your friends cannot see. You might want to explain to your friends or family that they just don't see his good side as well as you do, and he's not what they think. Then the steps continue.

REPEAT STEP 2. ISOLATION ...

And on it goes through all of the steps again ...

Thoughts about Isolation

Along with power and control soon comes isolation. The abuser will try to invisibly fence his partner off from friends and family and previous outside activities.

It is only a matter of time. Here is an example.

Just after graduation, Kristin spent a few days with her mother at a Maryland beach. Kristin's boyfriend relentlessly called and texted to interrupt those days. He wanted her mind on him alone. Not even her mother. Kristin's mom suggested she turn off her cell phone. College was behind her, and this time away was for relaxation.

Kristin smiled at her mom. "Oh, he'll stop." But he didn't.

If a victim's family members and friends grow weary of what is going on and give up on her, it is a victory for the abuser. He actually wants them to go away. Isolation is his goal. Fewer family and friends mean less competition.

We learned too late that Kristin's boyfriend interrupted every single relationship she had, no matter who it was with.

Mentioned earlier in this book, Samantha and Kristin were to spend the three-day 2005 Memorial Day weekend at Samantha's parents' beach house on the Jersey shore. But Friday evening, an undercurrent of texts and emails from Kristin's boyfriend began arriving on her phone. His messages carried into Saturday. He used every tactic he knew to sink the women's plans together. By that afternoon, he had convinced Kristin she needed to be with him instead of Samantha. He drove to the Jersey beach house and removed Kristin from the weekend getaway.

It is a perfect example of an abuser's isolation technique.

The following day, Kristin and Samantha spoke by phone. Samantha was rightfully enraged. Later, Samantha could not recall who hung up the phone first, but that was the last time they talked. She remembers telling Kristin, "Don't you see? You need to get some space from this guy!"

Kristin tried later that week.

The Truth: 33%

This statistic is real: 1 in 3 women become victims of serious physical violence at the hands of an intimate partner within their lifetime. Typically, it occurs between the ages of 16 and 24.

Doesn't 33% seem impossibly high? That is a nationally recognized statistic. But shouldn't it be higher still? I don't believe all women report when they are injured. Do you?

I do not believe numbers move people to action, but I use the 33% statistic. Note how that number is followed by the words "typically, it occurs between the ages of 16 and 24." But it also happens to 12-year olds and 60-year olds. No matter what age, the template (the steps) described on preceding pages holds true.

Even if you have never experienced physical violence with an intimate partner, the emotional and psychological warning signs described on these pages must seem obvious. How does anyone misinterpret them as anything but serious trouble in a relationship? But people do not make connections between those signs and what could happen to them. These are supposed to be loving relationships, but you can see they are not.

Kristin's friends saw controlling and manipulative behavior in her relationship. They spoke with her. Nobody knew how dangerous it would become. And that is the scariest part: people do not know. If you are reading this book, you know!

Kristin's closest friends wanted to attempt some kind of an intervention that final June 3, 2005 weekend. They wanted her to get some space from this guy. To use that time to evaluate the pros and cons of dating this man. They were simply too late. She was killed early the morning of Friday, June 3.

The best of intentions, without proper guidance and education, might not be enough. Timing counts for a lot too. If something feels wrong, *you have to figure it is wrong*.

And do something.

Seek help!

It Is Intentional

For a while, I wondered if abusers do not know what they're doing. But I have read enough and have spoken with enough professionals to have an informed opinion.

Nobody mistakenly or accidentally manipulates, controls, or abuses another person for any period of time without intending to do so. It is deliberate. The notion that the abuser did not mean to be doing this is the biggest lie every abuser tells.

It is not true.

It is intentional.

It is unfortunate when victims believe the excuses they hear from abusers and remain in unhealthy relationships. Many abused women sympathize with their abusers and, in doing so, make matters worse. They enable more abuse. More, meaning more frequent abuse and more harmful. It is ironic.

Identifying ways to take advantage of other people is learned behavior on the part of an abuser. It is gained from employing various techniques on victims and seeing which ones are successful. Whatever works is used again and again.

If a manipulative technique does not achieve the effect an abuser wants, the abuser will typically punish the victim. It is trial and error, rewards and punishments. The abuser "trains" the abused.

It is absolutely intentional. I have no sympathy for abusers.

Breaking Up

A relationship breakup can be a sad thing.

But breaking up with a controlling and abusive person can be extremely dangerous. Most domestic violence homicides happen after the victim has ended the relationship. That could be immediately after the breakup or days after, or even weeks or months later. This is a scary truth.

If a person is in an intimate partner relationship with someone who is extremely controlling or abusive, breaking up with that person is potentially dangerous. It is the most explicit message that the control that the abuser had over the abused is threatened or broken.

You can see why it becomes so dangerous. It needs careful attention and planning. Start with good advice.

Get in touch with domestic violence counselors or call the National Domestic Violence Hotline: 800-799-SAFE(7233) and get professional coaching. Do not believe you already know enough about how to be careful.

It is your life. Get help.

One version of how to break up with someone who is so terribly controlling came from the prosecutor of Kristin's case. She said, "I'd call him up on a Friday using someone else's phone. Or a phone where you cannot be reached later. I'd break up quickly. I'd get out of town for the weekend. Better still, a whole week."

Getting out of town for a week is not practical for everyone, especially a high school student. But it is not wise to break up in private. Not when you are in a relationship with someone who is overly controlling. Unfortunately, my daughter did not know better.

But you do!

There is the issue of saying goodbye one last time.

No! Never do it. I have heard the stories.

Never see that abusive person ever again if possible. I met a woman who spoke at a domestic violence seminar. After breaking up, her ex-boyfriend begged to see her one last time. He said he just wanted to say goodbye properly. She trusted this was okay.

They chose a mall parking lot for this meeting. He got into her car, yelled at her, then pulled out a handgun and shot her in the face. After multiple surgeries and therapies, she could be counted among the lucky ones for surviving. She lived but was blinded in her left eye from the wound.

Women who allow their exes opportunities to see them one last time put themselves in harm's way.

This includes my daughter.

Gaslighting

Gaslighting describes a form of psychological abuse when a victim is gradually manipulated into doubting her own sanity. The manipulation is caused by an abuser executing a plan.

Gaslighting is derived from *Gaslight*, a 1944 mystery-thriller movie about a woman whose husband manipulates her into believing she is going insane. Today, gaslighting continues to be used to gain a psychological edge over a victim.

Signs of gaslighting can include causing someone to feel no longer like the woman she used to be. Or feeling more anxious/less confident than she used to be and feeling every single thing she does turns out wrong. It can also cause a woman to think that no matter what goes wrong, it must be her fault.

In time, this abused person can eventually feel off-balance. She might sense something is not right but is unable to figure it out.

These techniques were perpetrated on my cousin's daughter. She was married and had three sons. Her husband would find subtle ways to alter items around the home so she would think she was losing her mind. Before bedtime, she might lay out the next day's breakfast items. But they were not there the following morning. It was as if her mind was playing tricks on her. Or that she had become detached from reality.

It is understandable how a person would find it increasingly impossible to make sound decisions and, eventually, lack confidence in herself. She might give important decision-making over to her closest confidant, her abuser.

That is the goal for the abuser: absolute control.

People who gaslight become experts in pushing all the right buttons. They learn their partner's vulnerabilities and use those against them. A gaslighting campaign can make her doubt herself, her judgment, her memory, and even her entire being.

What are common methods of gaslighting? The abuser feels the need to change something about the victim. Maybe it is the way she dresses or acts. If the victim does not comply, the abuser may convince her she is not good enough for him.

Mind games used by abusers can be cunning and stealthy, like trivializing how the abused person feels and playing with her emotions. Maybe it is telling her that family members talk about her behind her back. Maybe it is denying things that were actually said or done and denying knowing about them.

Many people who gaslight others have narcissistic personality disorder. They believe they are extremely important and that the world revolves around them. They are self-absorbed and do not have time or interest in others unless it serves a direct purpose for them. They are not empathetic and do not have the ability to understand what another person is feeling or experiencing.

Gaslighting is a powerful weapon in an abuser's tool kit. Knowing that gaslighting exists helps all of us to be more aware.

What Is a Healthy Relationship?

An obvious question.

At some point, we have to ask ourselves, "What about healthy relationships? What are they like?"

Allow me to answer from what I have learned. Everyone deserves a healthy relationship safe from violence and fear. Violence and fear are the complete opposite of trust and love.

Healthy relationships consist of respect, support, honesty, and an overall sense of freedom of expression. They are held together by feelings of open communication and shared decision-making. Healthy relationships include active listening and talking about feelings.

Decision-making is not one-sided. Partners have an equal say in what is acceptable and what is not.

But all relationships must come with some caution. Protect yourself and your loved ones from an abusive situation by learning the warning signs that can steer you away from permanent harm. Warning signs can save you from misinterpreting someone's dominant behavior as love.

This kind of love is not healthy. In fact, it's not love.

It is unfortunate we need to think twice when someone acts really nice to us, but it is necessary. When someone's actions seem "too good to be true," they just might not be true. It can be a cruel world at times and being a little skeptical can help you, and others, remain safe.

I am a huge believer in happy endings. I have always been a romantic at heart. I hope you have found my daughter's story, and this book, helpful. I hope you never experience what we have.

If you find yourself in an unhealthy relationship, be sure you get help.

Questions for the Author

Q: Not many who experience such a devastating tragedy write a book about it. Why did you write this book?

A: As you can imagine, what happened to my daughter profoundly affected her family and friends. Everyone was emotionally damaged from this horrific loss. I felt I had the ability to help prevent this from happening to other people if I told the whole story. From what I have witnessed, lives have been made safer when people heard about Kristin. They identified with her and learned from what she and her friends did not know back then.

Q: There is such power in this story. Why is that?

A: Kristin is a real person, and her tragedy is real. Her story stops audiences when they hear what happened, especially *why it happened*. They see themselves, or their friends, in Kristin. She is accessible to them. Some speak of her in the present tense with words like, "Kristin has been so helpful to me." If it helps, I'm all for it. She has become as real to them as she is to my family and me.

Q: Was it emotionally taxing to write about this tragedy?

A: I've given over a hundred speeches about what happened, so this was not my first experience describing Kristin's story. But it was the first time writing a book about it in such precise detail. The parts that describe what she experienced when she was attacked were distressing to put into words, of course. Ultimately, putting this on paper was cathartic for me.

This story has power to help people. As a book, it stands to help more people than I could accomplish in any other way. It is positive for me to be able to share it.

Q: Many who knew Kristin were harmed by this tragedy. Have you remained in touch with them?

A: In terms of harm, yes, everyone who knew Kristin was challenged emotionally. She represented a stunning loss. She was a bright light in all of our lives, and people like that are often irreplaceable.

We met with many of Kristin's high school and college friends at either her viewing or funeral soon after this horrible event. Most college friends later participated in our *Kristin's Krusade* 5K Run/Walks during the eleven years we conducted those. I think we do a good job staying in touch, thanks to social media. I appreciate the way her friends keep Kristin's memory alive in everyone's mind and heart. She'll always mean so much to them.

Q: Have you forgiven the man who did this?

A: I have been asked this question after some of my speeches. I look at this way: it's his life, and it will be his afterlife at some point. He will have to answer for his actions, but he will not have to answer to me. Forgiveness is between him and his maker. I prefer to stay out of that whole area.

Q: If you had the opportunity to ask the man who killed Kristin one question, what would it be?

A: Shortly after her death, I would have asked why he did what he did in such a merciless manner. Today, I feel differently. I would probably ask, "Knowing that you murdered someone so innocent and so defenseless—and in such a horrible fashion—how can you live with yourself?"

Q: Are you considering writing other books on dating violence?

A: If there were another book or two on this subject, one could be about the influential women who give large portions of their lives to the domestic violence issue. Someone needs to showcase the heroic acts they perform every day. They are guardian angels, and they save lives.

Another book could focus on serial abusers. What is so frightening is how sociopaths can live with no regard for the emotions of others. Their lack of conscience is inconceivable to me.

Q: The story with the locket is fantastic and complicated. Do you think it was Kristin reaching out from *the Other Side*, as you call it?

A: Yes, I do think it was Kristin. Not sure how. It was probably Kristin with some divine intervention behind it. When I think about the degree of complication, and what it took for it all to play out, I believe Kristin was involved. This story captivates people like nothing I have ever seen. I still get shivers about what happened.

Q: The "Dear Kristin" journals, are you still writing them?

A: Not as much as I did in the beginning, but, yes, I still love to speak directly with Kristin through these journals. I'm so glad I started those. I like to read what was written during that first and second year. It helped me.

Q: You mostly focused on women as the abused persons or victims throughout your book. What was the reason for that?

A: No matter what research statistics I have seen, women are more frequently abused than men. The ratio is dramatic. So, I used that larger group. Also, this made a natural flow from Kristin's unhealthy relationship and tragedy to speaking about women in particular. This is not to say men are not abused both emotionally and physically, but those cases are far fewer. I must also mention that abusive partners in LGBTQ relationships use the same kinds of power and control tactics as in any unhealthy heterosexual relationship.

Q: How is your family doing these days?

A: Time changes the hurt, but it's not going away. I'd say it hurts as much as ever; it just hurts differently. We think about Kristin every day. It doesn't take much to be reminded of her, then our emotions rush in, and we are hit hard by her loss.

We miss Kristin the most around the holidays and her birthday. But the date that gets the most attention is June 3, the day she died. That's the way it is. We try our best to focus on the good things in life that still lie ahead of us; not what happened in 2005.

Q: What are your expectations for this book?

My family and I believe this book will help people. We have accumulated powerful knowledge and advice. We felt it was time to share it. A large quantity of information in this book has been dispensed already in my speeches. I see how it helps encourage awareness and offers real steps to safer lives.

This book was the best way to crystalize what happened to our family and maybe move to some version of closure. I get no greater pleasure than when someone tells me they heard what we presented and are in a safer and happier state of life.

I have had women tell me they sought marriage counseling after hearing me speak. They didn't realize their marriages were so unhealthy until my speeches struck a nerve in them. In some cases, their spouses were not able to improve, and the results were divorce. They could not wait to tell me they were much happier.

Q: Besides publishing *When Dating Hurts*, what else are you doing for the dating violence cause?

I'm on the board of Clery Center (Strafford, PA). Clery's the leader in partnering with universities to create safer campuses. We launched *"Kristin's Krusade,"* an initiative focused on dating violence. We use the same name as my previous foundation's 5Ks.

With the publication of this book I will be looking to do TV, radio and podcast interviews; publishing newsletters; and maintaining a blog. I do my best to keep connected with domestic violence professionals to stay on top of the latest understandings about the dating violence issue.

Q: Any final thoughts?

I urge people to believe the truth about the prevalence of dating violence. We can never be too careful. Read through and accept the warning signs seen in this book. They are real, and they can be clues to danger in the works. One day you will definitely be in a position where you witness something that feels like an unhealthy relationship. Then it's up to you to do something.

Reactions to Bill's DV Speeches

Dear Bill,

Thank you for your connection. I just wanted to say thank you for what you do. Your daughter Kristin's story was my inspiration not only to leave my abusive boyfriend but to start my work to help others to leave their abusive relationships. I graduated from Saint Joseph's University in 2014 and my long term boyfriend that I had dated during this time, was emotionally and physically abusive, but it was not until I heard about your daughter and what she went through that I really came to understand that. I graduated from the University of Pennsylvania last year and one of my graduate internships was at the Penn Women's Center where I worked with other students who had been affected by relationship and domestic violence. I then brought this program over with me to my next job at a smaller college that really had no work being done in regards to dating violence and I know that in the time that I was there, I was able to help dozens of students.

I just really wanted to say thank you. I'm sure you hear stories like this all the time. But I know that without the work that your family has done around your daughter's tragedy, I would be in a much worse place right now, and I know I would not have been able to touch as many lives as I have around these same issues.

Bill I can't thank you enough! Not only for coming to Virginia to share your story with our team, but for also impacting my life in such an incredible way! I am on a mission to get this out to more of our associates. I'm anxious to hear some feedback from our team that was down there.

Again, thank you for everything!

Wawa note

Hi Mr. Mitchell, My name is ▓▓▓ and I'll be a sophomore at Saint Joe's next year. I'm in Alpha Phi and was at your talk and Kristin's Krusade. I know you probably get messages like these a lot, but I just had to tell you the way Kristin and your family impacted my life.

Let me be frank and say that I have never told anyone this, as I am a very open person but avoid details of my past that make me emotional. Until the summer before my senior year, boyfriends were never part of my life. My friends admired my independence and determination for success; however, by the end of my senior year, I had few friends, let alone ones that could admire any aspect of my personality-which become a stranger to anyone who had known me only a couple months before.

His name was Tim and everything that I loved about him, in hindsight, was pure manipulation and disrespect. Every characteristic (besides violence-but who knows what the future could have held) you stated during your speech perfectly described his controlling and over-bearing personality which turned me into a liar for the first time in my life and someone who I never wish to be again. The part that astounded the most was when you described the constant texts and calls with no time for family and friends-that was my life. Thankfully, my mom forced me to completely remove him from my life after a year of pure hell (dating on and off, lying to my mom and her having no trust in me, losing almost every friend I had, etc). A piece of me still was angry at her and cared for him until the night you spoke. I don't hate him but his irrelevance in my life is a gift I want to thank you for.

After that day, I never had the urge to text him or look him up on any of his social media. Places, music, and memories that we once shared no longer affect me when I come across them. Although we have never met, I want to thank you for helping me find myself again and to simply be happy. Until I transferred to Saint Joe's halfway through my freshman year this past fall, I haven't felt that continued true happiness since my junior year of high school and I'm at fault.

Thank you again from the bottom of my heart and I hope to meet you at Kristin's Krusade next spring.

Mr. Mitchell,
Thanks so much for sharing this with me. I recently graduated from Saint Joseph's University and attended your speech there last year with my sorority (Alpha Phi) . Also, as ironic as it sounds, I just realized as I am typing this that under my sweatshirt I am wearing my Kristin's Krusade Tshirt. I wanted to say how truly inspiring you (and your family) are. The legacy that you are building to commemorate your daughter is so beautiful and the awareness that you are creating for the cause is inspiring. Thank you for sharing your amazing words, I look forward to reading more.
Sincerely,
▓▓▓

> Hi Bill,
>
> Thank you for speaking last week. My friend did come with me! Although she didn't see a clear connection between her boyfriend and the talk, I think it shows that she is willing to talk about it with me. I believe the open line of communication is important, so that any future events and warning signs, I will feel comfortable having a conversation with her.
>
> Thank you for all you do!

> **I came and saw your lecture when you came to Saint Joseph's University earlier this year. Such a beautiful message, thank you for spreading awareness and tips. You're saving lives – Thank you!**

> Hello! My name is ▓▓▓▓▓ I am a marketing major at Saint Joseph's University and a member of the Alpha Phi sorority. I have participated in Kristin's Krusade the last three years and am reaching out to this organization because I would love to assist even more with this cause. My older sister who means the world to me was in an unhealthy abusive relationship. It started off as emotional abuse, which ultimately escalated to it becoming physical and the need to contact police. I thank god everyday that she escaped that relationship and I am so sorry about what happened to Kristin. That being said I would love to use my marketing and advertising education to help with this cause. If this organization had any volunteering opportunities that included marketing/advertising such as social media use, creating flyers, or even just getting the word out. Please let me know and I look forward to assisting in any way. Thank you!
>
> You can reach me on Facebook, or my email is ▓▓▓▓▓

Sent: Friday, March 31, 2017 3:13 PM
To: Bill Mitchell
Subject: Re: Hello from Bill Mitchell

Dear Mr. Mitchell,

I was so flustered and full of emotion after your talk and after meeting you and your lovely wife that I forgot to thank you both for all you do. I can't imagine that doing these talks and everything else you guys do is a cup of tea or walk in park but I just wanted to thank you guys for being so brave in doing so. I didn't know Kristin but coming from someone who went thru similar abuse, I can truly tell you how proud she is watching over you all and the closure you have given me and I'm sure many other survivors.

For me, the hardest part of the aftermath of the abuse is the feeling of still being isolated. I was isolated physically from friends and loved ones during my relationship but now I sometimes feel emotionally isolated. I feel alone even in a crowded room sometimes or even when I'm surrounded by my amazing and supportive family because it feels like no one understands what my abuser did to my emotions. Hearing your talk and speaking with both of you took some sort of weight off my chest that has been holding me down for two years and I can't express how much I appreciate it.

Also, I forgot to tell you that my mother gave me a bracelet after I went thru everything. It was the same quote you used at the end of your presentation. It's my personal favorite and I wear it everyday as a reminder of my strength. *"You are Braver than you believe, Stronger than you seem, and Smarter than you think."*

My parents and I will be in attendance at the 5k and look forward to seeing you both. Please let me know if there's anything I can do to help and be involved.

Thank you so so so much for you kind words and taking the time to reach out to me.

Like your Kristin said, "I cried a little...but I won't cry forever."

Thank you so much again from the bottom of my heart,

Hi Mr. Mitchell

I had the opportunity to hear you speak at our Berwyn office last year and was very saddened by the loss of your daughter and the tragic circumstances of losing her at such a young age. You are truly an amazing person to be able to take such a tragic event and share with others to prevent other families from suffering a similar loss.

I read the pages of your book and the whole time I wanted to know more about this amazing young woman the beautiful face and the smile of an angel. I wanted to read about how she came to be this incredible person that affected so many people in such a positive way. I wanted to hear in your words how you came to love your child so much and the painful void you carry today knowing that Kristin was robbed of a bright future. Every parent holds a secret dream of the life they want for their children.

What you have written so far took a lot of courage and as the mother of a 30-year-old daughter I can't imagine your courage and your strength. It must come from the love you have for Kristin. Hearing you speak and reading your story makes it clear that the bond the two of you shared will not be broken and that she has inspired you to save others from abuse.

> Hi there.
>
> Today, Kristin would have been 33. I'm so very sorry for your loss.
>
> I've followed the Kristin Mitchell Foundation, read the posts, have heard the grief over the years. And until recently, I've been a victim of emotional abuse, control, threats of physical violence, etc. from my soon to be ex husband.
>
> Seeing Kristin's beautiful smile, hearing her story.....it's one of the things that has helped me find the courage to say no. I don't deserve this kind of life. I deserve so much more. My children deserve so much more. Kristin's story helped me take the first steps I needed to, when I was so scared to do so.
>
> It's a private story, but when I saw that today would have been her birthday... I just wanted to share with you that your words and her story have helped change my life.
>
> That's all for now. Must get to bed. I hope my words fill you with happiness tonight, knowing that you have helped me. That Kristin has helped me.
>
> Xoxoxo and thank you.

From: ▇▇▇▇▇▇▇▇
Sent: Tuesday, April 25, 2017 10:30 AM
To: bill@billmitchellcreative.com
Subject: SJU Kristin's Krusade

Hi Mr. Mitchell,

My name is ▇▇▇▇▇▇▇▇ and I am a senior sociology and philosophy major at Saint Josephs's University and I am also a member of REPP. A few weeks ago I attended your talk on dating violence and attended Kristin's Krusade that Saturday. First of all, I would like to say that your courageous willingness to speak on this issue is not only admirable but also so impactful to so many young people who are struggling with domestic and dating violence.

During the time of your talk, I was dating a young man who I met online but I was unsure if I liked the path the relationship was taking. He was becoming increasingly manipulative and sneaky, and became angry and demeaning when I tried to explain to him that I did not like the way he was treating me. Though I recognized these behaviors as odd and off-putting, it was not until your talk that I realized that this is dating violence. I admit that I was becoming fearful when I was around him, as if I was walking on eggshells in order to not upset him, but I did not know how to handle the situation. Your talk gave me the courage to go home that night, send him a text to never speak to me again, and block his cell phone number. Not surprisingly he did not take the news well and came back at me with mean text messages, but that does not even matter because he is out of my life for good and I no longer have any connection or contact with him.

I would just like to thank you for asking the question, "Is this really the best you can do in a relationship?" This question made me realize that I do not deserve this treatment and there will be someone else out there who treats me with the respect I deserve. I will also be passing this information on to all of my friends, sister, and anyone else who is experiencing the trauma of dating violence.

I apologize for this email coming so late! I am finishing up my senior year of college and things have been hectic but I wanted to make sure I wrote this to you and Mrs. Mitchell.

So, please continue your work and know that you are creating positive change for so many young women. I am sure Kristin is very proud.

Thank you and have a nice week,

▇▇▇▇▇▇▇▇

Reactions to Early Drafts of this Book

Hello Bill,

I just read this. I am speechless. Tears are still rolling down my cheek. You can truly see the heartbreak, confusion, and numbness that you felt. I have never read anything that touched me this deeply. I am amazed by the strength of you, your wife, and your son.

You are such an incredible father. I can't even imagine the stress it takes to write this series. The fact that you have dedicated your life to ending dating violence is magnificent. You are a very special person and I feel grateful to have connected with you.

I would be honored to work with you and help your foundation in any way I can. Your message needs to be brought out into the world and I know it will. Yes, we will absolutely stay in touch.

Thank you again for sharing this with me.

I read every word. I never do that. There is not anything coming to my mind except, I am very moved. The fact that you do what you do helps me realize how strong you and your wife are. I am blessed to know you Bill. I am calm, my mind, not racing, not worried, not wondering about tomorrow. Just hoping that Heaven is all that I hope that it is, even more for your family, than for me.

8:57 pm

Bill,

Thanks for continuing this story.
So much of what happens after a tragedy is invisible, and so many people are affected unexpectedly. We need these stories.

> Dear Bill,
>
> I am overwhelmed. My heart hurts, I feel sick to my stomach.
>
> Yes...there is so much work to be done.
>
> Heading to mass and looking for God to give me some thoughts. Please give me a call this week.
>
> Peace ♥

> Bill,
>
> I started reading and couldn't stop. The detail is amazing. In future installments are you going to talk about the cellphone coincidence?
>
> I guess you will complete the locket part. In all conversations I'm not sure you ever told me about the light bulbs popping every night for almost two weeks.
>
> When my husband passed, my sister-in-law suggested I get an electrician since there must have been an electrical problem at my home. I knew differently. Bill (my husband) was sending me a message.
>
> Your dedication to the fight against DV is admirable. Please keep up the good work—and send me more installments.
>
> Take care.

> Sir, someone shared this on Facebook and it took me back. Kristin was a friend of mine. I even remember going to your house a few times. I have a daughter of my own now who is 3 years old and I truly can't imagine your strength, courage and selflessness to face this every day to educate others to prevent such a thing from happening to anyone else. You're truly an inspiration, for men like you will make the world better place.

Acknowledgments

Each of us has come a long way since our initial contact with detectives. I pray nobody ever gets a call like that one. It is our hope the journey described in *When Dating Hurts* helps us heal.

My deepest thanks to Raquel Bergen, Ph.D., Dr. Beverly Bryde, Colleen Lelli, EdD, and Beth Sturman for their generous encouragement throughout the writing of *When Dating Hurts*. These women have dedicated themselves to the domestic violence cause, and they continue to make real differences for people in need.

Great thanks to law enforcement professionals Detective Jim Carbo, former District Attorney Bruce Castor, Detective Sam Gallen, Detective Jim McGowan, and the prosecutor of Kristin's case, Assistant District Attorney "Charlotte Stark"—whose name was changed for privacy reasons. Through their kind words and precise actions, these heroic crime-fighters provided first-rate law enforcement beginning with that heartbreaking day, June 3, 2005. I salute their tireless bravery, generosity, and proficiency.

Special thanks to Jim Astrachan, Linda Dragonuk, Lou and Fran Gunshol, Patty Mahoney, Patricia Marlatt, Sharon McDaniel, Dave and Donna Thomas, Donna Watkins, Kevin Welsh, and Shelley Wygant. Their selfless advice, words of wisdom, insights, and other contributions to this book were essential in making this memoir full and accurate.

Thanks to my editor, Emerald Barnes, who provided brilliant recommendations to the entirety of *When Dating Hurts*. She surpassed the duties of editing, and took Kristin's cause as her own.

Extra-special thanks to those who contributed but cannot be named for both safety and privacy reasons. Their stories touched me deeply, and I am indebted to them. Their courage to share with me the hardest parts of their lives is taken as a privilege and an honor. I feel their pain, and I know they do ours.

Incalculable thanks to David, my son, and Ali, my daughter-in-law, for their input on structure and placement of events in this work. Their ideas enabled this narrative to take a more interesting and less-conventional flow. They have also been instrumental in ways to put *When Dating Hurts* in the hands of people who most need to read it.

Heartfelt thanks to my Mom—lovingly called Gaga (Grandma) by Kristin and David. Mom is a fan of my dating violence speeches and the creation of this book. Her blessings mean everything to me.

I owe my deepest appreciation to my wife, Michele. Together we have endured a parent's worst nightmare and have become stronger in faith and love having lived through this. Along with providing continuous moral support throughout the long process of writing and editing, her personal viewpoints about Kristin and the days after her tragedy gave *When Dating Hurts* a strong central theme: our family's journey.

The Mitchell family continues to see how the power of Kristin's story impacts lives. Many victims have recognized and safely left unhealthy relationships. That is why *When Dating Hurts* needs to be shared.

Note found in Kristin's belongings.

Stay in Touch.

You can stop dating violence in your community.
Join our community. Work to end dating violence.

Learn more about Kristin's story
WhenDatingHurts.com

The When Dating Hurts podcast series
is on most popular podcast players

Twitter
@WhenDatingHurts
#WhenDatingHurts

Facebook
Facebook.com/WhenDatingHurts

Questions or Comments
Email: BillMitchell@WhenDatingHurts.com

Be safe. A call to one of these organizations
is always the best place to start the conversation.

The National Domestic Violence Hotline
800-799-SAFE(7233)

The National Sexual Assault Hotline
rainn.org   800-656-HOPE(4673)

Love is Respect
loveisrespect.org   866-331-9474

WHEN DATING HURTS

Made in the USA
Middletown, DE
08 December 2022

16269781R00186